Crime Against Women

Crime Against Women

R.K. Dutta

Reference Press

4831/24, Ansari Road
Darya Ganj
New Delhi-110 002
Phone: 3260807
Fax: 3274173
E-mail: essess@del3.vsnl.net.in

First Published 2003

ISBN: 81-88583-03-0

Price: Rs.650/-

Published by:
Reference Press
4831/24, Ansari Road,
Darya Ganj,
New Delhi-110 002.
Phone: 3260807
Fax: 3274173
E-mail: essess@del3.vsnl.net.in

Printed in India by:
Mehra Offset Press

CONTENTS

Preface

The semantic meaning of 'crime against women' is direct or indirect physical or mental cruelty to women. Various kinds of violence against women are eve-teasing, molestation, bigamy, fraudulent marriage, adultery and enticement of married women abduction and kidnapping, rape, harassment to women at working place, wife beating, dowry death, female child abuse and abuse of elderly female etc. The alarming rate in the crimes against women can to a large extent be attributed to the lack of infrastructures for single working women who have to leave their families at an early age to work away from home. Sexual harassment and eve teasing are a common phenomena and sometimes even police is a party to all this. This lead to a deep insecurity among girls and women and does not let them feel emotionally independent. Instances of wife-beating and violence on women in several other forms like beating/burning them to death due to the fact that they did not bring adequate dowry or do not accept the role of a slave, are common. Marriage, in our system, is still considered to be an eternal bond and society views a woman with distaste if she tries to break this bond, whatever her problems and agonies.

Large families are inconceivable in the present socioeconomic set-up, but the birth of at least one son is important, in most families. A woman who does not give birth to a son is still rated as inferior to the one who has produced a son. Whether a woman wants it or not, repeated pregnancies may be forced on her and women are still tortured, divorced on this account and unfortunately, it is normally a woman who is responsible for inflicting this kind of misery on another woman. Obviously, in spite of all that is being said and done in the name of feminism or the upliftment of women and all the tall claims being made by the governments, the paths of women are still beset with several difficulties though since women cover half the sky, it should be one of society's primary concerns to look into the problems women are confronted with and to try to solve these problems.

The most effective strategies are likely to be those that support women to organise peer groups and mobilise community resources and public services, including women's health services. Such approaches enable women to overcome resignation to the legitimacy of the established order are important factor in the perpetuation of imbalances of power between women and men. These can be altered through conscious social policy and programmes that treat women as subjects who can and ought to shape their own destinies. Adoption of such strategies would move population policies far beyond their past treatment of women as instruments. If women are to implement their reproductive preferences, then it is essential that their empowerment occur not only within their personal spheres, but also in the broader spheres of the community and the state.

1

Violence in Family

The semantic meaning of violence against women is direct or indirect physical or mental cruelty to women. Violence against women can be as simple as eve-teasing or as grave as rape or dowry death.

Various kinds of violence against women are eve-teasing, molestation, bigamy, fraudulent marriage, adultery and enticement of married women abduction and kidnapping, rape, harassment to women at working place, wife beating, dowry death, female child abuse and abuse of elderly female etc.

However, for the present purpose only family violence against women is looked into. Most common family violence against women are husbands and in-laws harassment for dowry or any other reason, dowry deaths and wife battering: female child abuse and abuse of elderly female in the family are also included in the family violence against women. Although of late, more and more literature has build around what is called as the women's question there is precious little by way of scientific literature which would provide a satisfactory' answer to questions which invariably come up in any dispassionate discussion on family violence against females. Of course, much has been written on Hinduism and the caste-system. Considerable scientific attention has been paid to marriage and related practices. Likewise some perceptive accounts dealing with the practice of dowry are also available. A few researchers have attempted to assess social attitudes towards dowry. As far as coercion and violence emanative from the practice of dowry are concerned, researchers are constrained to proceed on little better than a few impressionistic accounts. In a study of dowry death, one-third of the deaths traced to fatal accidents, about a half were suicides or homicides, although unrelated to dowry, and dowry related deaths were 16 per cent.

The problem of dowry deaths has been analysed by looking into age, education, occupation, income, caste, family composition, ill-treatment and humiliation, patterns of brides murder, medical aid, abetment, role of police, conviction and motives in regard to 13 dowry deaths. Based on this, two propositions have been put forth: (1) the most important factor contributes to the bride burning is offender's environmental stress or social tensions which may be caused by factors endogenous as well as exogeneous to the family and (2) the economic situation in a women's husband's family contributes much to her adjustment soon after her marriage as well as to her humiliation and cruel treatment. And dowry deaths are found more in the middle classes and educated groups.

Criminologists and public at large almost completely ignored the emergence of wife battering as a problem until 1970's. By the mid of 1970's the remergent women's movement and made battering a central issue and given it wide publicity. During that period some empirical studies have been conducted on wife battering.

Some of the theoretical explanations for the wife battering are coercion theory, cyclical theory and the status inferiority theory. According to William Goode, use of physical force is an integral part of the institution of the family and is one of the means to maintain control in the family. He argues if force does not exist, the structure of the family system would be destroyed. In fact, Goode has used this thesis of use of violence as coercive form of social control for explaining violence between all members in the family.

Walker's cyclical theory of violence maintains that the interaction between husband and wife tends to follow a cyclical pattern attempting between (a) tension building phase, (b) the e plosion or acute battering incident, and (c) the calm loving respite. Over the time the first phase becomes more common and the third phase declines. The status inferioriy theory maintains that the rate of wife battering is greater when the wife has a more prestigious position than her husband.

Social bond theory explains the problem of Wife battering in a better way as it comprehensively takes care of all the factors like social norms and social organisation which socializes and individual, the personal characteristics of the fenders and individuals, the inter-personal characteristics of offenders and ecological factors.

High level of family conflict, stress and violence in society, family socialization in violence, cultural norms and sexual inequality are noted as causes of wife battering. Wife abuse is seen as a reaffirmation of male self-image as aggressor which has been internalised and encouraged during childhood. Child abuse in own families or parental violence, alcohol and childhood experiences in battering husbands are some of the factors of wife battering.

Moore looks into social, legal and psychological and personal factors to explain the causes of wife battering. Newman hypothesised that the conditions of the presence of alcohol, hostile dependency, extensive brooding on the part of husband, husbands, frustrations in his work and other activities, raising anger after verbal disputes, and the husband having been battered by his patents in childhood contribute to wife battering.

As far as explaining the wife's complicity in husband's battering is concerned four theoretical approaches have been analysed. (1) the traditional sex role socialization approach (2) the provocative wife, argument approach (3) the learned helplessness approach. (4) Persona, resource approach. The tendency of abusive relationships has been attributed to women's social life with men who were drinkers and gamblers. Inspite of battering wife stays back due to fear, economic status and children.

Those who are abused as children will more likely to tolerate abuse as adults; lack of economic independence and powerlessness affects decision to leave or seek help. Additionally, outside help is ineffective in coping with intrafamily violence and social constraints and training hamper efforts to change the situation.

To overcome the problem of family violence against females some policy suggestions have been made in the areas of criminal justice system, social service agencies, emergency room-staff and physicians, personal support for the victim, setting up of shelter, churches/religious institutions, media, mental health, marriage and family and children of battered women. However, there are some different opinions on some of the suggested policies. The root cause of family violence against women lie in the very nature of the family and of other aspects of society.

Consequently, shelters, counselling and prosecutions are unlikely to have major or lasting effect unless they are part of a larger process designed to change basic societal characteristics. These include the incidence of violence outside the family, social norms concerning violence, the use of the violence in child rearing and sexual inequality within the family and in society at large.

Violence by men against women, and specifically against their partner is not a new problem; it is assumed by some to have begun wit the first monogamous pairing. What is new however is public admission that violence against women occurs in a civilised society and the insistence by the government and well meaning citizens that such violence is no longer acceptable that we should discuss that problem and search for solutions which will put an end to such violence. In this regard that present paper attempts to look into the various policies an programmes in the country for the betterment of women

Legal measures

The fountain-head of legal policies is the Constitution of India. The Preamble clearly lays down equality of status and opportunity to all. All provisions of the, Constitution are applicable to both men and women. Some of the articles directly relevant to women are:

Article 14: The state shall not deny to any person equality before the law or the equal protection of the laws within the territory of India.

Article 15: (1) The state shall not discriminate against any citizen on grounds only of religion, race, caste, sex, place of birth or any of them.

(3) *Nothing in the article shall prevent the state special provision for women and children.*

Article 16: (1) There shall be equality of opportunity for all citizens in matters relating to employment or appointment to any office under the

(2) No citizen shall, on grounds only of religion, race, caste, sex descent, place of birth, residence or any of them, be ineligible for, or discriminated against in respect of any employment or office under the state.

Directive principles

Article 39: The state shall in particular direct its policy towards securing (a) that the citizens men and women equally have the right to an adequate, means of livelihood; (d) that there is equal pay for equal work for both men and women; (e) that the health and strength 4 workers, men and women and the tender age of children are not abused and that citizens are not forced by economic necessity to enter avocations unsuited to their age or strength.

Article 42: The state shall make provision for securing, just and human conditions of work and for maternity relief.

On the basis of these provisions Government of India has enacted 32 Acts dealing with women. Among them 11 Acts are directly concerned with women. They are: (1) the Equal Remuneration Act, 1976; (2) The Medical Termination of Pregnancy Act, 1972; (3) The Hindu Adoption and Maintenance Act, 1956; (4) The maternity Benefit Act, 1961. (5) The Prevention of Immoral Traffic Act, 1986 (earlier The Suppression of Immoral Traffic in Women and Girls Act, 1956); (6) The Hindu Marriage Act, 1955, (amended in 1976); (7, The Special Marriage Act, 1954; (8) The Dowry Prohibition Act, 1961 (amended 1984); (9) The Child Marriage (Restraint) Act, 1933; (10) The Minimum Wages Act, 1948; (11) The Hindu Succession Act, 1960.

Besides, criminal law also provides some special provisions for women. The procedural law that is Criminal Procedure Code makes some distinction for women in regard to search, seizure, arrest, imprisonment etc. In non-bailable offences bail is generally not granted but in case of women she can be released on bail even if the offence is non- bailable (Section 437).

If a police officer, or any other person acting under warrant of arrest, is required to enter an apartment to arrest a person, and such apartment is in the occupancy of a woman who, according to the custom does not appear in public, such police officer or person shall, before entering such apartment give notice to such women that she is at liberty to withdraw and shall afford her every reasonable facility for withdrawing and may then enter or break open the apartment as the case may be, according to provide of Section 47(2) of the Cr.P.C. In regard to search of women section 51 (2) of Cr.P.C states that whenever it is necessary to cause a woman to be searched the search shall be made by another woman with strict regard to decency.

Similarly, if a woman is required to be medically examined at the directions of a police officer in regard to the commission of an offence within the meaning of section 53(l) Cr.P.C., examination has to be done under the supervision of a female registered medical practitioner. Police officer has the power to require attendance of witnesses for making an investigation, but no women shall be required to attend any place other than the place in which such woman resides (Section 160 Cr.P.C.).

Death of a woman in mysterious circumstances leads to many doubts in the minds of the public. It can be accident or suicide or homicide. In this regard the scope of Section 174(3) has been considerably widened by a recent amendment carried out by the Criminal Law (Second Amendment) Act, 1983, and includes cases of death of married women under suspicious circumstances during the initial seven years of marriage. It has been made obligatory on the part of an officer in-charge of police station, specially empowered police officer, to send the body for examination by civil surgeon or any other qualified medical man appointed by the State Government for this purpose. Section 416 of Cr.P.C. protects women by postponing capital sentence if she is pregnant.

Similarly, the substantive law i.e. Indian Penal Code, which contains quite a few sections dealing with women. Although eve-teasing and molestation have not been spelt out in the code, depending upon the severity one may make use of section 294, 351, 352, and 354 of the penal code dealing with obscene acts and songs, assault, criminal force and outraging modesty of women; wife battering has not been included as an offence perse either in the IPC or in any other law. Harassment of the wife or daughter-in-law has become common with the sole purpose of extorting money as dowry. The women is beaten and some- times the beating coupled with harassment results in severe injuries. Such cases would be covered in 327 IPC. Cruelty on married woman has been made a substantive offence by insertion of a new Section 498A in the IPC by Criminal Law 1983.

According to the explanation 'added to the section, cruelty means: (a) any wilful conduct which is of such a nature as is likely to drive the women to commit suicide or to cause grave injury or danger to life, limb or health (whether mental or physical) of the women; The increasing reported cases of dowry-murders and the effective lobbying by women's organisations pressurised the government to set or (b) harassment of the women where such harassment is with a view to coercing her or any person related to her to meet any lawful demand for or any person related to her to meet any lawful demand for any property or valuable security or is on account of failure by her or any person related to her to meet such demand.

The provision is supplemented to substantive provisions of the and taking Dowry Prohibition Act, 1961 which prohibits, the demanding and taking dowry. An important change in the rules of evidence has been introduced by the insertion of a new section 113A in the Indian Evidence Act. According to ordinary rules of evidence, a fault has to be proved by the person who alleges. But there is a presumption about the existence of certain facts as an exception. Section 113A lays down an important rule in this matter:

(a) If a women commits suicide within 7 years of her marriage, and

(b) Her husband and relative have subjected her to cruelty. The presumption, in a question of abetment of suicide by husband or relatives, would be that such husband or the relative has abetted the suicide. Likewise law on rape has also been amended by adding new sections 376A to 376D, and 228A, that not only protects women but also her name. A few more important sections are 359 to 348 dealing, with kidnapping and abduction, 339 to 348 on wrongful restraint and confinement. 493 to 498 on offences relating to marriage.

In addition to these laws of amendments, a few more changes have takes place. In 1976, the Law commission introduced a highly controversial Bill regarding Marriage Laws, The commission recommended the introduction of "irretrievable breakdown of marriage" as aground for divorce. This also provided safeguards for women by empowering the courts to direct the husband to pay maintenance and alimony to his divorced wife. However, this bill did not take the form of an Act because of the opposition from certain quarters.

The increasing reported cased of dowry-murders and the effective lobbying by women's organisations pressurised the government to set up the Joint Committee of both the houses which submitted its report in August, 1982, and in 1984, the Dowry Prohibition Act was passed. The only important reform made by the Act is that the aggrieved person or recognised welfare organisation, women's organization can file a complaint before a magistrate even if the girls parents are unwilling or hostile to lodge complaints. Women's organisations have been emphasising a lot on the provision of family courts to tackle matrimonial disputes. In 1984, the Government of India conceded their demands and introduced a comprehensive Family Court Act, 1984. It conducts cases of matrimonial disputes quickly by providing for an informal procedure of conciliation.

In the past few years one of the very important movements in the legal field is public interest litigation. Recently the court has passed an order by which any individual or institution on behalf of the aggrieved can file a suit. Under this provision, many groups-women as well as public interest have raised issues of gender justice in the court of law.

Legislation and its proper implementation- are the two basic elements essential for every organised society. However, more often than not these law remain unimplemented. The more frequent reasons for non-implementation are the cumbersome laws, elaborate procedures and the inadequacy of the machinery provided in the Acts.

In regard to courts' action Desai and Patel state that "we do not have any convincing evidence to suggest that judges in lower courts, in High Courts or in Supreme Court are favourable to women's cause, since at various times different judges have proclaimed path breaking judgements." Heated debates were generated when the Andhra Pradesh High Court gave its judgement in 1983 on a petition by a well-known actress Sarita, challenging the restitution of conjugal rights by her husband. But to the great disappointment of women's groups, the Supreme Court reversed the judgement. The Supreme Court also set free the murderers-in-laws of Sudha Goel and those of Manjushree Sarda cases. In Sudha Goel's case the fair judgement of the HighCourt was being questioned in the Supreme Court. The judges in the former have been interviewed and even charged with contempt of A prominent legal women activist remarks "the zig zag course of securing convictions in cases of dowry deaths and the inability of the judges to spell out criteria for assessing the evidence in crimes of violence against women which must necessarily be different from those for assessing any other crime".

In case of state versus Basant Kumar, Ladkibai and Meena Kumari, the sessions judge held that "the accused had created such circumstances that Usha was left with no other alternative but to commit suicide. In most of these cases, to begin with, the offences are suppressed, and even when they are taken to court it is with great difficulty that they are proved". Hence under the Section 306 IPC all the 3 accused are sentenced to 10 years imprisonment. The judgement is important as it demonstrates the necessity of bringing charges of abetment to suicide where there is a known history of harassment so that the culprit does not gets away scot-free.

Recently in a property dispute case also, the high court judge has retained the right of property of a woman over the gifts given by the parents or relatives in marriage called 'stridan'. In USA the prosecution of wife battering cases are less frequent than arrests. Only 16% reach courts whereas in assault cases 75% reach courts. Prosecutors believe that these cases are best handled by social service agencies and prosecution is pointless since the victim typically withdraw the charges. These and other factors create a self-fulfilling prophecy that discourages even those who want to press charges, make arrests and prosecute cases. Wife battering cases reach court for trial are one-half of the general assault cases and one-fourth of the serious assault cases. Penalties are high even though the physical attack is typically more severe.

Policies and programmes of the government

Policies: One of the overriding objectives of the planning process is social justice. In the Seventh Five Year Plan following policies dealing with women have been explicitly mentioned.

Objective No. 3.8, states "human resource development also includes measure to improve health status and steps to improve the participation of vulnerable groups like scheduled castes, scheduled tribes women and disabled persons in the development process".

Objective No. 3.2, points out "the need to generate employment opportunities for educated youth in rural areas."

Objective 3.33 states, "to be effective the problem of urban poverty requires a multi-pronged strategy designed, among others to:

(a) provide gainful employment to the unemployed particularly women and youth. In 1986, a programme called self-employment programme for urban poor has also been initiated.

Objective 3.13 aims at increasing involvement of the voluntary agencies in the implementation of plan programmes.

One of the important features of Seventh Five Year Plan is acceleration of the voluntary adoption of a small family norm and a positive role of women in economic and social activity. This apart, universal elementary education with special emphasis on girls and nutrition programme for mother and child are also notable features.

Besides, 4 points of the new 20-point programme also refer to women. They are:

> Point 15: Accelerated programmes of welfare for women and children and nutrition programmes for pregnant women, nursing mothers and children especially in tribal, hill and backward areas.
>
> Point 16: Spread universal elementary education for the age group 6-14 with special emphasis on girls and simultaneously involve students and voluntary agencies in programmes for the removal of adult illiteracy.
>
> Point No. 3: Strengthen and expand coverage of integrated rural development and national rural employment programmes.
>
> Point No. 5: Review and effectively enforce minimum wages for agricultural labour.

An overall study of these policies reveal that the policy thrust has changed from welfare to socio-economic independence. And it can hardly be emphasised that the economic independence of women assumes pointed significance, especially to those who have been continuously harassed by in-laws or husbands. In the light of policies it would be of interest to see what programmes government has undertaken to make the women economically self-sufficient.

Programmes: Under the Government of India. Ministry of Agriculture, Department of Rural Development has been established. This department has implemented various programmes:

(1) The Integrated Rural Development programme (IRDP) is a major instrument of the Government strategy to alleviate poverty. Its objective is to enable selected families to cross the poverty line through a strategy of productive asset

endowment. In this regard to ensure better participation of women in the development process it was decided that at least 30% of the beneficiaries should be women". At the end of January 1987, it was found that only 13.13% women were benefited instead 30%.

(2) A national scheme of Training of Rural Youth for Self-Employment (TRYSEM) was launched as a centrally sponsored scheme on 15th August, 1979. The main thrust of this scheme is equipping rural youth in the age group of 18-35 years with the necessary skills and technology to take up vocations of self- employment in the broad fields of agriculture and allied activities, industry, services and business. In this also the policy thrust is that at least one-third of the' TRYSEM beneficiaries should be women. During 1986-87,38 lakhs (37.2 %) women benefited from this programme.

(3) Development of Women and Children in Rural Areas (DWCRA): In recognition of the fact that the women have been only marginally benefited under various rural development programmes, a Pilot scheme was envisaged in 1982-83. It was implemented in 50 selected districts all over the country and which gave a fillip to involvement of women in anti-poverty programmes.

Since reaching women in isolation was considered difficult the strategy envisaged for reaching larger number of women was through the group approach. Women belonging to families living below poverty were organised in groups of 15-20, who were given some benefits in addition to normal facilities available to them under IRDP. The more popular activities in DWCRA programme are tailoring knitling handloom and forest based industries. A core group was constituted by the Department of Rural Development to oversee the training requirements for the implementation of women's programmes.

During 1986-87, it was proposed to organise 7500 women's group and against this target, upto January 1987 only 4544 groups had been formed. One important feature of DWCRA is involving voluntary agencies in implementing its programmes by providing financial assistance to them. These grants are channelised through Council for Advancement of People's Action and Rural Technology (CAPART).

(4) National Rural Employment Programme (NREP) has been launched: to generate additional gainful employment for the unemployed and underemployed persons in rural areas; create productive community assets for strengthening rural economic and social infrastructure and improve overall quality of life in rural areas. In this programme preference is given to landless labourers. Among them, women are given her preference. In the year 1986-87 out of total employment generated, women account, for roughly 19%.

(5) Integrated Child Development Services (ICDS): At the centre Department of Women and Child Development (WCD), Ministry of Human Resource Development, coordinates the implementation of ICDS. The ICDS is based on the conviction that child development programmes can become catalytic agents for social change and serve as entry points for improving the quality of life of present and future generations of the disadvantaged and poor. It seeks to improve child survival health, nutrition, learning opportunities for pre-school children and their mothers. It initially had only 33 projects, as against nearly 1500 projects at present spread over length and width of the country.

The national machinery has been set up to develop policies and programmes for women. These consist of: (1) A coordination committee. (4) A women's welfare and development bureau. These projects for women have been sponsored by the Government of India.

Policies and programmers of voluntary agencies

Well-meaning citizen' and voluntary agencies have been playing a pivotal role for the cause of women. There are no less than 125 women's organisations in the country. Generally they have come out with a common policy of overall upliftment of women. Many of these organisations have schemes for employment generation through activities like making pickles, snacks, papads, stitching of garments, running creches etc. However, they are not free from liberal women's organisations' complain that these women work in inhuman condition and that they are used as cheap labour.

Experiences of 'Annapurna, are quite inpiring. In the textile, working class area of Bombay, women's cooperative 'Annapurna' (i.e. Provider of food) provides lunch and dinner services to its customers who are mainly migrant industrial workers. Women who are involved in this project are from poor and working class background.

Mobile creche for working mother's children runs a day-care programme for children (aged up to 12 years) workers. By now, it has 45 centres in Delhi 25 centres in Bombay and 3 centres in Poona.

Since 1975, .various women vs organisations help their members to get bank-loans for establishing business. SEWA, Ahmadabad runs its own Bank-The Mahila SEWA Sahakari Cooperative Bank. It has over 8000 shareholders and over 12000 bank accounts. It is totally managed by women. It has provide an alternative to exploitation of women by big traders and money-lenders. Self-Employed Women's Association, a registered trade union, has Organised women rag-pickers, head-loaders, junksmith, fish-vendors, bamboo-workers, bidi-workers, block-printer, used garments dealers and enabled them to get fair deal in their respective professions.

Many autonomous women's organisations that take up social problem like dowry, wife-battering, prostitution, rape are faced with acute problems regarding rehabilitation of women victims of violence. Even though their main activity is to fight for women's rights, they have to start developmental projects in the field of health, education and employment that would make the women self-dependent. Besides, a few organizations have been active in the areas of distress management and legal aid.

The growing realization about the low status of women and violence against them has resulted in various actions from different quarters. In regard to legal measures, path breaking judgements have been made, relevant Acts and Codes have been amended and needed Acts have been enacted. On the Government's side main aspects of women have been incorporated in policies and plans.

Several programmes like IRDP, TRYSEM, DWCRA, ICDS etc. have been initiated. National committees and women in distress cells have been established. And what is more, participation of voluntary agencies in implementing government programmes has been vigorously encouraged. On the other hand, well-meaning citizens and voluntary agencies have launched many programmes for the economic independence of women. Among them, a few voluntary agencies have embarked upon radical ideas and programmes to bring about a change in the status of women.

It was in 1984 that we in AWAG [Ahmedabad Women's Action Group], studied the incidence of violence against women in Gujarat. The figures available from the state Police indicated that three women died per day as the consequence of familial violence. We went into the details of a number of cases and arrived at the conclusion that the most important single factor that contributed to this was the readiness of the woman to accept defeat and to sacrifice herself. Her upbringing, her education, her surroundings, everything taught her to bear meekly and give up life when it became unbearable. This, we thought was wrong as it was also wrong for the family to harass her. We all have imbibed old values and these are responsible for the position of the woman in the family and numerous deaths of women.

In order to give high status to them we had to change their attitude to life by convincing them that they did not have to die and that bearing pain meekly is no virtue. We' also had to tell people in general that the old values that oppress women should be discarded. The identity of the woman has to be respected, she must be considered equal to man, she must get social justice. In order to do this we used the street-theatre initially.

A woman director directed a number of street-plays which were performed in Ahmedabad and all over Gujarat. Of the very first street- play more than sixty shows were performed within the first six months, i.e. from August 1984 to Jan. 1985, This had to be suspended for some time as riots broke out in Ahmedabad in Feb., 1985, We took stock of the inputs we had made and the impact generated, and released that though we did rouse the people and made them aware of the problems of women, we could not measure the impact our work. It was very widely diffused. It awakened the citizens of Ahmedabad and people of Gujarat to the plight of women in Gujarat but more intensive work was considered to be necessary.

Out of that search for intensive work, was born our 'Positive Awareness Raising Workshop. We have had a number of workshops over the years and in these we have shared with groups of thirty women each, our understanding of the status of women, violence against women and other allied issues. Women have opened their hearts to us and narrated their experiences. These experiences are used as illustrations in subsequent workshops and the women sitting around in their turn tell us about their lives. From these sessions we have learned a lot about women and their suffering especially the violence they suffer within the family.

The first noticeable fact that communicates itself to us is that familial violence is so widespread that one could term it as universal. In the workshops we use visual specially prepared to communicate basic concepts and ask the participants to interpret these and relate them to their lives. As soon as we introduce visuals depicting violence against women, the participants start exchanging meaningful glances and start simpering. Most eyes turn to that person who is known to be the daily recipient of beating. When we ask them to interpret these visuals they say that this is all too common, what is there to interpret. As whisperings in one corner and loud comments in another subside we are told how one of them is being battered, or how each of them receives a blow or a kick as surely as the sun sets. One of the communities, calls the daily beating. 'Paya dabano'.

The woman is expected to massage the husband's feet. When she is doing that she is rewarded by beating, While describing their daily routine a woman of the community said that this is the last happening of the day. Other women present expressed their agreement. When we repeat this before different groups of women, they seem to accept this fact of their lives as easily as they accept every thing else. There is no protest, no feeling of accepting anything that is not normal. It is as if an inevitable part of the process of living.

When the beating crosses a certain limit, when the woman's body can bear it no longer or when she thinks in the interest of herself and her children, she must find a way out, she does find a way out. In doing so women seem to act ingeniously, get assistance from neighbours or family members or some outside agency or even the police. Some cases are cited in support of this statement.

She used to suffer in a peculiar way. When she went out with her children, her husband would lock the door and go away. On her return she had to sit near the locked door for hours till he returned. Her children would join her when they returned from school. This almost became a daily routine and so she did not want to go to any of her neighbours' houses for shelter. Once, in consultation with the neighbours she decided to take a bold step. When the children left for school, she waited for her chance. When her husband went out to the community latrine, she got out, locked the house and slipped away. When she returned after two hours the husband was fuming and fretting. She was saved from being battered as the neighbours came up and reprimanded him for behaving similarly on a number of occasions. The husband, thereafter has not locked his wife and children.

It was the routine of R.Bibi to go early in the morning to a school where she was working. R.Bibi was a widow and this was the job she found with difficulty. She was certainly being brave in the sense that early in the morning she had to cross a patch of road that was uninhabited. Once she noticed a man sitting on the roadside and commenting on her when she passed by This chance happening appeared to be repeated and R.Bibi felt threatened. She increased her speed while passing by but that seemed to attract more comments. Then, one day the inevitable did happen. The man rose and come on to attack her. By the time. R.Bibi was well equipped. She had carried for the last few days, a small bag of cloth tucked in at the waist. In this bag she carried two large stones which were securely stitched in. When she noticed the man coming on she immediately pulled out her 'weapons', circled it in the air twice or thrice and let it go at the head of her assailant. R.Bibi proved a good shot, her missile hit him in the head, he went down and she ran. Since then, she has not been accosted by anybody.

Alcoholic husbands have been set 'right single-handedly or collectively by wives. Labhubahen of Ahmedabad City narrates her story of how she was to put up with the drunkard husband who behaved irresponsibly and how it was difficult for her to get medicines for her children. S he got fed up once and went away to her father in another city where she found a job as a housemaid. After a few days, the husband followed her and alleged that she was earning immorally. That was the proverbial last straw. Labhu picked up a piece of fuel-wood lying nearby and beat him up so badly that his arm was fractured. Since then she was not beaten but that did not cure him of his drinking habit.

He, also started contributing to family expenses from his salary. Manaki had a similar experience. Once her husband, who lived on her earning took away all her wages. On the way out, he met their daughter who was also bringing home her meagre earnings. He beat the daughter and took away everything. The girl went home- with tear-filled eyes and found her mother beaten and broken. She got so angry that she went straight to the police station and informed them that her father was drinking. The police took him in custody and kept him there for a week. He emerged a saner person, took an oath that he would not drink and kept the oath for two months. Manki's life became as unbearable as before. In Manaki's words, there is not a single part of her body that does not bear marks of beating. When it became too much, Manaki, who is a tribal, walked out from home and started living with another man who keeps her well.

In a village in Viramgam Taluka of Ahmedabad district a band of men lived on production and sale of illicit liquor. Whatever quantity of liquor they could not sell during the day, they would drink. Their small earnings were spent on paying the Police at the time of raids. The wives were very unhappy. They received the beating-, from drunk husbands in addition to the responsibilities of finding enough means to keep the family from hunger. Once they got together and decided to put an end to their husbands' business. They got out of home together at the time when the pots hidden from the eyes of the passer by would not be guarded. They took out each pot from its hiding place and broke it, spilling its contents. Having achieved their mission, they quietly returned home. When the husbands saw the havoc they did not know where to fix the blame. The business of illicit liquor was not resumed by the men.

A tribal woman Bhiloda Taluka, once reported how she decided to do away with the custom of covering once face with the end of the sari. We were elaborating on customs that keep women from the decision making process within the family and keep them out of the mainstream of life. At that time she said how she fought with the members of her family first and the villagers afterwards. She had challenged that she was prepared to go to the court of law as she knew that this was not the law of the country. In that workshop there was another woman who reported how she was asked by her husband to get out and get lost. She knew she had no other place to go to so she decided to jump in a well. But she did not do so. Instead she started building a hot that herself and hot that she chose a site exactly opposite her husband's house in their field. As she kept on building it bit by bit, the husband rallied and they were united again.

There have been cases of women deciding to change their way of life as a result of attending such workshops. Once we were having a workshop in a village in Viramgam Taluka, Ahmedabad District. During the first two days we thought Hansa, who sat at the end of the room tending her baby all the time, hardly listened to what we were saying. But on the third day during racapitulation time, when her turn came, she responded by telling us how on the previous day she had decided to stop covering her face. In the late evening she took her husband in confidence and kept her face uncovered from next day. The husband's elder brother objected and shouted a lot but she remained adamant. On her face there was a glow of achievement. Women have gained self- confidence and have responded bravely to their circumstances during the days of workshops.

We have heard of women countering violence by taking extreme steps. In a workshop it was reported how a girl was once being escorted by an 'uncle' of her husband. On the way it appeared that he tried to take advantage of the loneliness and the gullibility of the girl. He took her to a pump-room in a field and commanded her to submit herself to him. The girl must have felt trapped but soon found a way out. She requested him to look away till she undressed. As soon as he turned his back to her she picked up an iron bar that was lying on the floor and hit him on the head. She left him there as he laid unconscious.

In most cases, the woman is physically stronger than the one who beats her. Yet the beating is accepted as the woman has accepted her husband as her lord and master. She is taught that it to her lot to suffer while the master has a right to beat her. In order to decrease the incidence of wife battering and other violence on women we think that we have to d the thinking that she is an individual and an equal to man. Nobody is a lord or a master. An ablehbodied woman should not accept any beating. When we say all this, we initially seem to shock the women around us but surely there is a gleam of relief in their eyes.

They debate that if this was true and possible, would not their lives improve? we tell younger women not to bear any beating from the beginning of the married lives, we tell the older ones to start opposing it and take the help of the neighbours: if need be or even our help as an institution. This appears to work in some cases. So we are hopeful.

While expressing this hope we can not forget that despite the raising of awareness, the number of crimes against women in Gujarat has doubled in the last four years. The figures published by the Police for the year 1987, suggest that 6 women die per day in Gujarat as a result of familial violence. This increase is shocking and makes us wonder when and how women would be freed from such violence that is deeply entrenched in their lives.

Dowry Death

Women's oppression today, then has to be seen in a wholistic perspective, according to which "What links sati with dowry deaths, female foeticide, sexual harassment, sexual crimes is the fact of woman being regarded as a nonentity, a non-person" with no identity except that bestowed on her as some man's daughter, sister, wife, mother etc., These very forms of oppression of women are rotten fruits delivered by the vicious and decadent tree of Indian patriarchy. "' Even Britishers found dowry as a factor which could exculpate their colonial rule for impoverishing India and rationalise their brigandry.

In 1913 Sydney Brooks wrote, "The poverty of India is, it is true, abject and pitiable enough, but to charge it to British rule is grotesque. The social habits of the people their improvidence, their reckless expenditure on dowries and wedding festivities have infinitely more to do with it than any external agency has or can have. You might remit the whole of the land revenue, and abolish the salt tax and the custom duties, and India would still be abjectly poor, and famines would still occur." "The same socialization strategies that prepare boys to be soldiers and policemen also co-opt women as mothers, wives and sisters into that preparation process. The concept of structural violence, that which frames behavioural violence refers to the organized institutional and structural patterning of the family and the economic, cultural and political systems that determine that some individuals shall be victimized through a withholding of society's benefits, and be rendered more vulnerable to suffering and death than others.

That structural patterning also determines the socialization practices that induce individuals to inflict or to endure according to their roles. This latter aspect of structural violence is conceptually related to the fact that structural violence establishes the culturally accepted threshold for physical violence in a society. " This is an apt analysis, which could be stretched to our understanding of violence related to dowry. But we would still go beyond such an observation arguing that violence is not merely physical but mental as well. The trauma, anguish which the three sisters would have been facing before committing suicide, definitely does violence to their being. Violence is not merely an end product it is a process. Thus the whole process radiates violence.

The question which appears, who are the persons we are going to punish in the present case of suicide? Could the people who were demanding dowry be prosecuted ?If not, why not? Is there no redressal? Wouldn't it be having a viciously debilitating impact on the other two Sisters? Have not the recent Gwalior ostentatious wedding of children of Madhav Rao Scindia and Karan Singh contributed to dowry violence? The links are made nebulours, in reality they, are not. We have to use not merely sociological imagination but sociological intuition phenomenological in nature. Once we debunk this dowry phenomenon the culprits stand exposed. Unfortunately they are de facto above law as they happen to be Members of Parliament or members belonging to the elite sections.

Categorisation of oppression of women

We would categorise the oppression of Indian women into three manolateralistic forms. All these three take the form of victimisation namely, (i) Patriarchal victimisation: in this men are responsible for crimes like sexual harassment, wife battering, rape, dowry murders, and setting in processes like patriarchisation, genderisation, commoditisation etc; (ii) Patriarchally propelled self-victimisation: here the present suicide committed by, four girls of Kanpur and the suicides committed by brides figure.

In the former case it is the patriarchal forces which compelled the three sisters to Commit suicide notwithstanding their being educated. They felt "helpless" because " woman even today remains a slave, a vassal in short an entity with-no-entity. Having no patriarchally endorsed worth in herself, a woman is made to look for material consurnerables to enhance her value. Thanks to capitalism and our commercial media a woman today finds a lot of new commodities to do commoditise herself. But woman who has been made into a commodity, fit to be exchanged for patriarchy to prevail, fails to decommoditise herself with the help of other inanimate commodities, which in the ultimate analysis is nothing but commoditisation of the very process of existence manolateralistic to the core."

Whereas in the case of suicides committed by the brides, it is abetted proximately by the harassment and torture of the bride at the hands of her in-laws and remotely by the patriarchal compulsion of izzat for which the bride's parents are not willing to accept their daughter back, for only theirs daughter's corpses the customary saying goes-can come from her in laws house; and (iii) Victim propelled victimisation: here the publicly celebrated rift between mother-in-law/sister-in-law versus daughter-in-law to discredit woman as oppressor of her own sex figures. For instance, as Nandy notes that "...even man's cruelty toward women is no match for the cruelty of women toward women." "Indeed", observes A. R. Wadia that "the greatest enemy and the only one that ultimately counts of woman's 'Emancipation' is woman herself. To Renuka Singh "The worst deprivation of the 'deprived class' takes place when the woman Vs woman battle begins resulting in the loss of support of women for the cause of their own liberation"." K. L. Sharma observes, "It has been observed that it is women who obstruct the path of other women even more than men do; as is the case with mothers-in-law and colleagues at work. "What a pity", says S.C. Taneja, "that man has reached the moon and has made tremendous progress in every filed but has not been able to end the social evil of dowry.

And a more shocking aspect is that women are murdered by women themselves. Refuting the aforementioned superficial views we would argue that the intra-gender nature of women's oppression is a manifestation of the "scapegoat syndrome."" For instance, the mother-in-law who has herself been made a scapegoat earlier, searches for another on whom she can project the frustrations of her life-situation. And she finds in her daughter-in-law the object, who can be the target of her pent-up feelings.

We further maintain "that is unjust to say that in every crime or injustice against a woman there is a fellow women. This is the most decaying argument for intra-gender oppression, which tries to exonerate the male. This is so because we are merely perceiving the surface structure of reality. Only when we reach the deep structures of reality, we find not woman but man - his ethos, ambience, mores and norms-culpable. The mother-in-law and sister-in-law versus daughter-in-law phenomenon has roots not in a woman's mentality and her essentialistic characteristics they are illusory-but in the existing reality in which we have fixed her, where all the meanings of her life emanate not from herself but from man and his milieu." Thus we see that intra-gender oppression has roots in inter-gender oppression. "Through our sociological insight which pierces the facde, the picture which forms in front of us enjoins on us to perceive the problem of dowry in the broad framework of the male-dominated society and thereby seeing women as nothing more than a cog in the machine and thus being detrimental to their own genre."

Agreeing with such a view Ruth Vanita argues "every oppressed group perpetrates its own oppression. It was Indians who, at British orders fired on Indians. But in doing so, they strengthened British imperialist. Women who oppress women increase the power of men as group. Mother-in- law and daughter-in-law are forced to compete for the favour of a man on whom they are both dependent. If the dependence disappeared, so would the competition."

The data on dowry in Delhi shows an increase in dowry deaths between 1985 to 1987. There is a decrease for the same period, in dowry murders and cases registered under the Dowry Prohibition Act (DPA), 1961.Dowry deaths are on the rise while DPA remains a mute spectator. Physical violence related to dowry continues, while psychical violence transcends the hold of law as it remains unrecognised veiled under the private domain of a woman's life.

The preceding data shows failure on the part of police in not investigating these cases, which is why as few as 43,64 and 79 dowry death cases have been registered in year 1985, 1986, 1987 respectively. Even after having registered these cases there has been not even one conviction.' The official data which then tries to conceal the magnitude of the problem of dowry beleaguering women is just an ostrich like attempt to come to grips with reality. While women continue to be sacrificed on the altar of patriarchy, the Policemen grumble of not making, good money in Crime Women Cell at Police Headquarters and the district Crime Women Cells, though they extort money from the offender and his family as a price to exonerate them of their heinous deeds. So also Policemen curse the government for opening up Crime Women Cells—an outcome of androcentric training imparted to them without sensitising and conscientising them on women's issues. What more, then, can we expect from such a machinery except harming women and their interests.

Further, notwithstanding DPA being amended its scope stil remains limited in terms of "gifts". "No doubt dowry is given at the time of marriage by the bride's parent but that is not the end, it is rather a rehearsal for the gifts to be given to the bride throughout her life on different occasions like festivals, marriage anniversaries, birthdays etc.

Dowry, the menance, as originally devised, was thought provide post-marital security to an otherwise helpless bride. It was practised according to Hindu Shastra, the meritorious act off 'doan' or ritual gift is incomplete until the receiver is given a dakshina. Later, Kanyadan or the ceremony of giving away the bride became associated with 'Varadakshina', i.e., the gifts in cash or kind by bride's parents or guardian to the bridegroom. It Was a voluntary practise without any coorciol overtones, and was considered to provide financial protection to the bride during adverse times at a later stage.

The voluntary concept of dowry detoriated, and obligatory practise of the bride's father to give definite amount in cash and kind to the bride-groom crept in. This obtained social sanction and hence did not evoke any active sympathy for the bride.

Though the chivalry and human sympathy which inspired the enactment of the Prohibition of Dowry Act is appreciable yet in practise it wayward somewhere. The 1961 Act defines dowry as any property or valuable "secured, given or agreed to be given either directly or indirectly at, before, or after the marriage by either party as consideration of marriage". It however, has a loophole, a provision saying, that any present made at the time of the marriage to either party in the form of cash, ornaments, clothes or other articles will not be deemed as dowry, I unless they are made as consideration for the marriage to the party". Moreover, the offences could be taken note of by the Courts only when the complaint has been made by someone within one year after it has been committed.

The definition does not limit itself to the payment made by the bride's party. Both types occur in India amongst different communities. But the speeches on the Bill in Parliament referred almost exclusively to payments from the bride's side to the bridegroom's which alone embodies the plight of innocent girls and their fond parents. Dowries often drive girls to commit suicide so as to save themselves from the disgrace of remaining unmarried, and their parents falling into financial ruin and social humiliation.

Even the most ardent supporters of the Act are not hopeful of its effectiveness in curbing this evil, as provisions have been made for, gifts', which subtly affirm the continuance of this evil. Because only a few opined that there was nothing objectionable in such gifts provided if they were given voluntarily as has been waived in the Act.

Dowry is often a voluntary gift. It is its execution that is anti-social. But the act is not calculated to stop such execution, since the parties to it are not likely to admit it and thus invite punishment and invariably the dissolution of the marriage. It is only a third party, and disappointed one, that is likely to betray the transaction and prove to the satisfaction of the court that it was 'dowry' and not 'gift' that passed hands.

In many cases, black and unaccounted money play a major role. The entire transaction takes the shape of a huge bribe to buy the fond- daughter's future by arranging marriage alliance with the family of high social status. In the process, they ingraine the expectations of the prospective bridegrooms in the marriage market, thus the only cursed sufferers are the men of honest means and moderate incomes. This practise has forced educated middle-class girls to take-tip clerical jobs, of become teachers, nurses, sales-girls in order to earn for their dowry. 'This is particularly true in urban areas.

In general, the Act deals with the consequences, and not the causes. The marriages in which dowry is provided are generally arranged by the parents within their very narrow limits of caste and sub-castes, which puts the scarcity value on the eligibles to marriage. The value is unilaterally aggravated because the parents feel an inescapable obligation to marry off their daughters, but not their sons, before a date-line as they fix.

A grown-up and unmarried daughter is still a matter of adverse social comment, but not a son. In their feverish anxiety to marry off their daughters, the parents reluctantly succumb to dowries, ruin them- selves economically and demean themselves socially; while they play the waiting game with respect to their sons in hope of extracting maximum dowry. This social difference seems to be the primary cause of the payment of dowry by the bride's parents to the bridegrooms and not vice-versa. It would stop only when the difference is eliminated, and instead of parents arranging the marriages of their children, boys and girls are allowed to mix freely and choose their partners for marriage.

But in the communities where dowry prevails, boys and girls are I not allowed to mix freely, lest such mixing-lead to inter-caste marriage of pre-marital sex relations, which are forbiden in our traditional society. In the case of girls it is even more unacceptable as pre-marital sex may lead to pregnancy and would expose them and their family to social problems. However, as for the boys, they are free from this biological betrayal and, moreover, the male dominated double-standard society projects them as aminable weakness for the pre-marital or extra-marital affairs or sometimes admired as the legitimate privilages of the rich and mighty. These socially invoked male double standards are evolved from this biological difference.

Biological differences do not justify more differentials. No woman can be immoral without a man being equally so. To penalise the woman for immoral behaviour and to let the men go unscathed for the same act is really immoral. The biological difference can be narrowed by the effective use of birth-control methods to prevent unwanted birth in marriage or out of it. It should be a general equipment for all girls, married or unmarried. This reform does not weaken the moral sanction for pre-marital continuence and post-marital monogamy, which are, and must be common to both sexes. But if the practise deviatea from this be and is tolerated for men, it should be equally tolerated for women. There should be same standards for both of them.

Even for though the biological difference can be narrowed by the birth control methods, the difference caused by the developed psychological dependance in women has to be narrowed to achieve equality. Generally various studies conducted by many authors on psychological ingredients of women, confirmed that in social contact, women are more submissive at family level and this attitude continues even in marriage ir-respective of their educational level.

The etiology of dowry problems lie in the fact that marriage is a crucial event in one's life, be it a man or a woman. In traditional terms, marriage is basically a relationship between two families, however, the greatest anamoly in our society is that the marital partners either do not assert themselves or their assortion was not taken seriously by their respective families. This is more true in the case of female partners who remain silent observers throughout the rituals.

The study conducted by Upreti & Upreti(1982) in this area confirmed that in 50 percent cases the authority is in the hands of parents, that is, the view of the parents reigned in decision making regarding one is marriage. Hence, women's attitude towards marriage, and the parents influence over the women's decision regarding marriage are the predominant psychological factors in the dowry system.

In marriage, as it is already mentioned, is with reality the families who are knitted and not the individual's because most of the individuals do not have any say in their marriage, depite the fact that the spouses are fully aware of the parents astrocity. Hence, many girls remain unmarried or are forced to marry men much inferior to them in every aspect.

The connotations made by violence are always the physical violence because the disharmony caused comes to the purview of the social and legal system only after physical violence. But violence does exist even without physical violence which is unnoticed even though it is as destructive and inhuman as physical violence.

The image created by the Dowry Prohibition Act is that it comes into rescue only in extreme cases, because only in the extreme cases the physical violence is brought to the legal access. So it is well said that this Act deals only with the consequences and not the causes.

Evidently, it would be paradoxical to state something about the causative factors, rather than to improve the existing consequential approach with wider dimensions. So, the concept of psychological violence is introduced to differentiate the violence caused by physical of psychological means.

Moreover, it is also felt that these two types of violences caused by dowry problem exist amid the populations. The physical violence by dowry is more predominant amongst the illeterate non-working married women rather than the educated working women, whereas it is vice versa in the case of psychological violence. The violence caused by the physical or phychological means affects the physiology of human being, that is, where there is physical vollence there is physical inury caused by the act, whereas, when there is psychological violence i.e., conflict, there is also physical injury but this injury is not immediately after the stress (conflict), it is only evident after the persistant exposure of the stressor.

To a married Indian woman the predominant psychological violence on the conflict would be the marriage itself. As most of the marriages are attanged by the parents the dowry porblems creep into the newly married couple's life. Further, for the said reasons it is the husband's family members who exercise more control over him. Hence, the husband's family members have more access to influence the husband when there is a short fall in the dowry promises, which is very prevelant nowadays. By virtue of this, the psychological violence or conflict is caused. So, an attempt is made to appropriate a new concept - "Dowry-Psychological Violence".

The term Dowry-Psychological Violence is defined as "The stress or conflict caused by the in-laws for short fall in dowry to the bride by way of forciable restrain or intimadating the cognition of the husband". This definition is operationally defined from the definition of violence by United States National Commission. The present study is conducted with this information as the substratum. In the present study, it is limited to these conflicts between husband and wife aroused by the in-laws through restraining or intimidating tile cognition of the husband and which leads to psycho-social distress.

The studies reported in the present section are not directly related to dowry and psychological violence but are related to violence caused by the psychological factors on family and woman.

In examining the relationship between the social status of women and rate of wife beating in each state in the U.S., Kersti used data from the U.S. Census Bureau and elsewhere. The status of woman index was developed for each state based on economic, educational political, and legal dimensions. State violence rate were based on data from a representative sample of 2143 American adults. A curvilinear relationship was found between women's status and wife-beating. In a state, where women's status was lowest, wives were more likely to be beaten by their husbands.

Violence decreased as sexual equality in- creased to a point. In states where the status of women was highest, the level of violence against wives was also high. It is suggested that limited options to violent marriage keep battered wives in abusive relationship in low-status states. In states where women's status is high, increased conflict and violence may be a consequence of rapid social changes that some husbands find threatening. Data also shows, however that in state where women have the highest status, violence by wives against husband is equal to that of by husband against wives.

Filsinger & Wilson studied the relationship between interpersonal competence and marital adjustment. It was hypothesised that social anxiety is negatively related to marital adjustment. 179 inact married couples (average ages of husband and wives - 45 and 42 years respectively) completed questionnaire measure of both concept. Data were analyzed at both the individual and the couple levels. The hypothesis was supported, but social anxiety was primarily related to marital adjustment of self and not to that of spouse.

The types of causal attributions that violent husbands and the wives use to explain the husband violence with various targets were investigated by Shields and Hanneke. They standardized indepth interviews which were conducted with 85 violent husbands and 92 wives/partners of violent husbands. Data show a clear tendancy of wives of violent husbands to see the husbands violence as caused by factors internal to him. For all but one of the 6 significant targets for husbands, wives were more likely to see internal rather than external factors as the cause.

The only exception was for the target category wives were more likely to see the behaviour as externally casual. The husband displayed a marked tendnacy to see their violence as externally caused. Contrary to predictions, although neither husband nor wives were more responsible for their victimization, husbands did seem to be more likely than wives to blame female victims for their victimization.

Finn explored the stress and coping strategies of 56, 17 - 33 years old women who had sought help from a spouse—abuse treatment program. Ss completed a demographic information sheet, a stress scale, and a family coping strategies scale at initial referral. It was hypothesized that Ss would be under stress from a variety of environmental and interpersonal sources. Results suggest that violence occured when coping strategies were inadequate to mitigate the positive impact of stressor events. Stress came simultaneously from problems with money, jealousy, alcohol/drug abuse, and arguments. Ss were less likely than the general female population to utilize active, problem-solving behaviours and were likely to use passive strategies when dealing with problem situation. Findings show a moderate and consistent inverse relationship between stress and coping. When data were compared with data collected previously on abusive men by the author. It was found that a larger proportion of women than men reported stress in every problem area and both the groups were similar in the use of coping strategies.

The relationship between self-reported psychosomatic stress symptoms and dimensions of family and farm functioning among 126 wives of dairy farmers in New York State was examined by Berkowitz and Perkins. Ss completed a questionnaire assessing home and farm task, loads, farm complexity, intra and interpersonal role conflict, husband support and martial satisfaction. The psychosomatic stress symptoms included nervousness restlessness, insomnia, shortness of breath, and fainting. In general, stress symptomes showed little relationship to task loads, farm complexity, and intrapersonal role conflict. Much stronger relationships were found for interpersonal role conflict, husband support and marital satisfaction. Findings suggested the importance of family relationships in preventing or buffering stress in comparison to simple role-related task expectations of farm system.

Smith studied two basic questions, firstly, do family stress pile-up a meaningful concept for family stress theory and research? Secondly, what is the nature of the relationship of family cohesion and family adaptability to family satisfaction?

A sample of two hundred and twenty nine wife and husband pairs was taken. Family stress pile-up was measured with a family life events questionnaire that assessed whether variety of potentially stressful events had occured in the life of the family over the past three years, and how stressful those events were for the family.

Family cohesion and family adaptability were measured with FACES II. Family satisfaction questionnaire was measured with the Family Satisfaction Scale developed by Olson and Wilson.

A negative relationship was found between family stress pile-up and family satisfaction and it showed a linear relationship between family conesion, adaptability and family satisfaction.

The physical violence caused of dowry problem is comparatively less amongst the working women in compatison to the non-working women. Despite the fact that the in-laws feel that the income brought by the working women is a perenial source of dowry yet this does not exempt them from dowry violence, because of short fall of dowry at the time of wedding. This violence is of a different nature, as already stated earlier. Hence, it is presumed that the violence amongst this population is more oriented to words psychological than the physical aspect.

The tool used in the present research was designed by the author. It consisted of 35 items measuring 7 areas of conflict and stress. The areas of conflict were based on the work of Lock. The technique used in this questionnaire was commensurate scaling technique, in which the items are the source for two measurments, namely conflict and stress. That is, the level of conflict caused by the source items and the commensurate stress caused by this conflict is measured. The validity of the questionnaire was established by finding the percentage of relevance to areas of conflicts by dowry-psychological problems. It was administered to 50 working women. Initially 9 areas of conflict were choosen for testing, and of which 7 areas were choosen by the percentage of relevance response ranging from 78% to 97.33%. The other 2 areas percentage were 24% and 28% respectively.

The percentage-wise bifurcation of the 7 areas of conflict was : I - Leisure time -97.33%, 2. Relationships with the husband's family - 89.75%, 3. Financial Aspects - 85%, 4. Individualistic Behaviour - 83.25%,5. Child-rearing - 81.5%, 6. Social Behaviour - 80.75%, and 7. Affectional and sexual relationships - 78%. The face validity for the items of the 7 areas of conflict were established by interviewing 3 social workers, 7 psychologists and 15 working women. As per the suggestions' 'slight modifications were made in the items before the final questionnaire was prepared. The test rested reliability was established and was computed to be 0.831 after Spearman-Brown correaction formula.

Three point rating scales were used for both conflict and stress i.e., I - a source of Low Conflict or Stress; 2 - a source of Moderate Conflict or Stress; and 3 - a source of High Conflict or Stress and if a statement does not apply or is untrue N.A. or Not Applicable is used.

The concept conflict and stress were operationally defined in the Introduction section of the questionnaire itself, so as to enable the respondants to have better understanding about the concept and to restrain them from responding with their own understanding about the concept used.

Conflict - A problem, something you find difficult to cope with about which you feel worried or enxious.

Stress - Any type of mental or physical disturbances caused by the conflicts and which affects your normal functioning.

Each subject obtained two cores, one for conflict and the other for stress. The higher the score on the conflict/stress scale represents the higher conflict/stress for that source situation.

The percentage and coefficient correlation was used to process the collected data. The perusal of reveals the high correlation between conflict and stress amongst the married working women. This result substantiates the concept "Dowry-

Psychological Violence". That is, the conflicts (Psychological violence) invoked by the dowry problem induced stress amongst the choosen population. The stress detoriates an individual's mental and physical health, and when it is persistant it impairs the normal functioning. Hence, the stress which goes unnoticed during earlier stages it developes various hazards in the working women during the period of time. Despite the Dowry Act, which is oriented to the physical violence as consequence, does not protect this type of violence eventhough it is equally destructive for the society. Hence this type of uncovered violence needs prevention and rehabilitation.

The order of dominant conflict areas and their correlation to stress. The result reveals that 4 of the 7 conflict areas have significant correlation with stress. They are 1. Leisure time, 2. Relation- ship with husband's family members, 3. Child-rearing, and 4. Financial Aspects. It infers from these results that the conflict areas leisure time, financial aspects and child-rearing invoke high stress among the below 2 years of marriage group. Whereas, the other 3 conflict areas, inspite of the reasonable percentage of conflict response shows that is no significant relationship with stress. Hence, the conflict caused by dowry in 3 areas do not invoke stress.

The result that there is no significant relationship between the conflict areas and stress in the 2 years and above of marriage group but the rank order of conflict area is different from that of the below 2 years of marriage group, indicating the difference in conflict areas as the period of marriage increases. This can be attributed to the adaptability of the traditional Indian woman. That is, inspite of the conflict response, they would have learnt to resolve conflict, by which they can be devoid to excessive stress caused by the conflicts.

2

Divorce

Today, marriage faces many threats. It is facing pressures from diverse sources, particularly from inter-spousal relationships themselves, and the immediate environment. The disharmony in these relationships results in resorting to law courts. The extent the magnitude and the nature of the trial can best be examined by the outcome of marriage as it exists at present.

In Hindu society, marriage has been considered a sacrament. Although in the lower castes, divorce is sought through custome and convention, the higher castes obtain divorce by taking recourse to the law courts. The legal redress now available has made it possible for an unhappy couple to seek a way out of the lock in the wedlock. This trend appears to be an avert expression of a new conception of marriage. Largely undefined, it is the result of dynamic changes in the social environment.

There are two hypotheses with regard to the causes of divorce in Hindu society: Firstly, environmental factors are more responsible than the personality factors for divorce. Secondly, biological and social factors are more responsible than the psychological and economic factors for divorce. With a view to offer a useful analysis, an attempt has been made to bring about all such hidden facts to light, which may support or reject our hypotheses. We will confine to the analysis of causes of divorce, mapping out conditions under which individuals are more likely to terminate their marriage instead of continuing it.

Thus, the focus is relationship among characteristics of individuals, rather than individual's unique behaviour. That is to say, a given characteristic, such as wife's adjustment with in- laws is related to another factor such as husband's love for his wife. It would not be correct to say that in a particular case, divorce was caused by wife's irritable temperamnt or husband's domineering nature alone.

The factors affecting divorce rate are not necessarily the same which contribute to marital failure, since divorce is merely the opening of the doors to escape from failure. It is a symptom of failure of marriage. However, we believe that the causes of divorce are the same as the causes of disputes of unhappy marriages. Baber and some other sociologists have also given the same argument. We have, thus, attempted to analyse here the causes of divorce not only on the basis of interrogation of our respondents as to why they divorced but also on questions about the conflict between the spouses. We kept in mind that we were trying to find out how the divorce crises were viewed and experienced by the spouse. We wanted better knowledge about the kind of complaints made by the wife (and also by the husband) because it were these problems that they faced during the marriage.

The study of Choudhary reveals that the factors associated with marital stability of factors in dissolved marriages associated with one another may be classified into two broad categories: (1) Environmental factors, and (2) Personality factors. The former can further be subdivided into, (a) factors endogenous to family, and (b) factors exogenous to family. The latter on the other hand include individual's characteristics like domineering nature (or 'complex'), impotency, barrenness, mental deficiency, lethargic nature, etc. As regards to environmental factors, it is an established fact that the basic elements of personality are patterned during early years of life.

The results of studies by some western scholars like Burges and Cottrell' reveal that the environmental forces, to which the individual has reacted in childhood and adolescence, lead towards adjustive values in marriage. The possibilities of maladjusted behaviour also spring from the parents, marital conflicts. Individuals who suffer from parental disharmony or bad parent-child relationship reflect many concomitants of maladjustment in the dynamics of their personality.

The causes of environmental factors included with in the family are: role conflict (or authority), physical assault, chronic disease, poverty, age disparity, unduly large family, immaturity at marriage, and illicit relations. The causes outside the family are: dowry and wife's career. The personality factors on the other hand include domineering nature, irritable nature, lethargy, importancy, barrenness, and mental deficiency. All these factors contribute to the breaking of marital relation between husband and wife and ultimately lead to divorce.

Damle, Kuppuswamy, and Fonseca in their studies have categorized the causes of divorce differently. According to Damle, the main causes of divorce are: (1) childlessness, (2) obligations of marriage not properly fulfilled, (3) happy married life rendered impossible (which includes: husband either stays away or has another wife or mistress, and immaturity of the wife), (4) domestic disharmony (which includes: quarrels between the partners, ill-treatment of wife, family quarrels, and refusal of the wife to live with her husband, and (5) miscellaneous causes. Kappuswamy has reported cruelty, sexual defects, childlessness and infidelity as the major causes of divorce. Fonseca has diagonised the causes of divorce as infidelity, economic distress, personal defects, vices, imcompatibility, sex difficulties, health, and living conditions.

Williams Goode has explained instability, non-support, authority-complex, drinking, home life, values, illicit relations, and desertion as the chief causes of divorce. Goode describes these causes as different from those of legal grounds of divorce. Norton, Arthur, Glick and Paul have explained young age at marriage, low education, low occupation, low income as main socio-economic indicators which have been linked to marital discords. Elliot has analysed the causes of divorce as real versus legal. Levinger has said that cycle of life is inexorable : what rise's eventually descends; what grows eventually perishes. Closely knit interpersonal attachments too, sooner or later, dissolve.

It is common knowledge that legal cases of divorce do not necessarily reflect the reality of the marital conflicts. Goode writes that legal grounds reflect the fact that our legal system requires the 'innocent' party to prove that the other is 'guilty' in his/her marital behaviour. By the time the suit is filed, both husband and wife have usually agreed to obtain a divorce, and they simply utilize the grounds that are legally most effective and socially least accusatory against the other partner. What then are the real complaints of husbands and wives against one another? As stated earlier, several Indian and Western studies have attempted to uncover the complex web of their charges and counter charges.

Such listing of marital difficulties are worth examining, as they have been described as the true causes of the marital disorganisation. An experienced researcher knows that some responses given by the respondents fall easily in the categories developed by the researcher for classification but all answers are not given with greater specificity.

In our coding operation, for achieving the level of specificity for classifying the answer in one or the other category (developed by us), significance was given to the most important single complaint made by the respondent rather than his/her total response.

For example, if the female respondent (wife) stated that her husband deserted her because of his relations with other woman (illicit relations), this total response was not ended as two separate complaints. Therefore, if say, 25 percent of our respondents gave as a complaint "illicit relations", this does not mean that this was the "cause of divorce" in 25 percent of the cases. All those respondents listed under this head might still have other complaints. The average number of complaints were over-two per respondent and we had no way of weighing their importance in "causing" the divorce. We can merely say that 25 per cent of our respondents thought that this factor was of great importance in the breakup of their marriage.

Some respondents attempted to present a personality diagnosis of their spouses on superficially objective terms. Others felt that their partner personally betrayed them. A few never guessed that a divorce was impending until it happened, while others felt from an early period in the marriage that it would not last. It was not possible to classify each answer on several levels of meaning because each respondent varied in his/her grasp of these levels.

We were forced, then, to stay as close as possible to the literal statements of the respondents. We have classified the causes of strained relations between the partners leading to divorce into four categories: social, biological, psychological, and economic.

Strained relations between spouses may arise because of the difference in occupational status, income, employment of the wife or unemployment of the husband, etc. The martial relations also become strained because of the family environment (structure of the family), chronic disease, immaturity at marriage and wide age disparity between the spouses. All these factors create conflicting situation in the family. We will present each factor descriptively to assess whether they indicate any pattern and direction pertaining to behaviour and attitudes of husband and wife.

Role of authority

One important source of stress and conflict for the partners arises out of the fact that they may frequently be required to participate in a variety of social roles. For example, a women is expected to play the role of a wife, a mother, a companion and a life-partner. Different roles require different types of behaviour. In families where the traditional role patterns remain strong, conflict may arise when the wife attempts to assume a new role not consistent with the traditional role. Many husbands object to any assumption of authority by their wives in a field they (husbands) consider their own. When such role conflicts persist, marital instablility may be imminent.

Many men beat their wives on flimsy grounds. In some cases, the parents play a significant role in antagonising their son against his wife. They complain against her on trivial matters such as getting up late, being lazy and lethargic, lack of interest in cooking, beating children, disobeying in-laws, etc. The husband also finds himself in a difficult situation, particularly when he is accused of being a henpecked husband. It results in frequent quarrels between the spouses, and the wife is beaten by the husband at times. It leads to strained relations between the husband and wife. We found about 6 percent of such cases is which physical assaults were the main reason of strained relations.

Suppression of pronounced physical deformities or defects at the time of match-making is indeed a serious negligence fought with grave consequences. Quite often, such negligence is the result of the tendency to ignore such defects or keenness to find a match, specially a groom. However, some of these problems may developed after marriage, such as chronic headache, stomach trouble or venereal disease. Such diseases may prohibit the partners to have physical contact. In most cases, the wife is an unfortunate victim. She is too shy to make this fact known; she can not confide or talk it over, and the husband ill-treats her. She may carry a fear that this might bring her martial life to an end. But one can file a divorce suit on the ground of chronic disease which is proved to be of permanent nature and incurable. In our study, about 10 per cent cases were observed in which chronic disease 'was the main reason of strained relations between the spouses.

Family structure and inadequate home life

Decent living conditions play an important role in the success of marriage. Lack of privacy, poor living conditions in overcrowded, cramped joint families can be the major cause of disagreements between spouses. Differences resulting from expectations of goals, values and way of life can develop in strained relations of husband and wife. When privacy is threatened, the wife develops a defensive attitude which is irritable and becomes non-committal in her behaviour towards other family members.

This results in continual mental stress and resentment causing rifts and tensions in the marital relationship. Women coming from nuclear families find it exceedingly difficult to adjust in crowded and cramped living styles of large joint families. In our study there were about 10 percent cases in which it was found upon analysis that impact of the size of family was the primary reason for strained relations between husband and wife.

There were instances, where wide age disparity between the spouses had become the cause of strained relations. The emotional neglect of wife, or husband not taking his wife out for movies etc. affected the home and the home roles to the extent that they developed a feeling that they can't get along. We found 3 per cent such cases in our study in which the wide age difference between the spouses led to varied disagreements between the two.

Marriage unites two persons of opposite sex and enables them to, fulfil their biological need. On marriage, attitudes, and values with respect to the daily patterns of existence emerge. The sexual relationship is one such aspect of marital adjustment. This relationship was found to be severely affected by three factors in our study: (a) illicit relations, (b) impotency and (c) barranness.

No aspect of human behaviour is fraught with greater possibility of personal disorganization than unconventional and illicit sex relations. As Jacgues Barazun has pointed out, "there is a great deal of chaos in contemporary attitudes towards sex.

Rigid notions of sex conduct incorporated in our moral values and laws do not conform to the state of our language and literature, our present day advertising, or our public entertainment. 'Some people do not conform to the concept of chastity as written in holy books and embodied in our moral ideas. The premium on illicit sex conduct is secrecy, and if it is proved or discovered, it may become for a married man or a woman, a sure ground to a suit under adultery to seek divorce. Illicit relation was the cause of strained relations between the spouses as many as 24 percent of the total cases studied in our study.

A complicated and involved expression of personality, difficulty in sexual relationships concerns the problem of impotency. By impotency, we mean the inability of man for coitus. It is the physical incapability of either partner to consumate the marriage. The term impotency is usually applied to men and frigidity to women. Impotency as the cause of strained relations between the spouses in our study was discovered among about 9 per cent cases.

With all exceptions, about 10 to 15 per cent of all marriages in the world are dissolved on the ground of childlessness. For many barrenness is extremely difficult to accept with resignation. In some instances, the attitude and behaviour of parents and in-laws becomes an important aspect of the problem, particularly when the desire for children is strong. Further, it is possible for the husband and wife to blame each other for their childlessness. Then the relationship between the spouses becomes more strained. The partners generally have no knowledge of his or her sterlity. The Hindu philosophy has stressed on the necessity fo

A couple to have children. Infact, Hindu philosophy has laid more stress on having a child, it is considered to be one of the fundamental biological need fulfilled through marriage. It was found in our study that in 4 per cent cases, barrenness was the cause of strained relations between the spouses and ultimately the cause of divorce. Though, barrenness is no longer a legal ground for divorce, although it contributes to the failure of marriage to a large extent.

In the context of marital problems, analysing "personality" is often amorphous, unstable, and frustrating, unless there is a fairly reliable personality diagnosis made through some standardised diagnostic devices. We classified here, 'personality' as a psychological problem if the wife used terms which clearly indicated her belief that the fundamental problem was of personality. There had been two major factors, viz., irritative nature, and domineering nature which contributes to the failure of marital relationships.

Psychological aspects are related to temperament of an individual. It is the combination of genetic qualities in the individual that determines his/her emotional reactions. Temperamental qualities appear to be largely innate. Although they can be subdued, but cannot be eliminated. The person who reacts quickly and irritably can attempt to control the outward expressions of emotions but can not control indignation. Terman has emphasized that "unhappy couples are characterized by such temperamental traits, such as being touchy and grouch; losing temper easily; freighting to get their own way; being critical of others, being often in a stay of excitement, and alternating between happiness and sadness without apparent cause." Irritativeness and domineering nature were the two factors highlighted in our study. The study revealed that the irritative nature of the partners was the major cause of strained relations among 12 percent cases.

Another major personality factor in marital stress is domineering nature of the individuals. The husband shows no emotion about wife and home and exercises more control over wife's behaviour. He even uses techniques of nagging or sulking. The wife is not allowed to run things in her own way or to make decisions as she chooses, and instead has to cater to her husband's wishes.

Individuality or domineering attitude is the right of the person to be the active agent in his own life and select his own values out of the array which were available. Man is governed today by higher integrated systems specially those connected with social goals and value system and the like. These are very essential in playing social and marital roles. The incompatibility arising from such directional traits today are because of the rise and need of certain cultural imperatives. Changing concepts and ideas of the marital relationship require accommodation, integration, and equality in practically every sphere of life such as status, education, interest and outlook.

There is a consciousness setting in Certain values and 'style of life' which calls for ego-involvement. This ego ideal refers to the individual's conception of himself as he would like to be in contrast to what he 'really' is. For instance, individuals educated in the west try to acquire and cultivate a new mental outlook and social status. But this does not stop here.

Such an individual would like his partner to adjust socially and mentally to his 'climate' more for his social and psychological satisfaction, as his wife becomes an outward symbol of his inner craving. But with the log that already exists and where, the partner does not come up to his expectations, there is severe impairment of the ego. Consequently, although such marriage is on the decline it drags on because of a sense of honour." Domineering nature as the cause of strained relations between the spouses in our study, was found among 3 percent of the total cases.

Economic factors

In the present study, poverty, dowry, and the career of wife were the three factors found responsible for conflict between the spouses.

a) *Poverty:* The economic role-obligations of the husband are many. Broadly, we can reduce them to two: (a) providing money with which to support the household, and (b) helping to manage that money with some regard for the needs and desires of members of the family. A husband may fail in one of these or both. With respect to the first category 'non-support', 3 percent wives complained that their husbands did not perform the role of 'Provider'. In most cases, we could not get objective proof that the family was not able to make both ends meet due to husband's failure to provide. In 2 per cent cases, the wives complained that the necessary things could not be purchased when the level of living did not actually appear low. We confined ourselves, however, to the complaints made by the wife, since it was her world that we were attempting to explore.

Similarly, if the wife complained that her husband did not work or he did not bring his salary home, the responses were classified as 'non- supportor'. Generally, the disapproval of the husband in our society is that he fails as a provider' if he fails as manager. As manager, he may spend too much on entertainment, smoking, alcohol, etc. and thereby leaves insufficient money for household needs. We found two per cent of such cases in our study.

(b) *Dowry*: This is a social evil where a constant demand for more and more money from the bride's parents is made. The dowry is given/taken both in cash and kind. However, majority of persons were inclined towards taking dowry in cash. The amount of dowry was usually decided well in advance of the marriage. The dowry that the bride brought was sometimes considered insufficient when the in-laws discovered that the bride's parents were richer than they had expected. The bride was not allowed to keep any part of dowry that they brought with them except for a few pieces of jewellery. Their dowry was, in many cases, utilized to furnish dowry for her sister-in-law. All this had been the main cause of conflicts between the two families. Dowry as the primary cause of conflict was observed among 7 percent of the total cases in our study.

(c) *Wife's career:* We came across 5 percent of the total cases where wife's working career was found to be the main cause of conflict between the spouses.

In a traditional family, the typical pattern of husband-wife relation- ship is, "male dominance and female dependence". The husband primarily enjoys the superior position over the wife and the major decision-making roles are mostly the domain of the husband. The wife tactilly accepts a subservient position in the family and her role in the domestic sphere basically remains complementary. Nonetheless, the spousal relationship rests basically upon meeting the mutual expectations and obligations corresponding to the status of spouses within the family as well as outside it.

If there is any failure or conflict in fulfilling these expectations and obligations, marital relations between the spouses cannot remain unaffected. However, the time factor during which strained relations between the spouses are surfaced or exposed, depends largely on various concomitant factors, social, biological, psychological and economic. Marriage dissolution and divorce are not caused by a single factor. Divorce may be explained in terms of several factors, such as social, biological, psychological and economic.

Islam has made provisions of the dissolution of marriage. Marriage is regarded as a civil contract by Muslim Law and to that extent it can be dissolved by writing a divorce deed. But this is the last resort which primarily the husband has to take, when the wife fails to adjust herself. A man has greater rights than a woman in the mater of divorce in Islam. The man can, of his own accord, divorce the wife under certain conditions, ever against her will. But the wife cannot divorce her husband against his will, unless she has acquired this right by a Sigha (condition) of divorce at the time of the Nikah. The Sigha should be mentioned in the Nikahnama according to the Shias.

She can then demand a divorce (Khula) from the husband but this is also subject to the approval of the husband. According to Muslims, a divorce or dissolution of the marriage contract is meant for the purpose of avoiding the evil consequences of an unhappy marriage. As the Holy Quran says, "Either retain them with humanly or dismiss them with kindness". The contract of marriage may be dissolved in any one of the following ways : (1) by the husband at his will; without the intervention of the court, called Talak, (2) by mutual consent of the husband and wife, without the intervention of the court, called Khula or Mubarat, (3) by a judicial decree at the suit of the husband and wife.

1. *Divorce by Talak*: Any Mohamadan of sound mind who has attained poverty may divorce has wife whenever he desires without assigning any cause. A talak may be effected either (1) orally or (2) by a written document called a Talak-name. But under Shia law a talak must be pronounced orally in the presence of two witnesses. Talak communicated in writing is valid only when the husband is not physically capable of pronouncing it orally. Pronouncement of talak may be either revocable talak dissolves the marriage immediately on its pronouncement, while a revocable one does not dissolve the marriage until the period of Iddat has elapsed, and may at any time be revoked either expressly or implicitly by resuming sexual time be revoked either expressly or implicitly by resuming sexual intercourse. A talak may be effected in any of the following ways:

(a) *Talak Ahasan*: This consists of a single pronouncement of divorce made during Tuhr (period between two menstruation) followed by abstinence from sexual intercourse for the period of Iddat.

(b) *Talak Hasan*: This consists of the pronouncement made during three successive Tuhrs, no intercourse having taken place in between these periods. A Talak Hasan becomes irrevocable and completed on the third pronouncement, irrespective of the Iddat.

Sunni and Shia law, as to Talak Distinguished : (1) Under Sunni law, a talak uttered even under compulsion, fraud, under influence or paroxysm of anger is valid, while under Shia law, an intention to divorce is a necessary element and consequently a Talak pronounced under the foregoing circumstances is not recognized as valid and effective. (2) Under Sunni law, it is not necessary that a talak be pronounced in the presence of any witness while under Shia law it must be pronounced in the presence of two witnesses. (3) Under Sunni law, a talak may be effected either orally or in writing but under Shia law it must be pronounced orally unless the husband is not physically capable of pronouncing it orally.

Khula and Mubarat

A dissolution of marriage by agreement may take the from of Khula or Mubarat. A divorce by Khula (redemption is a divorce with the consent of the husband and at the instance of the wife, in which she gives or agrees to give a sum to the husband for the release from the marriage tie; in fact it is a divorce purchases by her. It is complete and irrevocable from the moment the husband repudiates the wife. A Khula divorce is effect by (a) and offer from the wife coupled with (b) a sum for the same and (c) acceptance of the offer by the husband. Once the offer is accepted it operates as a single irrevocable divorce (talak-t-bain) and its operation is not postponed until the execution of the deed of Khula. Mubarat (Mutual freeing) divorce proceeds from the mutual consent of both the husband and the wife. As the incentive comes from both sides, no return is required from the wife in this from of divorce. The offer may proceed from the wife or it may proceed from the husband, and once it is accepted the dissolution is complete, and it operates as Talak-t-bain (irrevocable divorce) unless it is contracted to the country.

A divorce affected by Khula or Mubarat operates as a release by the wife of her dower or part of dower but this does not affect the husband's liability to maintain her during her Iddat, or to maintain his children by her. Khula and Mubarat Distinguished : In Khula, the wife procures her release by payment of some valuable consideration, though if the wife fails to pay the consideration, the divorce does not become invalid. In Mubarat there is no consideration. In Khula the wife makes the proposal, while in Mubarat either spouse may make the proposal.

The Procedure of Divorce among Shias

The procedure that is usually followed in divorce is that the husband levels charges against the wife before the Mujtahid who calls the wife and tries his utmost to unite them, because in Islam divorce is the last resort. But in spite of his advice, if the husband is not ready for a compromise, he pronounces a Sigha of Talak (Holy Verse regarding divorce) before two witnesses, who should be reliable Adil. The above is the procedure for divorce if the husband divorces his wife.

If the wife becomes impatient of her husband and cannot bear to live with him, she may seek to get rid of him by giving back her dower, or any other additional sum that the husband may propose (Khula).

Usually the sum is a fourth of the dower of the wife. In Khula the husband and wife both appear before the Mujtahid and it is his duty to advise them regarding the bad consequences of a divorce, and two reliable witnesses.

When there is an inclination for divorce on both sides, nothing but the dower need be renounced and this is called Mubarat. In Mubarat also the above procedure is followed. These different types of divorces are subject to the willingness of the husband to grant her a divorce.

The Dissolution of the Muslim Marriage Act of 1939

The Act was passed in order to consolidate and clarify the provisions of Muslim law relating to suits for dissolution of marriage by women married under Muslim law, and to remove doubt as to the effect of the renunciation of Islam by a married Muslim women on her marriage tie. The Act came into force on the 17th March, 1939, and lays down the following grounds for divorce:

1. The whereabouts of the husband are unknown for a period of four years.
2. Failure of the husband to provide for the maintenance of the wife for a period of two years.
3. Sentence of imprisonment on husband for a period of seven years.
4. Failure without reasonable cause to perform marital obligations.
5. Impotency of husband.
6. Insanity of husband.
7. Repudiation of marriage by wife.
8. Cruelty of husband.

Can a husband remarry a divorced wife? According to the Shias, if a man divorces his wife and then marries her again, divorces her again, and remarries her and again divorces her, he in that case cannot remarry her without submitting to the ordeal of her being married to another person and divorced by him. The only can he remarry his divorced wife.

In Mohamadan Law, when a marriage is dissolved by death or divorce, the woman is prohibited from marrying within a specified time. This period is called Iddat, and is the term or period which must elapse before a new marriage is rendered lawful. It is a period of continuance imposed on a woman, on the termination of her marriage in order to establish the paternity of a possible child conceived earlier, during which a woman is expected to live a life of seclusion and abstain from all luxuries.

The observance of Iddat is necessary where cohabitation had taken place before the divorce. If consummation of marriage had taken place and the marriage is dissolved by divorce, then the duration of Iddat is three monthly courses, or, if the woman is pregnant, till delivery. If the marriage is dissolved by death, the period is four months and ten days, or, if the woman is pregnant, till delivery, whichever is longer.

If the marriage is not consummated, Iddat has still to be observed as in the case of death of the husband but not in the case of divorce. Thus Iddat is compulsory for a woman after divorce. During the period of Iddat a divorced woman is forbidden to marry another man. She cannot go out of the house during this period and if going out is unavoidable, she can do so only during the day and not at night.

Besides the necessity for ascertaining the legitimacy of a possible child, another important purpose for fixing a period of Iddat following a divorce is essentially to bring about a reconciliation between the husband and wife. It is the duty of every husband to maintain the divorced wife during the period of her Iddat and bear all her reasonable expenses during this period.

Maintenance and Custody of Children after Divorce

It is the duty of the husband to maintain the children after divorce also, whether the children live with the mother or with him. The mother is entitled to the custody of the children without distinction of sex until they are weaned. During this period which is limited to two years, the children cannot under any circumstances be removed from their mother's care without her consent. After the child has been weaned, its custody, if a male devolves on the father, and if a female, on the mother. The mother's custody of a female child continues upto its seventh year. After she attains that age, the father is entitled to her custody in preference to the mother.

The institution of divorce exists from time immemorial in various forms and in various ages. If marriage is a natural institution, divorce is a counterpart though considered undesirable by every one in every age. A very comprehensive view of divorce has been given by Bertrand Russel who wrote, "Divorce as an institution has been permitted in most ages and countries for certain causes. It has never been intended to produce an alternative to the monogamic family, but merely to mitigate hardships, where, for special reasons, the continuance of a marriage tie was felt to be intolerable".

The law on the subject has been extraordinarily different in different ages and places. Divorces are very rare in the shia community, for two reasons. Firstly, marriages having been initially so well-considered and settled keeping in view of all existing and contingent circumstances, the possibilities of divorce and very rare. In the second place, the traditions of faithfulness in marriage which prevail among the families are such that both parties, and specially the girls, are ready to put up with problems, however difficult, and some how make things agreeable. The general idea is that alliances should be well-considered and once established should be abided by both parties, as divorce defames both.

Similarly, the age of the respondents is also one of the factors for increase of divorce. Elder people generally still regard divorce as the greatest blot on the fair name of the family, while comparatively young respondents do not think so. Out of these 35 cases of divorce, 30 were initiated by the husband; only 5 were demanded from the side of the wife. This shows that girls were more averse to divorce—they were only a seventh of the number of persons seeking divorce.

As the reasons for seeking divorce by the husbands were based on the non-fulfillment of his expectations, the wife could also similarly demand a divorce on the same grounds. The main reasons in this connection were non-maintenance and negligence on the part of the husband, husband's second marriage and undesirable behaviour by the husband. The table further reveals that the main reason in this connection was an economic one i.e., non-maintenance. The other reasons pertain to the behaviour of the husband e.g. second marriage, negligence and undesirable behaviour.

The religious principles about divorce are very strict and the chances of permission to separate are very limited. The process of divorce is also difficult and requires considerable amount of time for arbitration and failing that consideration of the matter by the theological judges, before deciding on the divorce.

Society also disapproves of it and the divorce is a sort of slur for both parties, forboding an unsettled future. It is also not morally desirable, for it entails disintegration of the family and casts an unwelcome shown over the character of both. The impact of Hindu culture has also to a great extent, randered divorce an extremely undesirable course.

Conjugal relations are strained when there is a difference of opinion between the spouses on each other's responsibilities and duties as husband and wife, and when the demands and expectations of the wife or the husband are not fulfilled. Due to the paucity of funds, husbands are at times not able to fuifill the desires of their wives; this results in dissatisfaction and disagreement on both sides. Ultimately, things become unbearable and bring about disruption of the family. This especially happens when there are no children; filial love generally acts as a sort of check against separation.

These cases pertain to the present age, where modern education has changed people's outlook on life. The old spell of persistent unequivocal faithfulness under any circumstances is weakening and people are considering life in its stark reality. The tendency is to become more materialistic and less spiritual, giving rise to degradation of moral values. Another factor is the disproportionate education of boys and girls. Girls who are highly education of boys and girls.

Girls who are highly educated generally believe in equal rights for men and women and therefore fail to adopt that degree of humility required in their dealings towards their husbands. Their air of superiority begets dissatisfaction in the minds of their husbands who may expect unrestrained respect and unqualified and object submission on the part of the wife. Another factor is diminishing economic resources, giving rise to family difficulties and ants which are unbearable to modern girls, as they are generally fond of fashions which require liberal spending and are sometimes a source of nuisance to their husbands, with limited means.

Now fashions are not only common among girls but also among boys. When the demands of fashion of both collide, they give rise to a competitive struggle and ultimately to serious disagreements. Another factor is the growing system of keeping the bride as well as the bridegroom in the bride's family by wealthy people. In such cases a husband does not enjoy the same status of freedom as other, he is reduced to a position subordinate to that of his wife. This ultimately becomes intolerable and he contemplates either separating his wife from her family or separating himself from the wife altogether.

Social Implications of Divorce

The social contract aspect of marriage in Islam has many sides, the chief being sexual relationship. Other aspects include family life, procreation, bringing up of children, companionship, love, sympathy, co-partnership, coopera-tion and division of labour in family management. Thus, the relationship is based on gradually deepening foundation. Some religions treat marriage as a permanent relationship unbreakable throughout one's life so much so that if one dies, the woman specially is required to observe celibacy throughout her life afterwards.

In ancient India, upto the medieval period, the system of *Sati* (consigning oneself to the fire with the dead husband) was prevalent among Hindus, thus avoiding the sufferings which widows are subject to. Lord William Bentinck, with the support of certain India leaders, legislated against the Sati. Today the law disallows it though occasionally reports appear of a woman committing Sati on the death of her husbands. Educated and rational people have been supporting widow remarriage and the practice of Sati is practically unknown. Islam, being based on human nature, takes a more generous and liberal views of natural instincts and allows widow remarriage, it not only allows widow remarriage but makes a provision for divorce also. The latter appears to be a necessity in view of the fact that marriages, though contracted after a good deal of consideration and mutual understanding, sometimes prove unhappy. In such cases it is better to separate if both partners cannot live in harmony and the continuance of the partnership leads to misery. In such cases divorce appears to be the only solution. If marriage is a social necessity, divorce also appears to be an alternative necessity.

According to Islam, divorce is a necessary evil but is inevitable in the interests of both the parties who cannot mutually adjust themselves. Some thinkers are of the opinion that divorce brings about family disintegration. On the other hand, divorce in our opinion, is the result and not the cause of family disintegration and when a family is already disintegrated, separation appears to be the only remedy for the evil. The main social implications of divorce may be stated as follows: the future of the divorced woman, the problems of her maintenance, the support and rearing of children.

So far as the future of the divorced woman is concerned, it is not a very bright one. They are generally looked upon as ineligible for remarriage, first, because of social prejudice and secondly, because they may feel reluctant to remarry. Sometimes people do not want to marry them, preferring widows to divorced women. This generally happens among the Syeds, who do not like divorce for their girls and would rather keep them married without divorce. If, in rare cases, a divorce occurs, the woman remains unmarried. In other Qaums tradition is not so strict and they occasionally remarry although many of them abjure marriage.

It is the duty of every husband to maintain the divorced wife during the period of Iddat. He must bear all reasonable expenses of the divorced wife during this period. It has been found in some cases that when the husband divorces his wife he thinks that he has no duty to perform towards her. In some cases it has also been found that the divorced woman herself leaves the husband's house and goes to that of her guardian, who maintains her.

Respondents' Qaum and occupation regarding their views in connection with the maintenance of divorced woman during Iddat have been examined in this connection. It is the duty of the husband to maintain the children after divorce, whether they are with the mother or with him, because the children belong to the father, and he has the legal as well as religious right to keep them. Respondents' education, and age in relation to their views in connection with the maintenance of the minor children after divorce have been examined in this connection.

A similar difference of opinion appears to arise about the children also. There seems to be some kind of misconception in the minds of some respondents which may be due to the actual and practical circumstances. The position is that divorced women during their period of Iddat are legally and morally to be maintained by their husbands as the replies of the majority of the respondents show. There may be other cases in which the divorced wife is either abandoned or unprovided for by husband or where she, of her own free will, prefers to stay during the Iddat period with her own family. Then the responsibility is shifted from the husband to her guardian.

Those who put the responsibility for her maintenance during the period on her guardians belong to the latter category. So far as her maintenance after the Iddat is concerned, the husband is in no way responsive got it and she has to be maintained at her parents' place. The maintenance of the children is the responsibility of the husband but if he violates his responsibility or if the children are retained and withheld by the divorced wife or her family, they are naturally to be supported by them. In this way a divorce places a woman in a precarious position, throwing her from the family of the husband to her own family. Considering the problem of divorce in its various aspects, it is interesting note that one may be face with serious consequences.

1. In those cases where a permanent and natural distinction towards each other has developed divorce is a necessary evil but may ultimately prove to be good in itself.
2. If only one party is unmanageable, and the other party is the sufferer, it is desirable in that case also to reconcile the unmanageable and end the sufferings of the other person.
3. There many be cases in which a divorce is sought based on selfish motives and for conjugal exploitation, which is a sin. In such cases, divorces must be checked and controlled. Adventurous are not wanting who get themselves married to innocent girls to avail themselves of the dowry and other monetary gains. After gaining their object they seek the first opportunity to leave the girls to their fate. This is highly condemnable.

Thus, a divorce has legitimate as well as dark sides. A divorce is not regarded as a very desirable objective by any society as it besmirches the chapter of both. A divorced man or woman is not highly respected by society because of the stigma attached to it. However, it is not necessary that a person who has not been able to adjust himself or herself with one will not be able to adjust himself or herself to any other, particularly when that person has gone through the consequences of disintegration of the family and he or she has been reduced to a precarious position. Those who do not learn the lesson in the first instance may be careful about their behaviour on a second occasion. In this way, a divorce has its educative value and teachers proper behaviour through its bitter lessons.

However, society in general does not favour divorce, for it causes family disintegration as well as social disorganisation.

Hindus on the whole abhor it and their views have influenced India Muslim society as well. Islam allows divorce but only as a last resort and as a necessary evil. Hindu culture and society teach a woman to look upon her husband as a "deity" to be worshipped by her. Her precepts enjoin her to be so full of devotion and service to her husband that a divorce is unthinkable.

Dowry is not plain buying and selling. Neither it can be waived away in simplistic terms. It has no religious significance but only the sanction of a society that has reduced a woman to an un-productive position and has considered her a gift to man to be sent to him in the most splendid packaging possible.

Today the custom remains as a visible symptom of a deep malaise in society, inextricately knitted up with individual esteem, social pride and prejudice, a symbol of the position of women, the respective roles attribute to men and women and the institution of marriage itself. In a society which is highly divided into social stratification wiping gout a custom which is being practised since, ages, cannot easily be wiped out so easily. The fact remains that in Indian society, so much importance is placed on getting a girl married that parents of unmarried girls are willing to meet almost any demand in order to get their daughters married.

In fact, as long as men and marriage are over-rated in a woman's life, there will be a price to pay if not in dowry, than under other nomenclature. Till women are viewed as individuals worthy of respect in their own right, manifestations like dowry will not cease. Bride is given gifts at the time of marriage, everywhere in the world but the gift settled as dowry before marriage and which equally strangely remains her personal property. Some consider a present to the in laws, a gift to the bridegroom before, at the time and after the marriage. Some see it as premortem inheritance from the bride's family, some as an insurance policy for the pride against any economic crimes. It has also been described as 'Stridhan'. According to Mura Sundaram, "Dowry is disguised, replete with hypocracy picked in pretensions, hidden in a man of social and religious superstition and anarhanisms, thereby guised as a moral system."

Importance of Dowry

Dowry system was not a part and parcel of Indian system. Dowry was introduced with the passage of time. The practice of dowry could be traced to hoary notions of giving valuable gifts to one's daughter at the time of marriage. Notions about the inequality between the sexes from the bed-rock of dowry through which a balance is sought to be brought about in matrimonial relations.

The milieu of newly married a girl faced in the household of her husband has been outlined earlier. In case she has brought along sufficient dowry, she is treated well and with difference. On the other hand, if she has brought a meagre dowry, she is treated indifferently. Dowry is considered the just due to the man and complaints arise when the girl or her family are unable to afford what is demanded.

In Indian society, so much importance is placed on getting a girl married that parents of unmarried girls are willing to meet any demand in order to get their daughters married. For a woman, marriage is a passport to even such a basic thing as being acknowledged as worthy individual.

Ironically enough, women bring a productive member of society but is still accepted only as a bonus alongwith the more 'Valuable material' Assets. She is not sold but buys for herself martyrdom and slavery. Dowry is variously seen as a gift to the bride, strangely settled before marriage and which is equally and strangely does not remain her personal property. Some consider it as a present to the in-laws, some as a means to set up a new home. Some people try to identify it as 'Stridhan' which is not so.

Causes of Dowry

In recent years, the dowry system in India has spread both horizontally and vertically. Horizontally in the sense that it has spread to such regions and communities which, until recently, did not have it and which, in fact, had the bride price system. Vertically, in the sense that there has been a sharp increase in the amount of dowry demanded and given.

Some amount of wealth always changed hands in Indian marriages. This may be bride price in the form of cash or kind, or dowry know as 'Stridhan' among Hindus and as 'Mehar' amongst Muslims, in the from of cash, utensils, jewellery, etc. It was willingly given and accordingly accepted as part of Stridhan. It was not extorted or demanded as in case of dowry.

Educational inequality between males and females for a variety of reasons, a greater proportion of males than females in Indian are educated. Although literacy is not the same thing as education, the different in the proportion of literacy among males and females has been increasing steadily. For example, in 1901, the production in difference of 9.7 per cent. But in 1981, the proportion of literates was 46.7 per cent among males and 24.9 per cent among females, resulting in a difference of 21.8 per cent. It is axiomatic that greater the difference between the educational attainment of prospective brides and grooms, the larger are the dowries demanded and given.

Although, it is difficult to produce hard data, it is common knowledge that there exists, economic inequality among marriageable males and females. Education being equal, males with moveable/immovable property, demand a larger dowry. Likewise, males with an education that is likely to enable them to earn more money, demand a larger dowry. Medical and engineering graduates fall in this category.

Status of women in many parts of the world must have been one of more bondage until the advent to modern ideas of freedom and equality. According to a recent issue of the Economist, in most of the 19th century, a British husband and sole rights over his wife's property and their children. He could chastise her out without a penny. Not until the married Women's Property Act of 1982 could see own, anything separately. Even then, she had no claims on his wealth.

In our own country, out attitude to women has been ambivalent indeed. It has been full of contradictions. Hinduism has evolved over the centuries integrating the beliefs and attitudes of diverse racial and cultural groups. There is no single Hindu view of women valid for all time. The ancient law-given "Manu" proclaimed that, "where they are honoured, there the God rejoice, and that where they are not honoured, there all rites are fruitless." If the Hindu law-giver was harsh in some respects, they were liberal and far in advance of their than in others.

The Dharmashastra nowhere mention the giving or taking of dowry and its is doubtful if there is sanction for burning or torture of widows. The Mahabharat says. " He who sells his son or gives his daughter for a price, goes to hell." The idea of Dharmpatni cannot obviously imply bondage or subservience for the wife. It means the pursuit together of a whole life. Manu said, "Let there be mutual fidelity ending in death alone.....This in a few words should be recognised as the highest law of duty for man and wife. Dowry has no religious sanction and it is not very old. In fact, it seems a recent phenomenon grown out of greed. It is also interesting to note that brides are often driven to suicide, not by the husband but by the mother-in-law or other close relations.

Dowry is not of very ancient origin. It assumed abnormal proportion in later times only. Among the ancient Hindu, the custom of dowry did exist in simpler form though under different names. This custom of giving presents at the time of marriage of custom prevails in India unheadedly. Parents of the girl give presents to the bride. The rational behind these presenting of gifts is the affection of the parents towards their children but in due course of time the said custom has grown rigid and became associated with social status and family prestige leading to great social evil. Everyday we read in newspapers, many a cases of Bride burning or dowry deaths for bringing insufficient or no dowry. These is hardly a day when newspapers do not have several reports of murders by dowry seekers. This social evil has taken a worse turn.

Prohibition of Dowry Act

An act to prohibit the giving or taking dowry has been enacted by Parliament on 20th may 1961 viz. "The Dowry Prohibition Act, 1961" which makes giving, taking and abetting of dowry punishable u/s 3 of the said Act, which lays that any person after commencement of this Act gives or take or abets the giving or taking of dowry, he shall be punishable with imprisonment for a term which shall not be less than six months but which may extend to ten thousand rupees or the amount of the value of such dowry, whichever is more.

Provided that the court may for adequate and special reasons to be recorded in the judgment, impose a sentence of imprisonment for a term of less than six months.

(2) Nothing Sub-section (i) shall apply to, or in relation to-

(a) presents which are given at the time of a marriage to the bride (without any demand having been made in that behalf):

Provided that such presents are entered in a list maintained in accordance with the rules made under this Act.

(b) presents which are given at the time of marriage of the bridegroom (without any demand having been made in that behalf).

Provided that such presents are entered in a list maintained in accordance wit the rules made under this Act. Provided further that where such presents are made by or on behalf of the bride or any person related to the bride, such presents are of a customary nature and the value thereof is not excessive having regard to the financial status of the person by whom or on whose behalf such presents are given.

Offences under this Act have been made cognizable and non-compoundable for certain purposes. Some special provisions to supplement Dowry Prohibition Act 1961, to cope with cruelty to married women culminating in Dowry Deaths by suicide or murder to helpless married women have been introduced by Criminal Law Amendment Act 46 of 1983.

By introducing a new section 498 in I.P.C cruelty to a woman by her husband or any relative of her husband has been made punishable with imprisonment for a term which may extend to three years and also with fine. Provision has been made for inquiry by Executive Magistrate and for Post-mortem in all cases when a woman has within seven years of her marriage committed suicide or died in circumstances raising a reasonable suspicion that some other person has committed an offence.

Amendment in Indian Evidence Act

It has been drastically amended to provide that where women have committed suicide within a period of seven years from the date of her marriage and it is shown that her husband or any relations to her husband had subjected her to cruelty the court may presume that such suicide has been abetted by her husband or by such relative of her husband under Act, 1983.

Dowry and Cruelty against Women

Bride price was devised centuries ago and was thought to be demeaning to human dignity and the honour. A sure form of marriage that was characterised by the custom was considered unacceptable. In fact dowry seems to be just another manifestation of the age of opportunism that we live in with exploitation as the watchward.

What better way of making easy money than to ransom, conditioned and decidedly proportioned to the amount paid to add insult to injury today in accordance with the today's progressive norms of society, a girl must not only be well-education, but also a worthy working girl is preferred. And if parents are not exhausted enough by this, there is the request for decent marriage. This is why that the birth of a girl if treated with a calamity in an average Indian family. The menance of dowry in all its insidious forms is essentially an urbanised evil originated from material greed.

Justice Krishna Iyer has pointed out that many a times women are sent to the lock up on charges to deprive them of property share or to get rid of them from the scene, when they become inconvenient.

Wife beating syndrome is quite common in India. It is clearly associated with social pattern of the society where family fued excessive alcoholism and frequent demands of subsequent dowry installments are quite common. Any bye-passer can hear a wailing, a quiet wailing, moaning and groaning through the closed doors can be heard in most of the Indian homes. Wife beating is in fact one of the most accepted crimes committed against women. It exists most in slums and amongst working class. In fact, now it is gradually creeping amongst middle class and rich families.

Violence in the family exists generally in a situation where the woman is totally in a situation where she is completely dependent on the person who physically assaults her. It is a strange situation in which women and often the children too, live in fear ad terror, particularly when the woman is completely dependent on the person who physically assaults her. It is a strange situation to which the women and often the children too, live in fear and terror when the victims approach police and police in turn normally discourage them.

The fact remains that after reporting the matter to the police, the women concerned knows that she to go back to same house with a cruel husband obviously waiting for her and if the man knows that a complaint has been made, he may get even more violent. Then there are children who may become husbands, target if the mother protests too much. An Indian woman would rather accept cruelty against herself than see it perpetrated on her children.

The life of a beaten woman is isolated and under constant fear. So far as this has been an unspoken problem, hidden behind shame and embarassment. A problem, for which there is yet no solution, no place for the women to go, no understanding, no legal support.

The law dealing with wife beating has been defined in Sec. 498 A in these words, "whoever being the husband, or the relative of the husband of a woman, subjects such woman to cruelty, shall be punished with imprisonment for a term which may extend to three years and shall also be liable to fine". But the question arises, is who will bell the cat? Nobody is going to volunteer to walk to a police station to lodge a complaint about a neighbour or a relation beating his wife and even if one goes to the Police Station, it is doubtful whether police will take the eudgles and investigate the matter with required promptness and dedication.

Violence in the family rarely arouses the social concern it deserves. Aggressive behaviour on the part of the husband towards his wife is largely overlooked and even tolerated owing to traditional notions arising from the patriarchal family structure. Violence against women can be sub-divided into two broad groups:

(a) they may fail victim to general crimes (theft, murder, cheating, etc.) or to crimes specific in relation to women (molestation, assault, rape, etc.) and

(b) they may be subjected to violence in the family which may or may not attract official notice.

Suddenly, violence against women is on the rise in the land of Manu, where women are honoured, there the gods rejoice. Today, the frequency of newly married woman being burnt to death in many urban areas is rapidly rising. This has caused an alarm and lower agencies have come in her heavy criticism for their failure to prevent this. Law is supposed to control and harmonise individual and group behaviour. Is it biased against women or does it have shortcomings inherent in it because of which those who commit crimes against them go unpunished? In order to project the status of women, the Widow Re-marriage Act, 1956, the Hindu Marriage Act, 1955 and the Hindu Succession Act, 1956 may be readily cited in this regard. The practice of dowry has also not escaped legislative attention in 1961, the Dowry Prohibition Act was included in the Statute book. Originally giving and taking dowry was a non-cognizable offence, but through a subsequent amendment the offence has been made cognizable.

A view has also been taken that law enforcement agencies have been somewhat dragging their feet in processing such cases. The police should be doubt probe more thoroughly into the death of a recently married woman and the prosecution should be more vigorous and courts more innovative in the interpretation of the law.

However, the point should not be lost sight of that all these agencies function under a set of given rules and come into the picture well past the preventive state. Whatever prevention influence they exert is mostly indirect. As such by streamlining them, we may be trying to remove the defect without paying due attention to the underlying cases, and hence a significant solution seems beyond sight.

The Dowry Prohibition Act has been variously described as a negative, limited penal and impractical Act, one which has not achieved its objective. According to Sec. 2 of the Act "any property or valuable security" given at the time of marriage, unless made as consideration for marriage will not be termed as dowry. The Act does not include any of the womens' objects like Sofa-sets, Television, Refrigerators, Cars, Jewellery and such items which accompany or even precede a bride into her home. The concept and definition of dowry itself is thus narrow and limited.

The Dowry Prohibition Act, 1968

Sec. 4 of the Dowry Prohibition Act lays down penalty for demanding dowry: "If any person demands directly or indirectly from the parents or other relations, or the guardians of a bride or bridegroom as the case may be, any dowry, he shall be punishable with imprisonment for a term which shall not be less than six months, but which may extend to two years and fines which may extend to Rs.1,00,000". Provided that the court may, for adequate and special reasons to be mentioned in the judgment, impose a sentence of imprisonment for a term less than six months.

Under Section 3 taking and giving dowry is similarly punishable.

Criminal Laws

Indian Penal Code, Section 498 deals with a husband of a woman subjecting her to cruelty. Whoever being the husband or the relative of the husband of a woman subjects such woman to cruelty, shall be punished with imprisonment for a term which may extend to three years and shall be punished with imprisonment for a term which may extend to three years and shall be liable to fine.

Explanation—For the purpose of this section cruelty means:

(a) Any wilful conduct which is of such a nature as is likely to drive the woman to commit suicide or to cause grave injury or damage to life, limb or health (Whether mental or Physical) of the woman, or

(b) Harassment of the woman where such harassment is with a view to coercing her or any persons related to her to meet any unlawful demand for any property or valuable is on account of failure to meet such demand.

Code of Criminal Procedure Sec. 174 - Sub-section (3):

(i) when the case involved is a suicide by a woman within seven years of her marriage; or

(ii) the case relates to the death of a woman within seven years of marriage in any circumstances raising a reasonable suspicion that some other person committed an offence in relation to such woman; or

(iii) the case relates to the death of a woman within seven years of her marriage and any relative of the woman has made a request in this behalf; or

(iv) there is any doubt regarding the cause, of death; or

(v) the Police Officer for any other reason considers it expedient to do so.

He shall, subject to such rules as the State Government may prescribe in this behalf forward the body with a view to its being examined, to the nearest Civil Surgeon or other qualified Medical-man appointed in this behalf by the State Government, if the state of the weather and the distance admit of its being so forwarded without risk of such purification as the road, as would render such examination useless.

Indian family is generally viewed as an arena of love, cordiality, gentleness and solidarity. The religious texts and commentaries are cited to support this contention. However, there has always been a dichotomous difference between normative pattern ordained in the religious texts and the actual behaviour pattern. Further, there were two codes of conduct: Shishtachara, normative pattern of the elites and Lokachara, pattern for the general masses.

Grihya Sutras give us an excellent insight into the ceremonies and rituals associated with the home life in ancient India. The vernashrama-dharma scheme of life clearly indicate the singnificance of Garhastha over other stages of life. The

Dharmasutras of Gautama and Baudhayana hold that there is really one ashrama viz that of the householder and that the other ashramas are inferior to that of the householder, Gautama further declares: 'the householder is the source of all other ashramas'. Manu reiterates the same sentiment under a different contexts just as all big and small rivers find support in a resting place in ocean, so men of all ashramas find support in the householder'. The householder was expected to give charity liberally and to clear three debts he owed to Gods, Risis and Ancetors by jajna, study and progeny.

Family as an institution in ancient India laid down the principles which regulated the relationship between husband and wife and parents and children. A man as a husband had certain responsibilities towards his wife. A husband was to act as a provider and was called upon to cohabit with his wife. Failure to perform such roles and responsibilities would attract punishment.

The husband was also required to provide identity, leadership and physical protection to his wife. Along with these duties a husband had certain rights and privileges. The husband has complete control over the mind and body of his wife. Without his consent a wife had no right to perform even a religious act. Husband had the right to use physical corrective methods over his erring wife which was the same as those possessed by a teacher over a pupil or a father over a son, viz., he could administer beating with a rope or a thin piece of bamboo on the back but never on the hand.

Kautilaya also endorses husband's right to beat his wife of refractive nature. He allows the husband to beat his wife, either with a bamboo bark or with a rope or with a palm of hand on her hips. A wife on the other hand had only duties. The foremost duty of a wife was to honour and serve her husband. She must always stay with him even in adverse situations.

The wife was completely secluded from outside contacts. It was only with the permission of her husband, that she was permitted to move out from her husband's house. Failure to observe these restrictions attracted censor, social degradation, humiliation and punishment.

The husband-wife relationship was not based on love, affection, mutual give and take and on equalitarianism the relationship was marked by authoritarianism and submissiveness. Wife was not only secluded from outside contacts but was looked at with suspicion.

Kautilaya, while advising the King for his safety contended that the king should make necessary arrangements for his personal safety firstly from his wives only then he would be able to maintain the security of his kingdom Kautilaya further demanded from the king: 'when in the interior of the harem, the king shall meet his queen only when her personal purity was vouch-safed by an old and reliable maid servant.

Such dictates establish the fact that wife was not relied upon. When tile relationship between husband and wife is marked by suspicion, the question of developing close, personal and intimate relationship does not arise.

After having described in brief the nature of husband-wife relationship that prevailed in ancient India, let us now highlight the main sources of intra family tensions, particularly between the spouses.

Polygyny

From very ancient times one of articles of faith was that a man was born with dents, that he owed three debts to gods, sages and ancestors and that by performing religious duties, studenthood and by procreating sons he freed himself from those three debts respectively. Rg Prays : Kautilaya also gives greater importance to children. He even prescribes punishment to those who become ascetic but are still in the age of compilation. These contentions can be further supported if we look at the goal of the life of a woman. Vishnu Dh.S declares, that the goal of the life of woman was to get married and procreate sons.

In case of her failure to bear a male child, the husband was allowed to go for polygamous relationship. The ancient Indian literature on Polygyny is not unanimous. Another school of thought allowed polygyny for the sake of getting a male child. Manu and Yaj both allow a husband to marry another woman if his previous wife gives birth to female children only. The third school does not allow a man to seek additional wives on flimsy grounds. Ap.Dh.S declares that when a man has a wife who is endowed with dharma and progeny he shall not marry another wife.

Kautilaya Lakes up a conciliatory approach. He allows second marriage under certain conditions that is, he has no male child and can financially maintain them. No doubt, Kautilaya was not against Polygyny, nevertheless, he did visualize the negative consequences.

There was a rivalry and competition among different queens of the king. For the purpose of winning over his love, some type of medicinal drugs were applied to the person of the king to secure his love. Kautilaya cited a number of cases in which the king was killed by his own queens because of jealousy and rivalry. Ramayana stands as a testimony to this fact that polygyny was a major source of tension in the family.

We find a number of instances in which the vows of marriage fidelity were violated. Sex violation was one of the main criteria of tension between husband and wife. The adulterous behaviour pattern on the part of a man and a woman was severely sanctioned. Caut. prescribes that a wife who violates the chastity must undergo a penance.

But she should be kept under guard and be given food. Vasistba opines that the wives of Brahmans, Kastriyas and Vaisyas who commit adultery with Sudra may be purified by a penance in case no child is born. While talking about the abandonment of an adulterous wife Vasistha says that only four types of wives are to be abandoned viz. one who has intercourse with husband's pupil, husband's guru, who attempts to kill her husband and who commits adultery with a man of degraded caste. These references clearly indicate that a woman was not to be abandoned the ground of adultery except in cases where she had extra-marital relations with a man of low caste.

The later authorities deprive a woman found guilty of adultery of rights and authority but allowed her to be accepted back after her menses. A woman becomes pure from adultery when she has her monthly period after adulterous relations, but if she conceives in adulterous intercourse, she may be abandoned.

VedaVyasa says that a wife who is guilty of adultery should be kept in the house but void of her rights of associating in religious and conjugal matters and of her rights over property and be treated with scorn, but when she has her monthly course after the act of adultery, the husband should allow her the usual rights of a wife as before. Santi-parva and Manu are more harsh to a woman who has intercourse with a low caste man. She is to be punished by the king with being devoured by dogs. These references clearly indicate that adultery on the part of a wife did not give an absolute authority to the husband to abandon her unless she had such relations with a low caste the consequences of the act is conception. Further no punishment have been specified for the husband for violating marriage fidelity.

Kautilya's stand on the issue of adultery is somewhat different in which he specifies different type of punishments for both men and women. While talking about sex deviance he demands constraints over the organ of senses which he has labelled as six enemies-lust, anger, greed, vanity, haughtiness and over-joy. He cites number of cases where failure to put restraint over he organ of senses have led to doom not only of the king but also his kingdom. For adulterous relation Kautilaya holds a man more responsible than a willing woman. Kautilya specifies punishment for adultery, when a woman voluntarily yields herself for adultery her cars and nose shall be cut off or she be required to pay a fine of 500 panas and the adulterer shall pay double the above fine.

Kautilya also specifies punishment to those who conceal the act of adultery. Kautilaya contends: I when a man falsely accuses another of having committed whereas in reality the latter is guilty of adultery the complainant shall be fined 500 panas. He who lets off an adulterer by receiving gold shall pay a fine equal to eight times the value of the gold received. Punishment for adulterous relations with a person of low caste attracted capital punishment. Kautilaya opines that any woman who yields herself to a slave, a servant or a hired labourer shall be put to death. On the other hand if a man of high cast commits adultery with a woman of low cast the punishment was not that severe. Kautilaya contends that a man who commits adultery with a woman of law caste shall be banished with prescribed mark branded on his forehead or shall be degraded to the caste of the woman. The adulterous relations among the lower segments of the society were perceived differently. In such cases Kautilaya opines that a Sudra who commits adultery with a woman of low caste shall be put to death while the woman shall have her ears and nose cut off. It seems that adultery with a nun was not taken that seriously. Kautilya contends: adultery with a nun shall be punishable with a fine of 24 panas while the nun who submits herself shall also pay a similar fine Punishment for adultery varied according to the status of the man and the woman; Kautilaya specifies differential punishment when he contends:

A Kshatriya who commits adultery with an unguarded Brahman woman shall be punished with the highest amercesement; a Vaisya doing the same shall be deprived of the whole of property, and a Sudra shall be burnt alive bound round in mats. Whoever commits adultery with queen of the land shall be burnt alive in a vessel. From the references cited it is clear that Kautilaya prescribed different punishments for the same crime.. The members of the twice born were accorded lesser punishment for adultery in comparison with the lower segments of the society. Kautilaya does not only hold the women responsible for adulterous behaviour but specifies more sever punishments for men who were treated as a party to such relationship.

The most important feature in Kautilaya's writing on adultery is that he advocates that the circumstances and conditions under which adultery is committed have to be taken into account while determining the guilt of the party. The women who submit themselves willingly were looked down upon. We notice that Kautilaya makes a provision for lesser punishment to those who were forced into such type of relationship ? It if for this reason that he demands adultery should be proved keeping in view the statements of the parties as well as circumstantial evidences. Kautilaya while talking about the causes of dissension allows a woman to cause the death of her violator with poison who had violently carried her off at night. In an other context Kautilaya is of the opinion that in a family in which a father had sexual intercourse with his daughter-in-law or a brother with the wife of another brother, there would be quarrel between father and son and brother and brother. Kautilaya has made these types of observations for the sake of eliminating seditious ministers, never the less, it indicated the prevalence of adulterous relations. For the purpose of sowing the seeds of dissension in an other context Kautilaya advocates that a mendicant women may tell a chief who is fond of his wife:

This chief, proud of his youth, has sent me to entice your wife, being afraid of him, I have taken with me his letter and jewellery, your wife is free from sin, secret steps should be taken against him, and I am very anxious. For the same purpose Kautilaya says that a woman, disguised as the minister's wife may tell the prime-minister: 'the King is troubling me, and an ascetic woman has brought to me a letter and jewellery'. It is obvious from these contentions that adulterous relations were motivated for the sake of lust, love and wealth and they were the weaknesses of man amid women.

Adultery committed during the long absence of the husband has been perceived differently by Kautilaya. He opines that a relative or a servant of an absentee husband may take his wife of loose character under his protection. If her husband on return, entertains no objection, both the protector and the woman shall be acquitted. If he raises any objection the woman shall have her ears and nose cut off while her keeper shall be put to death as an adulterer.

Adultery was quite common and to check such type of sex deviance differential punishments were prescribed keeping in view the social status of the adulterer and adulteress. Kautilaya specified punishments for both men and woman but advocated that instead of depending upon the resultant situation one should take into account the circumstances which led to adultery. Consistent with the rule of hypergamous marriages a man belonging to lower caste having adulterous relations with a woman of higher caste was accorded highest punishment.

Additionally, adultery was a source of family quarrel, tensions and dissensions. In short, extra-marital sex relationship were looked down upon and were one of the main causes of conflict between husband and wife. Kautilaya has only specified punishments for such behaviour pattern but has not indicated the future of such women as specified by the Smrti writers who indicated that adultress women should go through certain penances but should be accepted back after her monthly course.

There was another source of tension between husband and wife which related to their personality configuration. We have already stated that the marriage of the children came under the domain of elder kinsmen and the parties were married, particularly the girls, at lower age group. As individuals they may develop their own likings and dislikings and which may not be congruent with the life partner or may develop liking for some one other than one's own life partner. Further, by living together they may come to know about the weaknesses of each other or failure to come up to the expectations of the other which may lead to conflict, hatred and enmity.

Kautilya, while talking about enmity between husband and wife states: A woman, who hates her husband, who has passed the period of seven turns of her menses and who loves another, shall immediately return to her husband both the endowment and jeweller she has received from him, and allow him to lie down with another woman.

A man, hating his wife, shall allow her to take shelter in the house of a mendicant woman, or of her lawful guardians or of her kinsmen. This statement of Kautilya highlights the following facts:

(1) There were occasions when husband and wife used to hate each other (2) there were chances where a wife would love someone other than her husband, (3) men and women

were not treated at par (4) In case a wife hates her husband she would return endowment and jewellery to her husband and would allow him to have sex with another woman.

On the other hand when a husband hates his wife she would be put under the custody of someone but there was no provision that she could go with her lover and could have sexual relations according to her liking.

3

Dowry Death

Dowry related violence in contemporary society can be understood as an issue arising out of the socio-cultural construction of the images and the role of women in the institution of marriage. By the same implication, to solve such problems, one cannot turn to private solutions but one has to adhore to social policies and institutional alternatives. In this paper an attempt will be made to review the state of knowledge base in the field of family violence, with a specific purpose to understand the nature, extent, and factors associated with dowry related violence.

The problem of family violence, especially violence towards women, is not a new one and evidence about the incidence can be found throughout historical records of any culture. However, awareness about the extent and nature of these issues came to the forefront during 1970s in USA as a result of the National Family Violence Surveys.

In India, it was only during the early 1980s, in the wake of dowry and related problems, that crimes against women came to be recognised as an important social problem.

The urgency of family violence as an area of research for sociologists and the difficulties involved in studying such a sensitive area, and the low base rate of samples available are responsible to some extent due the limited level of the critical development and the, constraints of causal models put forward to explain family violence. As far as India is concerned, scholarly literature on violence in the family is virtually nonexistent. Even the statistical indices used in this country do not give us any estimate of the incidence of violence toward women.

Research studies on family violence in the west started with an initial focus on the incidence, patterns and factors associated with the phenomenon. Later, in the 1980s, their focus shifted to questions about causal models to explain family violence, consequences of violence for victims and evaluations of various treatment and preventive pro- grams designed to help the victims. While early studies adopted single-factor approach to explain domestic violence, with the gathering of evidence in the later period, the approaches became more and more eclectic.

The Feminist, Marxian and other critiques on the status of women, primarily sought to explain the roots of family violence as connected with structural and ideological roles of men and women and their asymmetrical power relationships both inside and outside the family. In capitalist countries, according to their argument, women's oppression is not only derived from their role as a wage earning labourer but also as a mother, wife, domestic labourer and child rearer. Very little emperical research, however, has emerged from these perspectives, as they were usually abstract in nature.

Of the several theories developed to explain and verify factors associated with family violence and wife abuse, on by some have relevance to our present discussion. They are;

resource theory, exchange theory, structural-stress theory, and Straus's behaviourist systems model.

A resource theory proposes that a person with more resources at his command plays a dominant role of man in the family and conversely a husband with fewest resources resorts to violence to compensate his loss of dominant role. Whereas according to exchange theory, the use of violence by a person is guided by the extent of cultural tolerance by using violence against women in a society and by the principles of costs and rewards for that behaviour. If legal and social sanctions would make such a behaviour risky, then individuals would think twice before resoring to violence.

According to the former theory, violence is a product of socially structured stress such as low income, illness, unfulfilled expectations etc., and violence is used in such contexts if its use is an accepted response to stress. The broad line of argument of the latter theory is that violence is learned and reinforced in the socio-cultural context and that violent spouses normally have violent home backgrounds.

Furthermore, Gelles and Straus noted that the social organisation of the family itself make it a violent-prone interaction setting with its characteristics such as intimacy, privacy, stress, inequality with regard to age and sex of the members, and ratio of time spent in the family living.

The above perspectives throw some light in understanding dowry related crimes. For instance, the crimes appear to be a product of socially structured expectations about dowry giving, the inferior status of woman and consequently the low bargaining power of the woman and her parents, the growing urban consumerism among lower and middle class sections of the society and the lack of effective legal and social sanctions against such crimes.

However, as these theories were developed in the west, they were primarily confined to the issues of violence between spouses or one actor using violence against other members of the family such as children, grannies etc. Dowry related violence on the otherhand, is peculiar to our country and largely in a culture-specific behaviour, where, besides the husband, normally his kin also join together in persecuting the bride. The culpability of girl's parents also cannot be ruled out in some cases.

Moreover, it is not yet clear from the available studies, whether dowry is a causative factor or a factor which precipitates the already simmering dissatisfaction in other areas of marital life of the couple, thereby leading to harassment of women for more dowry.

A few studies have made a mention of dowry related violence as a manifestation of lower-class frustration. In view of the non-representativeness of the cases studied, such statements need further verification. It is infact also necessary to study the predisposing factors in the family such as the low income, the unemployment, the family pathology, and the personality disorders of family members to verify whether problems relating to dowry cause or contribute to violence toward women.

Therefore, it is still too early to come to any valid generalisations about the nature of this phenomena and at present only a general assessment regarding the situation can be made from the available data.

First, a definition of dowry related violence is necessary for several reasons. Research in this area is based only on official reports of cases that come to public attention. To a large extent agencies like police, courts, anti-dowry cells etc., construct the 'incidence' of dowry related violence according to the definitions they use, which may vary, obviously leaving many undetected or uncovered instances of such violence. Therefore, a uniform definition of dowry related violence will have consequences not only for estimating extent, forms, and causes of dowry related violence but also help researchers studying the phenomena to identify subjects and to draw samples from a much wider population of cases.

Nominally, violence can be defined as an act carried out with the intention or perceived intention of physically hurting another person. The hurt maybe emotional injury or even material deprivation. This definition also includes harassment, cruelty as well as death caused by such behaviour. Thus; persistent demands for dowry, even though unintentional; against the woman or her kin, leading to the C, oppressive conduct by the spouse and/or by the in-laws toward the woman resulting in her harassment, death, or in commission of suicide by her can be termed as dowry related violence.

The social context

Evidence suggests that the institution of dowry is closely associated with the rise in industrial capitalism and the commercialisation of economy and consequent wealth-based status competitions. Dowry is serving as a means to a family to make a public display of its social status on the occasion of daughter's marriage.

It is tied to such economic organisation of society where men are owners of resources, and active contributors to the economy and where women secluded from productive work are confined to the dependent roles of wife and mother.

In India after Independence there has been a marked increase in the social and economic inequalities as a result of the superimposition of the market economy and capitalist development on pre-capitalist structures. This led to the emergence of new sections of elite and status competitions among them where dowry, expenditure, rituals and conspicuous consumption assumed importance. Western education, and access to education and employment with a more positive bias towards the males, coupled with the growing urbanisation made men socially and culturally superior to women thereby aggravating the dependency status of women. "Thus a marriage is.... a comparative weighing of status factor that is built into the process.... a woman takes heavy dowry along with her to minimise her dependency status".

Dowry understandably is not a one time payment at the time of marriage. Instead, it opens up a series of expensive rituals, gift giving, customary honour to groom and his kin which continue even long after marriage on different occasions. Added to this, the marriage expenditure has also to be borne by the bride's family.

Now a days, dowry is mostly paid in cash to the groom's parents and as a consequence the bride usually will have no control over the dowry she brought along. As a result, after misappropriating dowry, the in-laws may feel that they can make further demands to the girl for additional dowry.

In fact, majority of the girls parents are not opposed to dowry and other payments in principle; complaints arise only when the parents are unable to meet or afford what is demanded. With the entire mass media oriented towards promoting the mind- less consumerism, marriages are made and broken for such items as cars, scooters, TVs, refrigerators, and washing machines..... A boy who does not get any of these is ridiculed by his friends and colleagues and inability to bring these things may give rise to the bride being harassed, sent to her parent's place, or even burnt to death.

The social pressures thus built up, play an important role and parents of the girls yield to the demands made by the groom's family since they are aware that there lies behind the demands, the usually unspoken weapon, 'unspoken because it does not need to be spelt out, is harassment of the bride after marriage...'

Thus the larger framework of dowry custom, its patterns of practice, and the ambivalent public attitudes about the practice provide aground for expectations, considerations, and obligations for interacting families. Such a frame work is therefore potentially stress-laden because actions of individuals and families are evaluated and tested in this context and families failing to fulfil'or not falling in line with, expected norms will have to face anger or frustration from the other party.

Identifying the specific contexts of dowry practice that give rise to persecution of woman is rather difficult as crises in marriage may be because of several other factors such as personalities of the spouses, their compatibility, unrealistic expectations, differences in socio-economic backgrounds of the spouses, alcohol, jelousy etc. As mentioned earlier, dissatisfactions over dowry can either result in the presecution of the bride or aggravate the already existing marital discontent unrelated to dowry. Dasgupta and his associates observed that dowry related problems usually arise out of three contexts such as failure to pay the remaining part of dowry, inability to fulfil extra demands made by the bridegroom's family and the general dissatisfaction of groom's family about the gifts or items given by the girl's parents.

Several other reasons may also contribute to exacerate this problem. The fact that the bride is young, less educated, dependent and is a stranger in the husband's family, besides the external constraints, make her feet entrapped after marriage, leaving her with two options either to escape the persecution from husband and in-laws, or to seek help from outside.

Sometimes the girl's parents may make false promises or part payments of dowry fearing that the girl may remain unmarried, resulting in delayed payments or failures to pay the -remaining part of dowry. Hypergamy and high dowries are both ideologically and functionally linked. Moreover an element of unpredictability cannot be ruled out in the demands made by groom's family, there by causing confusion and distress to bride's parents. Estimates of incidence range regarding dowry related violence toward women is difficult to glean from the available census data. The statistics provided by the Home Ministry regarding dowry deaths helps us to some extent in assessing the prevalence of this phenomenon in our country. Apart from these officially reported cases, there are a number of cases which could have gone unreported.

The nature of dowry related-violence

Investigations exploring dowry related harassment and deaths are not many. At present, journalistic articles, though they have methodological limitations, form an important source to assess the nature and extent of this phenomenon.

Almost all the available studies mentioned above are based on 'caught cases', i.e. the cases that came to the notice of police or social service agencies and on sample populations which are relatively small and non representative.

The low base rate, the private nature of the family, and the area studied being sensitive make it difficult, if not impossible, to explore this phenomenon, arid to draw valid and reliable conclusions. We shall keep in view these observation's while surveying the available studies.

Victims of dowry related crimes have certain common characteristics. Law Commission has identified certain factual components of 'dowry death' such as the brides are mostly young, dependent, less educated, and that in a majority of the cases the death or suicide of the bride are reported as accidents kitchen in.

Several studies indicated about the age, dependent status and lack of education of dowry victims. Similarly Gautam and Trivedi found that the women were mostly young, less educated, dependent on husbands or in-laws and that the deaths were mostly due to bum injuries. The means adopted to murder or harass the bride are diverse. If the mode of death is through bums, poisoning, or drowning, the nature of harassment of the bride may take such forms as causing physical and mental torture, humiliation, confining her to a lonely place without giving food etc., Administering electric-shocks, nagging, branding, and bettering have also been reported as methods employed to torture the bride.

The methods adopted by brides for commission of suicide Were reported as burning, hanging, drowning or-taking poison. In a majority of deaths due to bum injuries, the use of kerosene has been reported either for commission of suicide or murder of the bride by in-laws.

Persons participating in dowry related violence against the bride are found to be mostly husband, mother-in-law and sibs of husband. According to Gautam and Trivedi, in a majority of the cases the husband and the mother-in-law of the victim had played a leading ròle in planning and executing the crime. It appears from the data that the marital disharmony or dissatisfaction relating to dowry surfaced largely during the early years of marriage. However, it cannot be construed as specific to victims of dowry related violence, since studies in other cultures also indicated that eruption of Violence in a marriage usually took place in the early years of marriage.

As regards dowry related Crises in a marriage, the building up of tension on the bride probably would be gradual, the husband's family making such persistent and determined demands for dowry on the girl that ultimately suicide becomes the last refuse for her. After a period of, say 5 to 7 years however, the marriage seems to be less prone to such Crises.

Most of the dowry related crimes and harassment are well planned executed within closed doors of a house by a group of members of family. As such gathering evidence about such crimes is rather a difficult task and several other sources of evidence have to be used to corroborate the commission of crime. Though the neighbours notice harassment of a bride they may rarely take serious interest considering such matters as 'private or family affairs'. Public out cry against illtreatment of a bride though heard occasionally, may not happen every time. Even law enforcement authorities may consider them as domestic disturbances thereby paying deaf ear to complaints made by the kin of the woman.

In many instances where husbands were obvious offenders, the dying woman might hesitate to make a statement before the police or the magistrate against her husband or even in-laws considering the fate of her children after her death and for fear of bringing bad name to her family.

As at present the available data is inadequate to understand the nature and causation of dowry related violence. There is growing a need for more systematic studies, using comparison groups wherever necessary, exploring such aspects as the socio-economic and demographic backgrounds of the interacting families, personal characteristics of victims and their husbands, nature of specific contexts that give rise to additional demands for dowry and persecution of the bride, awareness among the subjects about the legal measures protecting women from violence and the available support systems in the community to help women in such crises. Such data can help us assess dowry related violence in a proper perspective.

Since dowry-related crimes and other forms of violence against women one a area product of socio-cultural context, besides exploring linear relationships between forms of such violence and other variables such as types of dowry demands, socio-economic background of victims or of interacting families etc., there is a need to develop an integrated theoritical frame work by evolving concepts and theories to understand contexts of dowry related violence and a grounded theory approach, will be useful to develop such framework from empirical observations.

The main conclusion that can be drawn from the comparative and cross-cultural perspectives on family violence is that, there seems to be a fairly close correlation between the existence of legal and social sanctions against the use of violence toward women and the incidence of women battering. Therefore, suitable legal sanctions can prevent, or reduce the incidence and intensity of violence toward women by making such behaviour costly and less rewarding to the husband or his kin.

Protective provisions relating to violence towards married women were incroporated into the Indian Penal Code 1860, adding a new section, 498-A "cruelty by husband or relatives of husband", which among other aspects, covers dowry related harassment of the bride. Other measures were; addition of a new section, 198-A to Criminal Procedure Code 1973, to take cognizance of an offence punishable under 498-A upon complaint to police by the close kin of the bride, and an amendment of Sec. 174 (3) in the same Code to empower police to investigate cases of unnatural or suspicious deaths of women. Similarly according to the new section 113-A of Indian Evidence Act 1872, regarding violence toward women, the burden of proof has been shifted from the prosecution to the accused.

The Dowry Prohibition (Amendment) Act 1984 made the offence cognizable and widened the definition of the term dowry. At present the minimum penalty for accepting dowry and for abetting the offence is a five year sentence and/or a fine of Rs. 15,000.

The lack of control of the bride over dowry property and misappropriation of dowry by groom's family have been sources of conflict between families which frequently resulted in the persecution of the bride. Recently the Supreme Court in its majority judgement laid was wife's exclusive property and that the husband and in-laws of the woman being trustees of such property, an action for criminal breach of trust would lie against them if they did not return her this property.

A possible effect of the judgement will be th gradual wiping out of demands for dowry as husband and in-laws would sooner or later realise the futility of making such demands, since the property could no longer be appropriated by them and at best they would only be trustees to it. Taking and giving dowry has been declared as violation of government servants conduct rules for Central Government employees. The Family Courts Act passed in 1985 is ideally suited to tackle the conflicts relating to dowry in families.

Women's oppression today, then has to be seen in a wholistic perspective, according to which "What links sati with dowry deaths, female foeticide, sexual harassment, sexual crimes is the fact of woman being regarded as a nonentity, a non-person" with no identity except that bestowed on her as some man's daughter, sister, wife, mother etc., These very forms of oppression of women are rotten fruits delivered by the vicious and decadent tree of Indian patriarchy. Even Britishers found dowry as a factor which could exculpate their colonial rule for impoverishing India and rationalise their brigandry. In 1913 Sydney Brooks wrote, "The poverty of India is, it is true, abject and pitiable enough, but to charge it to British rule is grotesque. The social habits of the people their improvidence, their reckless expenditure on dowries and wedding festivities have infinitely more to do with it than any external agency has or can have. You might remit the whole of the land revenue, and abolish the salt tax and the custom duties, and India would still be abjectly poor, and famines would still occur." "The same socialization strategies that prepare boys to be soldiers and policemen also co-opt women as mothers, wives and sisters into that preparation process. The concept of structural violence, that which frames behavioural violence refers to the organized institutional and structural patterning of the family and the economic, cultural and political systems that determine that some individuals shall be victimized through a withholding of society's benefits, and be rendered more vulnerable to suffering and death than others.

That structural patterning also determines the socialization practices that induce individuals to inflict or to endure according to their roles. This latter aspect of structural violence is conceptually related to the fact that structural violence establishes the culturally accepted threshold for physical violence in a society. " This is an apt analysis, which could be stretched to our understanding of violence related to dowry. But we would still go beyond such an observation arguing that violence is not merely physical but mental as well. The trauma, anguish which the three sisters would have been facing before committing suicide, definitely does violence to their being. Violence is not merely an end product it is a process. Thus the whole process radiates violence.

The question which appears, who are the persons we are going to punish in the present case of suicide? Could the people who were demanding dowry be prosecuted ?If not, why not? Is there no redressal? Wouldn't it be having a viciously debilitating impact on the other two Sisters? Have not the recent Gwalior ostentatious wedding of children of Madhav Rao Scindia and Karan Singh contributed to dowry violence? The links are made nebulours, in reality they are not. We have to use not merely sociological imagination but sociological intuition phenomenological in nature. Once we debunk this dowry phenomenon the culprits stand exposed. Unfortunately they are de facto above law as they happen to be Members of Parliament or members belonging to the elite sections.

Categorisation of oppression of women

We would categorise the oppression of Indian women into three manolateralistic forms. All these three take the form of victimisation namely, (i) Patriarchal victimisation: in this men are responsible for crimes like sexual harassment, wife battering, rape, dowry murders, and setting in processes like patriarchisation, genderisation, commoditisation etc; (ii) Patriarchally propelled self-victimisation: here the present suicide committed by, four girls of Kanpur and the suicides committed by brides figure. In the former case it is the patriarchal forces which compelled the three sisters to Commit suicide notwithstanding their being educated.

They felt "helpless" because "woman even today remains a slave, a vassal in short an entity with-no-entity. Having no patriarchally endorsed worth in herself, a woman is made to look for material consurnerables to enhance her value. Thanks to capitalism and our commercial media a woman today finds a lot of new commodities to do commoditise herself. But woman who has been made into a commodity, fit to be exchanged for patriarchy to prevail, fails to decommoditise herself with the help of other inanimate commodities, which in the ultimate analysis is nothing but commoditisation of the very process of existence manolateralistic to the core." Whereas in the case of suicides committed by the brides, it is abetted proximately by the harassment and torture of the bride at the hands of her in-laws and remotely by the patriarchal compulsion of izzat for which the bride's parents are not willing to accept their daughter back, for only theirs daughter's corpses the customary saying goes-can come from her in laws house; and (iii) Victim propelled victimisation: here the publicly celebrated rift between mother-in-law/sister-in-law versus daughter-in-law to discredit woman as oppressor of her own sex figures. For instance, as Nandy notes that "...even man's cruelty toward women is no match for the cruelty of women toward women." "Indeed", observes A. R. Wadia that "the greatest enemy and the only one that ultimately counts of woman's 'Emancipation' is woman herself. To Renuka Singh "The worst deprivation of the 'deprived class' takes place when the woman Vs woman battle begins resulting in the loss of support of women for the cause of their own liberation"."

K. L. Sharma observes, "It has been observed that it is women who obstruct the path of other women even more than men do; as is the case with mothers-in-law and colleagues at work."" "What a pity", says S.C. Taneja, "that man has reached the moon and has made tremendous progress in every filed but has not been able to end the social evil of dowry. And a more shocking aspect is that women are murdered by women themselves. Refuting the aforementioned superficial views we would argue that the intra-gender nature of women's oppression is a manifestation of the "scapegoat syndrome."" For instance, the mother-in-law who has herself been made a scapegoat earlier, searches for another on whom she can project the frustrations of her life-situation. And she finds in her daughter-in-law the object, who can be the target of her pent-up feelings.

We further maintain "that is unjust to say that in every crime or injustice against a woman there is a fellow women. This is the most decaying argument for intra-gender oppression, which tries to exonerate the male. This is so because we are merely perceiving the surface structure of reality. Only when we reach the deep structures of reality, we find not woman but man—his ethos, ambience, mores and norms-culpable. The mother-in-law and sister-in-law versus daughter-in-law phenomenon has roots not in a woman's mentality and her essentialistic characteristics they are illusory-but in the existing reality in which we have fixed her, where all the meanings of her life emanate not from herself but from man and his milieu."

Dowry Death in India

In 1980s, urban areas in north India has seen a growing number of murders of married women, variously called dowry murders or bride burnings. The burning of wives is neither an extension of nor culturally related to the notorious practice of *sati*, the voluntary immolation of Bengali widows on the funeral pyres of their husbands. The resonances are startling—the burning of women, the thin line between suicide and murder—but the differences are significant because they point to a serious further devaluation of women in present-day India in spite of a century of progressive legislation on women's rights.

Sati was socially countenanced suicide because the widow was perceived as having failed in her ritual duties to ensure the longevity of her husband by using her special female power or shakti; bride burning, however, is murder and equally culpable by social and legal standards.

The method of dying or killing, that is, the immolation of women in both cases, is also a false parallel. The rituals that are prescribed for sati are adequately described elsewhere; suffice it to say that it was public act that generated social awe, status, religious merit, and even material gain for the woman's kin and affines and made her sati, or the virtuous wife in death.

Burning a wife, a ritually auspicious person, is perhaps more appalling than the less sensational ways of doing her in (poisoning, drowning, strangling, shooting, or bludgeoning, among others) but is chosen chiefly for the forensic advantage it has over the others. It virtually destroys the evidence of murder along with the victim and can easily be made to look like an accident. It is also relatively simple to commit. It occurs in the kitchen, where the lower middle-class housewife spends a large amount of time each day. Pressurized kerosene stoves are in common use in such homes; a tin of fuel is always kept in reserve.

This can be quickly poured over the intended victim and a lighted match will do the rest. It is easy to pass off the event as an accident because these stoves are prone to explode, and the now ubiquitous but highly inflammable nylon sari easily catches fire and engulfs the wearer in flames. Signs of a struggle simply do not show up on bodies with 90 or more per cent third-degree burns.

The bereaved widower, who has equipped himself with a cast-iron alibi, is soon in the marriage market again looking for a new bride with perhaps a more handsome dowry. Often it is the mother-in-law, with or without her son as accomplice, who will obligingly commit the murder. Dowry serves as the foundation on which explanation for discrimination against women have been built; it has the conceptual richness to satisfy a variety of analytical tastes over time. The colonialists stressed its cultural roots in a benighted Hinduism; Marxists see it as an economic institution, feminists view it as gender discrimination for daughters did not traditionally inherit land. Today, the dowry system is seen as the prime motive for two other crimes akin to infanticide widely prevalent in the subcontinent. Female infant neglect reflected in the worst adverse female to male sex ratios in the world today, and the abortion of female fetuses made possible by the abuse of recent advances in fetal diagnostic technology. Until recently, billboard advertisements in Bombay, for instance, made an unabashed appeal to pregnant women to take the expensive and some what risky amniocentesis test. It importuned them to spend 500 rupees now on the test in order to save 50,000 rupees in the future on a daughter's dowry.

The cause of bride-burnings or dowry death in India was, indeed, dowry and indubitably a cultural problem. This alleged fact has found wide support expressed in both detailed historical and anthropological analyses of female infanticide, the oldest and most widespread form of murder believed to be related, even in other cultures, to the practice of dowry. Dowry, an integral part of Hindu high caste culture, appeared to be a timeless and pernicious custom that constructs women as a financial liability to their natal homes as infants and in their marital homes as brides. Its ban, by an act of the Indian Parliament in 1961, seems only to have entrenched the custom deeper.

There were glaring contradictions in the explanations. Culture was blamed on the one hand, but so were Westernization, which brought in gross materialism, greed, and a desire for consumer goods and modernization, which put a cash value on everything and commercialized human relationships. Here was the puzzle: Was this violence against women related to the ancient custom of dowry or was it a product of acculturation to Western and modern culture? But why then in the West, where dowries were once common, had the practice all but disappeared? Clearly culture does change; what made the culture of dowry gradually disappear in the West and change for the worse in India?

When examining the evidence, particularly the colonial evidence on infanticide, the explanation that had hoped only to deepen and endorse began to unravel. Statistical evidence on sex ratios in the subcontinent point to a serious anomaly in the logic that underpinned the colonial verdict on the dowry system and made their figures suspect. On close inspection a startling fact emerged. Several families from Hindu lower castes and religions, such as Islam and Sikhism, which did not follow the practice of dowry and even received bride price (bride price is paid in cash and/or gods to the bride's family by the groom's family), were found guilty of committing infanticide, so it was awkward to insist on either dowry or upper caste pride (as pronounced in the case of Rajputs [powerful landowning and ruling castes in North India]) to be the cultural justification of so heinous a crime.

The convenient lie of branding dowry as the motivating culprit, or finding barbaric practices particularly among the upper caste Hindus, was begun by colonial bureaucrats in the mid-nineteenth century. Parliamentary inquires about the improverishment of the India peasantry had to be answered satisfactorily. It was expedient to lay the blame on culturally sanctioned "improvidence" and wasteful ceremonies and rituals, chiefly marriage celebrations and dowry, than to reverse the colonial land revenue policies that had uprooted the old system and transformed the basic relationship between peasants and their land.

These official documents generated by colonial bureaucrats are laced with information that flatly contradicts their own assertions, and the net result was that the one clear fact about the nature of this timeless custom of dowry dissolved into a murky half-truth. The politics of the process of describing and attributing meaning to the cultures of the colonized became more important to understand than their unhappy social consequences. Dowry in its menacing form for some women, as we know it today, was patiently the artifact not of an organically unchangeable and permanently constituted Hindu or Sikh culture but of acculturation in colonial time and space. This change, fortunately, did not occur evenly across castes and classes, and today, the majority of Hindu families practice what might be seen as a precolonial form of dowry. It is this process of change— sporadic, uneven, and regrettably irreversible—that this study endeavours to reconstruct from the very documents that claim otherwise.

After a careful rereading of colonial sources, dowry could be called on of the few indigenous feminist institutions in an overwhelmingly patriarchal and agrarian society (since the term feminist is hotly contested, I do not insist on it). In the late nineteenth and early twentieth century, dowry was not the enemy but rather an ally of women, acting as an economic safety net in a setting where women always married outside their natal villages (village exogamy is still almost mandatory) and where they did not normally inherit land. This institution was invented by women for women and the resources that were given to women were substantially under their direct control. Items for a daughter's dowry were accumulated gradually for each daughter not just by her immediate family, but by the entire village, which shared in an intricate web of reciprocal obligations; very few items were purchased, since most of them were produced at home, bartered, or received as part of the reciprocal gift exchange among village families.

Nor were daughters perceived as an economic burden. The dowry was the only independent material resource over which women had partial, if not total, control. It was viewed by a woman's natal family not only as a matter of pride but also as a means of securing for her the best possible match, while providing her with recourse in an emergency. Dowry can be reckoned not only as the index of the appreciation bestowed upon daughters in their natal villages and the measure of their status in their conjugal villages, but the practical concern of familiar to unsecure for their daughters a husband from a comparable family in which her children would be raised. How then did such a strongly spun safety net twist into a deadly noose?

The time span studied covers the mid-nineteenth century to the present. The place is the Punjab, in the northwestern part of the subcontinent, a varying and often partitioned space. In 1851, the Sikh Bedis were found guilty of female infanticide. This discovery became political capital for the British and justified their two unsanctioned bitter and bloody wars against the Sikh ruler of the Punjab, Maharaja Ranjit Singh, that led to the annexation of the Punjab only two years earlier. The righteousness of British aggression was further underscored, in their own estimation, by the fact that Guru Nanak, the founder of the Sikh religion in the fifteenth century, was of the Bedi caste. The present-day Indian states of Punjab and Haryana (which was part of the Indian Punjab until 1966) continue to have the most adverse female to male ratios, or 879 and 870 per 1,000 males respectively in the 1981 census. Female infanticide is treated as an aberration of the past because the British government set up a department to deal with it in 1870 and closed the department in 1906, claiming total success in their campaign to suppress the practice and make the Punjabis less improvident about dowries. They were wrong on both counts: Sex ratios have steadily worsened nationwide in the twentieth century.

In 1901, there were 972 females for every 1,000 males, while in 1971 and 1991, the ratios have declined to 930 and 920 females per 1,000 males respectively. The practice of killing female infants may have become less prevalent, but it was substituted by the less detectable practice of medical or nutritional neglect that achieved the same end more slowly.

It was the current sex ratio in India and comparable ratios in Pakistan and Bengladesh that aroused my suspicion that female child mortality has little to do with dowry or Hindu culture, since the partition of the subcontinent had been on religious lines and removed Hindus from west Punjab and cast Bengal in 1947. Since dowries do not figure prominently in Muslim culture, why were the sex ratios not all that much better in these two Muslim nations? This suspicion began the quest for a new culprit and the reappraisal of this intriguing cultural whodunit.

The rest of the investigation was not startling. Female infanticide was found among all castes and classes of people and the rationale for it was to have a planned family with the right number of children of the two sexes, in a convenient birth order. The bias in favour of boys was also universal, whether Hindu or Muslim or Sikh, and whether urban or rural. The British did not exactly manipulate the numbers to build the case against hypergamous, landowning castes; they merely ignored the numbers that contradicted that clean-cut explanation, which seemed to strike at the roots of the culture of the Hindu ruling classes, while their own policies strengthened the bias against women.

By a careful rereading of colonial records not only on infanticide but also on variety of seemingly unrelated matters, such as land revenue, peasant indebtedness and foreclosures of agricultural property, it is possible to establish that the meaning of dowry changed drastically in the colonial period in qualitative and quantitative terms and that is skewed gender inequalities further.

The records that indict the custom of dowry as the cause for killing female infants are littered with clues that lead to the history of a changing custom rather than the characterization of it as a practice frozen in time and supported by the ruinous extravagance and the tradition-bound behaviour of a caste society. This gradual but radical transformation in the meaning, practice and effects of the dowry system in the Punjab, and by implication elsewhere, was triggered by the changes in the colonial political economy and the extension of political and social control in areas where the practice existed.

When the British encountered the practice of dowry in the Punjab, they collected opinions on the nature of the custom. None of the reports describe dowry as gifts that could be demanded by the groom's family. They found it to be a collection of voluntary gifts of clothes, jewelry, household goods and cash bestowed on the bride by family and friends at the time of the wedding. In forty-nine separate volumes of customary law of an equal number of districts in the vast territory that constituted colonial Punjab-present-day Pakistan and Indian Punjab, Haryana, Jammu, Delhi and Himachal Pradesh—this definition of dowry has been reiterated as many times. Nowhere was it treated as the prerogative of the groom and his family to demand specific consumer goods and large sums of cash for the groom's business, education, or mobility; it was voluntary and depended on the pecuniary circumstances of the bride's parents.

The British charge of "improvidence" was not based on the expense for dowry but on wedding celebrations. These latter costs were strictly itemized and evaluated in cash for three economic tiers in society and became part of the bureaucrats' handbook for enforcement. Wedding expenses did not mean only a daughter's wedding expenses; many cases cited as evidence of proficacy in the handbooks of refer to the weddings of sons.

Yet the concerts about the escalating pressures of enhanced dowry in the late nineteenth and the twentieth centuries suggest that changes in this period affected the nature of this institution. The upward spiral in costs continued; cash and an ever-increasing range of consumer goods that became available in the Punjab as imports from Europe made the increase especially steep.

Demands for cash at the time of betrothal, lavish feasting and entertainment of the wedding guests, gifts for the family of the groom, expenses for the celebration of annual fasts and festivals, and the birth of children and their naming and tonsure ceremonies changed in time the nature of the daughter-parent bond. This trend has steadily aggravated in the postcolonial period and in its extreme form it has been the cause for violence against women and, more recently, the burning to death of wives who brought inadequate dowries.

What we are dealing with is not just a dowry problem but a pathology or a syndrome rooted in history and gender inequality in a patriarchal society. Colo-nialism and patriarchal values became meshed in an alliance against women, even when the avowed purpose of legislative reform in this period was to uplift the status of women in Indian society. Because the issue of violence against women is not merely an academic puzzle, but a matter of life and death, a reexamination of contemporary evidence in the light that history and feminist theory shed, is urgently warranted. In other words although dowry is the centerpiece of this study, it cannot help but illumine the pervasive commercialization of social relations in general and the central event in women's lives—marriage—in particular. This will help in assessing the loss of women's economic power and social appreciation even as they gained in legal and political rights through the process of changes unleashed in this period.

This complex interaction of local customs, such as dowry and colonialism has hardly been suspected to exist, let alone been adequately analyzed.

The widely accepted denunciation of dowry undergirds a host of corollaries that have blurred the thinking on the triangular relationship among marriage, gender, and property, which needs to be discussed in some detail. It also pushes to the fore other, perhaps, bigger questions. Did colonial policies often create, or aggravate, the very problems they sought to ameliorate? "Social evils" was the common designation for Indian customs such as sati and thuggee (the practice of thugs, a criminal caste), "discovered" by the East India Company collectors and magistrates and described as part of the exotic and "barbaric" culture they encountered.

Systematic legal and police measures were taken to eradicate these practices. It was in this context that Indian women and their status in Hindu society became a central preoccupation of the colonial powers. Were the social evils, such as accelerating chronic indebtedness, increasing drunkenness, and improvidence in the Punjabi countryside, the unwitting consequence of rules and regulations of the new regime rather than the consequences of Hindu or Muslim culture? What influence did the colonial codification of customary law (rivaj-i-am) and its implementation in the new colonial courts in the Punjab have on various customs, particularly on the definition of the rights of women and the notions of dahej (dowry) and stridhan (women's wealth)? These questions are explored in detail in the larger study to plumb the depths of social change and disruption under British rule.

Now we have to explain the politics of two key terms, culture and colonialism and their interrelationship on which the arguments rest. Neither represents a permanently constituted entity; both are continually contested and negotiated sets of power relations, and history has constructed their meanings. Moreover, native and culture and British colonialism were in dynamic relationship with each other and not without mutual, albeit unequal, effect on each other. In other words, it would be as narrow-minded to construe Hindu culture or tradition as a timeless, frozen entity as it would to think of the more than 250 years of British rule in India as a fully imagined and executed vision that can be called British colonialism. Both continually changed in the process of interaction and acculturation.

Colonialism in mid-nineteenth century Punjab could not be mistaken for the colonialism that Bengal experienced when it was first overtaken in 1757; differing strategies produced different results in the two places. Colonial investment in the Punjab, although accom-plished at little cost to the British, greatly expanded agriculture production. By building canals, communi-cations and railway lines, this ultrafertile grain-producing region was linked to a thriving international market. The British extracted wealth from the countryside through heavy taxation and exports of wheat and other raw materials to Europe.

Although this development was self-interested, it brought prosperity to this region along with enormous changes in the peasant's way of life. There was also an intensified colonial interest in understanding, describing, and ultimately reforming the varieties of cultures encountered among the subjugated people; this interest was not academic or philanthropic but political. The stubborn tendency to interpret indigenous culture as an organic entity with immutable values, symbols and belief systems was plainly self-serving.

That the culture of the colonialists was dynamic and ever-changing and Indian culture was static, timeless and inflexible were representations enable bureaucrats to devise means of social control in addition to political and economic domination. It was colonialism's professed mission to improve civilize, and regenerate Indian society, but this could be done only after the serious flaws in the culture were located. The abominable status of women became the ground on which this legitimacy was founded. Anthropology was invented to study the unchanging structures (kinship patterns, marriage rules) for societies without history.

When Bengal was the lofus of the colonialists' concern, vivid accounts of sati fulfilled this role admirably and fattened the volumes of the Parliamentary Papers in the late eighteenth and early nineteenth centuries. Descriptions of female infanticide made horrifying reading in subsequent years from the provinces annexed later. The discovery of, and operations to control and abolish, female infanticide in the North-West Provinces Punjab and Oudh caught international attention through the same media. It goes without saying that their horror was genuine, as is ours, even while we endeavor to explain the political purposes the suffering of others often serves. What is extremely interesting is the construction of the crime as a cultural artifact, and how a colonial agenda was served by social reform.

Miller and Panigrahi accept the cultural construction unquestioningly. Miller goes further and says that culture provides the motivations for infanticide, whether they are seen by the people involved as ritualistic,...economic,...or ecological... It is culture that "invents" the reasons for which some children who are born are not desired. Second, it is culture that sketches the outlines of the group that is to be the target of infanticide: whether it is to be only boys, only girls, first sons, daughters beyond the first, children born on Thursday, children born with teeth, or children with crippling deformities.

This argument involves a sleight of hand that conflicts material and ecological reasons under the rubric of culture and is therefore difficult to refute. Miller, in an uncritical application of the classic "work equals worth" argument, shows how the masculine sex ratios of the north and the balanced sex ratios of the south of India can be explained. Swidden and wet rice cultivation, with a high demand for female labour in the south, leads to inclusion of females in property-holding and land being given as dowry, giving women the social advantages of being in the work force, which leads to an (emotional?) appreciation of daughters and balanced juvenile sex ratios. The opposite is true, in her view, in dry-field plow cultivation areas in the north, where women are excluded from production (which is patently inaccurate) and given dowries of movable property only. The high cost of raising and marrying daughters leads to discrimination against them, which explains the masculine juvenile sex ratios.

It is predicated mainly on census figures and data from postcolonial ethnographics, which have descriptions of marriage costs that shows have grown in response to the forces at work in the nineteenth and early twentieth centuries. In the Punjab, for example, bride price and dowry simply exist and it is therefore untenable to argue that women's work in the fields alone determines the mode of marriage payments.

Briefly, what happened under colonial rule to the Punjab countryside is recorded in a succession of revenue settlement reports. The British had pioneered the permanent settlement in Bengal presidency in 1793; its revolutionary feature was that it transformed land, in which all classes and castes of people had varying rights and shared unequally in its produce, into private property that could be bought, sold, or mortgaged.

This created (very crudely and quickly) a class of zamindars with immense holdings on the one hand and landless peasants on the other. This is because the revenue payments were fixed in perpetuity and due on a certain fixed date every quarter. These amounts and dates had little sensitivity to seasonal variations in the quantity of produce or to delayed harvest times, both of which depended on the caprice of the weather. In a bad year, there would be no recourse but to mortgage or sell the land to meet government demand, which was set at a higher, more "efficient" level than the past rulers had deemed fair. This created absentee landlords, for traders and money lenders from Calcutta could now buy this land in government-sponsored auctions or foreclosures of mortgaged land. An army of landless peasants roamed the countryside for food, shelter and wage labour. The economic and social havoc this caused in Bengal has been adequately dealt with in the works of a large number of historians and economists.

In the Punjab, which was conquerred after two aggressive wars between 1840 and 1849, the British tried to find a less disastrous revenue policy than the one they had perused in once-rich Bengal. They settled on a ryotwari settlement by giving titles to the land directly to the peasants (ryots) who tilled it.

This method might have been less disastrous except for except for two components: the fixed amounts and dates for payment of land revenue and the newly created ability of peasant proprietors, who were in this case more numerous with small holdings, to alienate their land through mortgage or sale. These components proved as disastrous as any attempt to "rationalize" customary man/land relations that the British had hitherto undertaken.

Money lánders in the past had advanced small loans, and the object was never to let a debt be paid off entirely, keeping the debtor as a permanent customer. The new breed of truly avaricious money lenders, with a new appetite for appropriating the debtor's land rather than the repayment of the debt was also a creation of colonialism.

With land as collateral and with prices of land rising, the peasant was able to borrow far more than he could ever before: up to 70 per cent of the value of his land. He borrowed either in a bad year or in a year when the harvest was late, chiefly to pay his taxes on time. Chronic indebtedness became the other side of the coin of prosperity for the vast majority of these small peasant proprietors. The figures on foreclosures on the lands of the people who were not seen as the best cultivators, namely Rajputs, and of the self-exploiting jat, tell a painful story.

Interests rates went up from an already high level around 18 to 24 per cent to an exorbitant 24 to 40 per cent range, with various other tricks and deceits built into the loans secured with land titles to hoodwink the illiterate peasant. Prices of land went up too, particularly as monetization of the economy moved along apace with the building of canals, roads, railways and market facilities, and the price of grain increased as exports rose.

Apart from the colonial government, the grain merchant and the money lender, not the peasant, were the most direct beneficiaries of this trend. They no longer wanted to sustain the traditional symbiotic relationship with their peasant debtors; they now wanted as quickly as possible to foreclose on the mortgaged property and hire the former proprietor as an ill-paid day labourer. The corresponding increase in holdings of bania and khatri (commercial castes) who were the money lenders and merchants was a dramatic overall 40 per cent loss for the traditional peasantry within the first twenty years of the ryotwari settlement.

Canals were not entirely beneficial either and brought two tragic consequences that were difficult to dealt with—malaria epidemics and infertility to irrigated lowlands due to an increase in the salinity of the soil. The opening of the Western

Jumna Canal in 1840-41, for example, raised the water table and made some of the contiguous eastern districts, such as Panipat and Karnal, a barren waste of water-logged, saline land that looked like "snow-covered fields". For thirty years, there was no resurvey or reassessment of land revenue, and appeals from the distressed peasants were not heeded. Acts of last resort—desertions, vagrancy, immigrating to a fertile district, and serving as bonded labour—became routine. This, eliminated the difference between the security of rights in land that sons inherited and the "movable property" that daughters inherited as dowry.

The dowry became a prize for men as much as their inherited rights in land had been. If anything, a dowry was the more versatile in a situation where land was barren. The other unfortunate effect of the canal was the spread of water- and vermin-borne diseases, such as malaria and typhoid, that claimed dark colonial plot—just tragic and unintended ecological and etiological disasters that undermined the ability of the peasants to pay their fixed dues. So, indebtedness and poverty grew in the midst of the new prosperity.

A sample statement from the dozens of reports from revenue officials gives us a flavor of the peasant's lot in 1872-80, after three decades of British rule in the Punjab. A Mr. Sharer was dispatched to examine the complaints of the peasants in Karnal district. His investigations showed that the water table had risen sixty feet, barely two or three feet below the surface, causing the tract of land to become totally barren.

Punjab and how it affected social exchange. This quiet desperation built pressure to exploit customary ways of obtaining cash or gold or silver to buy land elsewhere, or to replenish a herd—and dowry was a logical place to look. The will to obtain larger dowries from the families of daughters-in-law, to demand more in cash, gold, and other liquid assets, becomes vivid after leafing through pages of official reports that dutifully record the effects of indebtedness, foreclosures, barren plots, and cattle dying for lack of fodder. The voluntary aspects of dowry, its meaning as a mark of love for the daughter, gradually evaporates.

Dowry becomes dreaded payments on demand that accompany and follow the marriage of a daughter. Women appear to have resisted giving up their ornaments to the very last, when the situation became utterly dire. Jewelry would be the last thing a peasant had to offer when in arrears over revenue and had to save his land from the auctioneer's block.

The social effects of this indebtedness were enormous. It made the raising of daughters into a kind of economic burden that never existed before the new revenue settlements. Wedding expenses of both males and females could be curtailed and so could funeral expenses, but dowry became the lever that a woman's affines grasped with tenacity.

The ritual calendar and the harvest calendar in peasant society are intimately linked: betrothals, marriages, tonsure ceremonies, sacred thread initiation ceremonies occurred at "auspicious times" and were celebrated on the small profits of the harvest. British revenue policies never permitted capital accumulation, but kept the peasant at his wonted subsistence level. Inflexible British revenue payment timetables proved often not to synchronize with nature—a late monsoon would mean a late harvest and that would drive the marginal cultivators to deplete their savings or to the moneylender's door to meet their payment schedules.

These short-term loans frequently became life-long debts because land as collateral gave the money lender the incentive to make his conditions of repayment as difficult as possible. The next thing the peasant would need was a further loan to marry off his pubescent daughter because the profits of the harvest were now pledged to the money lender.

What this spiral of events boils down to is that a daughter's marriage, which customarily could not wait too long past her puberty, became the last straw that broke the camel's back. A son's wedding cost as much as a daughter's wedding (and this is true even today in Punjabi urban and rural families), but a son's wedding could be postponed. While funeral expenses could be trimmed, wedding expenses that could be borne by the bride's family steadily climbed because of reasons that will emerge presently. The crucial fact, however, was that neither daughter's weddings nor funerals could wait; other ritual events could be postponed, particularly the son's betrothal or wedding day. So it was not the cost of the wedding but the constraints of time that made a daughter's wedding an exploitable condition in early colonial times.

A daughter's wedding, therefore, necessitated a loan more often than a son's; and a possible demand for a bigger dowry from her in-laws would occasion an even b igger loan. In desegregating a farmer's debt, the amounts that pertained to a daughter's dowry were seen as inexcusable improvidence. This kind of circumstantial evidence against dowry finally indicated it as the killer.

The British increasingly understood the devastating ramifications of their own revenue policies but they preferred to blame the culturally based dowry system, rather than their own rational reconstruction of the land holding and revenue system. The notoriety about dowries quickly gained currency, and women were the lossers in both natal and affinal families.

Women in Society

One advantage of dowry is that it facilitates the marriage of some girls who could not get married otherwise. The Government of India has not yet formulated definite ideas on how to deal with this social practice. Nirupama Rao narrated the story of her parents who were living in poverty after getting their four daughters married. Her father, now retired, was working in the P&T department, and living in Mysore. As dowry was a regular practice in their community, her father was continuously in debt to get his four girls married. "There was a stage when I decided I would never get married. But then I had to think of my younger sister, if I had refused marriage they would have had difficulty in getting her married. As I have seen how much my parents had to suffer to see us married I would never dream of accepting dowry for my two sons."

Vijayalakshmi, who had to delay marriage till she was thirty-two as her parents could not afford a dowry, ended marrying a widower who did not take any dowry. "It is high time the evil of dowry disappeared. No woman can have respect for herself if this practice prevails." A young undergraduate, felt there was no great point in women saying they do not approve of dowry. "Young men must come forward and say they will not accept dowry. Once they are definite about the evils of dowry no one can perpetuate this custom which has degraded woman's status."

In all areas dowry is considered unfavourable. Only in the Northern and Central regions, a larger percentage of women are in favour of this practice. In these two areas, the practice of dowry is so ingrained that they consider it a necessity to give daughters their rightful gift when they leave home. Asha Grover justified her opinion in favour of this custom saying, "The dowry I get at the time of marriage is something I can take with me to my new home with pride. Though as a daughter I am eligible to my father's property, one cannot wage a battle with my brothers in demanding my due share since my parents will have to spend their life time with them. As such, a woman's right for property is only theoretical. In practice a women will get nothing if she loses her right to a dowry."

When we consider the stratification of society socio-economically, the lower strata seemed to be more favourable to the practice of dowry than the other two groups. This underprivileged section is out of touch with current thinking. They only think in terms of the little money they give during the marriage. The practice of dowry as it exists among the higher castes of India is unknown among the lower strata. Very often among the scheduled castes the expenses are equally shared by the bride's and the bridegroom's party. In many hill communities it is the man who gives a "bride price" to be allowed to marry a girl. The acute harassment which high caste middle class families face to get their daughters married is never seen among the lower classes.

It is encouraging to note that the percentage of women favouring dowry is gradually reduced with progressive levels of education. This reveals that the trend in social practices is primarily determined by education in all stratas of society. Mixed marriage was considered to be a marriage where caste, religious, or linguistic considerations do not come in. Caste as a barrier to marriage is gradually dying off especially in urban areas since people are more aware of the personality characteristics which are important in making marriage a success. The uprooting of families from their ancestral homes, free intermixing of communities, and trade and occupation not necessarily determined by caste background are all factors which have diluted the importance of caste.

A favourable attitude to mixed marriage has come about with better education. The higher the educational level of women, the higher the score for favourableness. Mainly women below college education are narrow minded and rigid about caste differences. Women with lesser education invariably come from conservative families where caste still determines the mode of life, habits and practices. It is very difficult for them to conceive of a society where caste does not exist. Marriage being the basis of family life is fitted into a particular caste pattern when the husband and wife belong to the same caste. A bride and bridegroom belonging to different castes would create innumerable problems it is believed.

When women begin to take up employment their attitude to caste gets less rigid. Approximately 20% more working women are favourable towards mixed marriage than housewives. No working women more often have strictly arranged marriages which conform to all regulations and norms of society. Working wives are more exposed to the outer world which promotes love marriages. The difference in attitude between housewives and working wives towards mixed marriages. Though there is larger approval for mixed marriages among the better educated and working women, only a few of the rest show a positive approach to the abolition of caste barriers in marriage. Very few said that they would encourage their children to marry outside the caste. The usual words were, "If my son or daughter wants to marry outside the caste I have no objection." The women who themselves had a mixed marriage were more positive in their approach to such a marriage.

As the pattern in India is still of arranged marriages, caste considerations become a major factor. It is only very rarely that arranged marriages turn out to be mixed. The new trend, especially among the educated, for love marriage completely overshadows caste considerations. When intellectual and emotional compatibility come in, caste becomes secondary. As caste and language produce great differences in habits, customs, and in life style, unless men and women are educated, the squeamish attitude towards caste will not completely disappear.

Divorce was not heard of in traditional families. In ancient India the belief was such that men and women once united by God should not be separated. With growing individualism one thinks of what is acceptable to oneself, not in terms of what is acceptable to society. This attitude obviously makes room for divorce. A divorce is a legal process a couple goes through in order to change their obligations and privileges towards one another and which restores the freedom to remarry. The chief grounds for divorce are lincentiousness, adultery, incompatibility and desertion, communication of venereal disease, excessive drinking, leprosy, religious conversion and impotency. In western countries, according to Alfred Kinsey and Dr. Dumas, adultery is common and it is even accepted by society. Some feel that it helps the marriage to relieve pressure on one's spouse who has to provide the sole source of attention, affection and physical love. The present study shows that only the higher socio-economic class tend to think of divorce as somewhat favourable when required.

The middle and lower socio-economic class are more traditional in their approach and are not fabourable towards divorce under any circumstances. The primary reason for this might be the financial dependency of the female on the male. If they are separated, the family will suffer. The care of children will be hampered. The girl will be a burden on her family again which is not a happy situation in the presence of sisters-in-law in the family. So women are expected to suppress their grief's and stay back with their husbands for the prestige of their family and also to conform to society's expectations. Many times it is unfortunate that the woman is viewed as the cause of the divorce because she is considered to be the person for making adjustments always. If she deviates a little, then she is considered to be at fault. In the upper class the attitude to divorce is almost half on either side of the continum. Some feel it should not be undertaken while others feel that is not worthwhile to waste a lifetime if married life becomes unhappy.

Approval of divorce is directly linked with the educational level of women. As the educational level increases, more and more women approve of divorce if conditions of married life are not congenial. This is especially true of professionals because of their financial independence. They have the confidence, are less tradition-bound and willing to accept change. On the whole the acceptance is slightly over 30% and for professionals the percentage of acceptance is double that of the average for the whole sample. Men and women become more and more individualistic with education, affluence and independence. The divorced woman is naturally more liberal in her attitude to divorce. Among the respondents we had two women divorced twice and two divorces unhappy in their second marriage also.

Those who favoured divorce gave numerous reasons for which a divorce could be considered justified. Some of them are severe problems with in-laws which make a girl's life miserable; a cruel and aggressive husband; an alchoholic husband; sexual infidelity; husband's failure to support his wife and children; when the girl and her parents are harassed for more money; and when the husband takes another wife or deserts his wife.

Surprisingly, mental illness or any disease were not mentioned as legitimate reasons for divorce. Those against divorce were firm about the need to preserve a marriage against all odds. The objections against divorce were that men and women in their foolishness cannot break up homes and leave children in the lurch; women who are dependent on their husbands would have no place to go if marriages break up; a women who leaves one man will never be able to settle down wit another if she has children; divorce is just not acceptable to the Indian ay of life; and as woman always makes the greater adjustment she should preserve the marriage partnership without magnifying little problems.

Mrs. Vimla Jain said, "I would rather remain unmarried than marry a man who has left his wife," echoing the views of most Indian women.

Marrying a divorcee is objectionable to most Indian women but the attitude is changing with education. Society looks down upon divorcees, hence a divorced male or female finds it very difficult to get a suitable match. Often too much emphasis it put on a person's married life rather than on the individuals's merits. Even among the highly educated only around one-third favour marrying a divorcee. Among the rest, less than 20% third favour marrying a divorcee. Among the rest, less than 20% have a favourable attitude.

Miss Raji Viswanath had an interesting explanation for her preferring a divorcee to a widower. She said, "A divorcee must have separated from his wife after a quarrel or a misunderstanding. He cannot have fond feelings for the wife whom he has decided to separate from. On the other hand, a widower must have loving memories of his wife. Such a person will never be able to give any love to his second wife. So I prefer a divorcee to a widower."

There is not much regional variation in the attitude towards marrying a divorcee. But according to the difference in the socio-economic status it is found that the lower socio-economic classes are more favourable towards marrying a divorcee than the middle or higher starta. Women of the lowest social order often overlook social restrictions for the necessity of survival. As we go up the social ladder. People become more tradition bound, especially the middle-classes. Women prefer to maintain the *status quo* than go against tradition and get ostracised.

Only 50% of women accepted marrying a widower. The respondents who favoured this said, "A widower should be willing to compromise. He must not be too old or narrow minded. He must know the practical problems in a second marriage and must be willing to adjust and accommodate." Many women felt a widower could be trusted but not a divorcee.

In some cases a widower is accepted for various reasons. The girl may be poor or have some physical defect, and in some cases may be quite old. Women with college level education in the top starta are more favourable towards marrying a widower than others. In the lower level as well, very often for economic reasons a woman may be willing to compromise. In the upper starta marrying a widower does not seem to be unacceptable.

The middle class is more conservative, and more prove to follow the traditional pattern of marriage. This is the group that is most tradition bound and unwilling to take a chance and accept a new practice. Only out of dire necessity will they compromise.

The respondents revealed a number of reasons for not wanting to marry a widower. He might be an unlucky person, and it would not be wise to link one's fate to his. Also if it could be avoided why should one consider an already married man? Most felt that a widower should marry only a widow as both are in a similar situation.

Children from a previous marriage could also create problems. Whatever a woman may do for a widower and his children, a woman becomes a stepmother which is not a very enviable position. Some respondents felt that a widower remarries out of necessity and not for love. Also, the second wife has a superstitious fear of the spirit of the first wife.

Thus, although women in general accepted widow remarriage, they are not very favourable towards marrying a widower.

A widower's re-marrying is accepted by society, as he needs help to manage the house. But widow remarriage is looked down upon as a betrayal. The restrictions become more binding in the more conservative groups. However, over 70% of the whole sample approve widow remarriage. The percentage increases as the educational level and socio-economic status improves.

The reasons for opposing widow remarriage were many as stated by the respondents. They felt they were handicapped rather than benefited by a second marriage. Many felt that the second husband can never take the place of the first. He will never accept her children as his own. So why create more problems? Some women strongly protested against widow remarriage arguing that a woman should marry only once to safeguard the interest of the home and family. Mrs. Prasad said with much pride, "A Hindu woman marries only once. It is a man who needs to marry repeatedly." Some felt that a widow should not marry if she had the means to live or the earning capacity. Kamala, a working woman in the lower income group, said, "What guarantee is there that the second husband will not dies prematurely? If one's husband dies a woman should learn to take up a job and make a living. One cannot forget within a short while the man with whom one has lived and go around looking for another man after his death. The new husband may take me but will he take my four children also?"

In contrast to this some women approved widow remarriage. They gave strong arguments in its favour, saying when a man can remarry, why not a woman? If a man can remarry and forget the past why should a woman sacrifice the rest of her life for a mere memory. Hence the feeling is that it is better that a woman should remarry and settle down rather than be a lose end. She and her children will be better cared for if she remarries and has a proper home. The favourable attitude towards widow remarriage is seen more among the educated and the working women.

Those who accepted widow remarriage conditionally said that widow remarriage is good only if the widow is young or has no children. Indian women in general are more concerned about the children rather than their own interest. The fear that a widow's children will not find a sympathetic father is deep rooted. Many women were of the conviction that marriage is for a lifetime and if it ends prematurely, it should be accepted as one's karma.

For Indian women, especially the less educated, to whatever starta they may belong to, marriage is a divinely ordained partnership for the good of the family, home and children rather than for personal pleasure and happiness. The idea that a woman should make a greater sacrifice than a man is deeply ingrained. They feel economic emancipation gained by employment outside the home is more important than looking for opportunities for remarriage. That it why we see many widows and divorcees taking up gainful employment especially after the death or separation of the husband. Among educated women, feat of loniliness and the need for companionship motivate them for remarriage.

In Indian families childlessness is considered a curse. If there are no children usually the woman is considered responsible. Whatever the case may be, adoption of children is considered an issue to be sorted out in each of these families. Over 50% of women are on favour of adoption but they usually prefer to adopt relatives than orphans. The advantage of adopting relatives is that they know the background and would definitely have greater affection because of blood relationship. Some favour adopting orphans because there would be no other claim later and also one can bring up the child the way one likes without interference. The attitude towards adoption did not vary according to socio-economic status or education or the type of family background. However, it was found that the middle class was more conservative than the other two starta. The woman in this study asked to air their views about sexual freedom for men and women.

It is found that in all classes, the attitude towards sexual freedom is unfavourable. Only slightly over 10% were favourable towards this in the overall sample. In the high socio-economic class 18% approved of it. Even among upper class educated women, the percentage approving of sexual freedom is only about 20%. When the educational level is low, even in the high socio-economic starta the percentage drops to 6%. The women of the middle socio-economic level are uniformly conservative in all levels of education.

In spite of education and wealth, Indian women are basically orthodox compared to their western counterparts. Women would rather be conservative than exercise freedom which may result in a unstable life. The more freedom one enjoys, the higher is the divorce rate.

The average figure for the sample as a whole is 11%. This is low compared to the statistics available in western countries. Among the three starta surveyed, the lower socio-economic group approve of this more than the other two groups in spite of the fact that the same group put greater restrictions on girls during their early years. After marriage due to environmental reasons some of them are forced to change their attitudes to life and life situations.

The woman of the lower starta make concessions in their standards about sex practices often out of economic necessity.

Hafisabi, a prostitute, defended woman's right to sexual freedom. "I have been doing this job for the last 20 years of my life. I have come to believe that any means is justifiable if it is to fill one's belly. When my husband drove me out and took another wife no one came forward to help me. I ran away from the village to earn any living and support myself and my daughter in this big city. I could not find employment in a house as a servant or as a cook as I had a child with me. An old lady whose acquaintance I made started me on this profession."

Any woman who has broken away from the tetherings of normal domestic life becomes liberal in her attitude to sexual freedom. She realises there cannot be different standards for man and for woman. Sexual freedom is more often approved by emancipated women belonging to the progressive younger group, by woman unhappy in marriage, sexually frustrated, widowed, or separated. A woman who finds complete fulfilment in her marital life rarely advocates sexual licence for women.

Mrs. Meneziz strongly felt that women must enjoy the same liberties which a man enjoys. "I would say it is my husband who had made me immoral. I lived seven years with him without seeing day of happiness. He drank, gambled, went to women, squandered even what I earned. I moved over to mother's house with my two boys four years ago. Now I have no compunction to go with any man if he gives me money. With my salary alone I cannot support my two boys and pay for the maintenance of my mother who is dependent on me. I would rather live this life of sin than go back to my husband." Rama Devi, a prostitute, blamed her husband for showing her the easy way to sell herself for money. "My husband compelled me to sleep with the men he brought home because they were willing to pay him. Now he stays home with my one year old daughter when I roam the streets at night." When asked,

"Doesn't your husband mind your going to different men?" Rama Devi snapped, "Why should he? He gets money for drinks and he is happy. If I find a man who will support me and my child, I will give up this occupation and run away."

Women who have gone through marital insecurity or economic distress often find sexual liberty a convenient tool to make a living. The degradation they have gone through makes them take a very loose attitude to sex.

On the other hand, a woman's personal failure to have a successful married life might make her take a very rigid attitude to sexual freedom for women. Herabai, the mistress of a rich businessman, had a tragedy to reveal. She comes from a family which has practised prostitution for generations. She never wanted to be a prostitute but she had no choice as she was introduced into the profession by her mother when she was hardly 16. After living a life of vice for over 15 years she met Mr. M who took her as permanent 'keep' and brought her over to Calcutta. He maintains her and provides for her needs. She has two children, a girl and a boy. She would never want her daughter to undergo what she has gone through in life. She hopes her daughter will get married into a good home and live the life of a normal woman.

Some women with lax morals becomes so out of necessity. They are the victims of social discrimination, oppression and ostracism. They are the products of a rigid conservative order which discriminates against women because of their sex. Such women, be they widows, victims of forcible child marriage, deserted women, or illegitimate mothers, find the cover of sexual licence very convenient to sustain themselves in a society where they are not wanted. Now let us see why in our society women in general do not approve of sexual freedom for men and women. Mrs. Rao declared, "Woman makes a home. If she becomes immoral the home will go to ruins. A woman with character not only retains her dignity but invariably influences her husband to be straight. Both men and women have to exercise sexual restraint it they have to preserve the home."

A graduate in literature said, "Woman cannot use the same yardstick as a man to decide her sex values. Often sex means so little to a respectable woman, and it is love which matters—an emotional experience involving her so completely that she gets totally immersed in her family life. Just because man in basically polygamous, woman cannot waiver sexual restraint and follow him. Standards of permissiveness for men and women are bound to be different."

Mrs. Sethi disapproves of sexual freedom for women. "I believe in women getting education, taking up jobs, earning for the family but not going wild sexually simply because men also enjoy sexual freedom. Our society has remained stable because of women's regard for their home, family and reputation." The concept of pativrata—a woman's complete loyalty to the man she marries—is deep rooted in the minds of Indian women, and they are convinced that sex should be limited to the marriage partnership. They are not eager to compete with men in this respect. "So what if men enjoy sexual freedom" is the attitude of many. The average woman is more concerned with playing the role of an ideal mother, a wife who will remain pure even if the husband errs. She is against taking sexual liberties for her personal gratification.

When the social status is high and the woman is well educated and young she takes a liberal view towards sex. Even if social norms are broken she feels less alienated. Money and position compensate for other values.

A majority of woman had not known any male closely enough to be classed as a boy friend. Although around 17% mentioned a boy friend, the degree of intimacy they had with the male friend varied considerably. For some it was just an adolescent crush, looking into each others's eyes or stealthily holding hands. In others it was their first and last love as they had loved the man and married him. Those who have enjoyed sexual freedom before to not necessarily marry the man with whom they had an affair and remain romantically inclined to men even after marriage. There were a few who had boy friends regularly for the sake of fun. More women in the educated group had boy friends, probably because women of this group get an opportunity to mix with men in college or at their place of work.

Approximately one-third of the professional women had boy friends in the upper and middle socio-economic starta. In the lower socio-economic starta, even when the educational level is only up to high school, slightly over 20% had boy friends. However, the proportion is very small in comparison to the western countries. Yet, for a conservative and tradition oriented society like ours, even this proportion is surprising. In the urban complex, many social restrictions and taboos have less effect because of environmental factors. Young people study together where they get plenty of opportunity to mix. When residential areas are crowded, one gets an opportunity to come into contact with men. Among women of the upper starta, where western standards are often adopted, having a boy friend, sometimes even after marriage, becomes part of life. In the lowest lot, young women coming from unhappy homes or separated girls easily fall prey to sex.

Indian women are still conservative about premarital sex. Only the better educated women belonging to the upper socio-economic starta make some concession in this matter. They are the educated group who are economically independent. They have probably been free with men, loved and married the man of their choice. If not married they probably would like to move with men and make their own selection.

Some women feel there is no harm in being sexually intimate with the man one loves and proposes to marry. Educated women are well acquainted with family planning methods and are capable of protecting themselves against undesired pregnancy. 93% of respondents do not approve of premarital sex.

The professionals in this group scored the highest percentage with 25% favouring sex before marriage. These women felt it was better to establish sexual compatibility before marriage rather than regretting it later. Education gives woman the freedom to decide what she needs, and this is especially true for the professionally qualified. The middle and lower classes fit into a more conservative pattern compared to the upper class.

Except for the highly educated women of the upper starta, sexual freedom before marriage is not socially permitted. Even the question of a girl openly dating a boy does not arise, and it is usually done stealthily without the knowledge of the family members. Rekha Naik put this question, "When we are not even allowed to talk freely with boys where does the question of sex experience come in? I am now 19. I go to a college for women. Except for a few of my brother's friends with whom I talk, I have not known any boy intimately. If I have to see a movie or go to a restaurant I usually go with my girl friends."

In the lower levels of urban society, because of the severe uprooting which most of the families go through people tend to become less conservative. Morals become lax especially if the girl is a little educated or is employed and economically independent. An unmarried girl working at a milk booth has had sex experience. She was ashamed to admit that often she got money from men she slept with. She had very little choice in the matter. The meagre amount of Rs. 110 she earned from her job was insufficient to support her mother, two brothers and two sisters. Her widowed mother was not rich enough to marry her off. A divorcee, said she had sex experience before marriage with a man whom she wanted to marry very much. Unfortunately her family never approved of the match. She was forced to marry a man of her parent's choice. The marriage was never happy, and after four years she separated.

In general, the Indian woman grows in a conservative background where woman does not enjoy sexual freedom. Even sexual licence in men is not really accepted because of the importance attached to sexual restraint before marriage both in men and women. Does the Indian woman mentally accept the idea of sex before marriage? Is she trying to bring a change in favour of sexual freedom for woman?

The Indian marriage continues to be a sacrament, a partnership for a lifetime. Chastity and virginity are still held with the greatest respect. Marriage in most cases initiates a woman into sex. She has neither the right nor desire to sex before marriage, and the more conservative the group the more fixed this idea becomes.

4

Physical Violence

Women who are married at a younger age are at higher risk of physical violence. The women who got married at younger age were more victims of physical violence by their husbands in contrast to those who got married at later age. Further, it was noted that there was a progressive decrease in the percentages of victims of physical violence from lower age at marriage category to higher age group. Out of 60 respondents who got married below the age of 18 years, 45 per cent were the victims. In contrast to this who were married after the age of 21 years, only 24.71 per cent were the victims of physical violence.

It is also interesting to note that median age at marriage of victims of physical violence was lower than those of non-victims. It can, thus, be concluded that those women who married at lower age were at high risk of physical violence in comparison with those who got married at later age in the Indian society although the age at marriage is increasing yet in the rural areas it still remains quite low that is, 17.81 years. Therefore, class and situational factors may play an important role in determining the age at marriage which in turn may be associated with violence because young couples are under lot of stress to adjust to new role responsibilities.

A few studies indicate that wives of younger age group are at higher risk of abuse as compared with those of older age group because older women are not prone to file assault charges either because of traditional attitudes or because of the possibility of divorce. The results of National Family Violence Survey conducted in America indicate that all forms of marital violence occur most frequently among those under 30 years of age. The rate of marital violence among those under 30 years of age was found to be more than double the rate for the age for 31 to 50 years.

The data for the present study were tabulated to find out association between the age of the wife and her being victim of physical violence. The respondents were distributed into four age categories. There was a progressive decrease in the percentages of victims of physical violence from lower age category to higher age category. Among the victims of physical violence 45.45 per cent were below the age of 30 years. In contrast to this those who were in the age group of 50 years above, only 18.18 per cent were the victims.

Similarly, if the median age of the victims of physical violence is compared with non-victims, it was noticed that median age of victims was 35 years in contrast to 39.24 years median age of the non-victims. In short, an inverse relationship was found between the age of wives and their physical abuse. In other words, physical violence against wives of younger age group was more frequent as against those of higher age groups. The data of the present study support the findings of studies cited above.

Wife abuse can occur at any age but the data on age indicate that wives of younger age are at higher risk of being abused. It may be due to the fact that younger couples are still learning to make adjustment with each other and addition of children in the family puts enormous demands and stresses on the younger people.

Presence or absence of children in the family is likely to affect the quality of relationship between husband and wife. Further, presence of more children in the family would create problem of management and proper training of the younger ones. Researches on the impact of children on marriages consistently show that the level of marital satisfaction and marital adjustment goes down after the birth of the first child.

An additional child would imply a decrease in time for parents to pursue, their own interests. Further, each additional child increases the work load and conflicts. In the traditional societies like India, child care still remains under the domain of mothers and for any deviance on the part of child it is the mother who is blamed. Further, more children put a lot of stress on the limited resources of the family.

Among the victims of physical violence it was found that the rate of violence against mothers who had five or more children or no child was more than double the rate for those who had one or two children. Keeping in view the number of children it was noted that there was a progressive increase in the percentages of victims of physical violence from one to two children category to women having five or more children or with no child. In short, it can be concluded that a large number of children in the family become a source of conflict resulting into violence against wife or mother.

The highest percentages of physical violence was found in those house- holds which had no child. It may be attributed to their younger age as well as wives' inability to have children because children are valued in the Indian society and those women who are unable to bear a child are ridiculed.

In the patriarchal society like India, greater importance is given to the male child. The female child is not only considered a liability because of associated dowry problems but mothers who give birth to female children only do not get much respect in the family as compared with those who give birth to male children lately with the help of amniocentesis the couples would like to know the sex of the child. In case the foetus is of the female sex, they go for abortion. A study of 8000 cases of abortion showed that 7999 of them involved a female foetus. The high female foeticide reinforces the sex preferences prevalent in our society. The victims of physical violence were almost equally divided in the categories of those who had only male or female children of both the sexes. In the present study sex of the children in the family was not found to be associated with wife abuse.

Wives living in extended and joint households are required to make adjustments with a large number of kin in contrast to those who are living in nuclear households. Further, patrilocal residence and patriarchal structure of the family places women into subservient position. The men are more likely to act as sons rather than husbands. The parents-in- law and other kinsmen continue to have greater affiliation with the sons as compared with daughters-in-law.

A number of cases have been reported where because of backbiting, the husbands have maltreated their wives. Hence presence of a large number of members in the family not only creates the problem of adjustment but they also act as instigators for wife abuse. Although there was no marked difference in the percentage of victims living in nuclear and extended households, yet among the victims a relatively higher percentage (36.67) were found to be living in joint and extended households in contrast to those living in nuclear households (32.94). Similarly, among the non-victims no marked difference Was found with regard to their pattern of living arrangement. Hence, the composition of household was not found to be associated with wife abuse.

From the foregoing discussion on the demographic correlates of wife abuse, it was found that the younger age at marriage, young wives and those having no child or a large number of children were at higher risk of being victims of physical violence. However, no association was found between the sex of the children as well as living arrangement and wife abuse. Based on the results of this exploratory research the following hypotheses can be formulated for verification in future researches.

1. The younger the age at marriage of the women, the greater is the possibility of their being battered.
2. The younger the age of wife, the greater are the chances of her being victim of physical violence.
3. The greater the number of children, a woman has the greater is the possibility of her being victim of physical violence of her husband.
4. The absence of child is likely to result in wife battering.

An individual's social milieu not only influences his social position, network of relationships and contents of learning but also his social behaviour pattern. Social behaviour is a function of the life situations which may be physical, economic, social or cultural or an interplay of these elements. It is assumed that persons having differential life situations would react differently to the same stimuli. It is, therefore, essential to explicate the role of these social variables for understanding the quality of conjugal relationship. The social variables considered for the present study are educational and occupational status of the respondents, their social class background, their caste and religious background, their attitudes regarding traditional gender roles in the family and their value orientation in favour of use of violence for the resolution of conflict. Formal education helps an individual to know what is happening outside one's immediate surroundings. It also facilitates him to develop rational outlook towards life. Education widens the horizon and makes the individual more knowledgeable. Education also helps an individual to get jobs of high prestige and with high economic returns. Further, higher education enhances one's social prestige. Efforts have been made to find out association between the level of education one has and the quality of interpersonal relations.

A few studies indicate that the less education a person has, the more likely he or she is to approve of and support violence. Some other studies, however, contradict their findings and on the other hand, they are of opinion that couples with the lowest educational levels are less prone to violence than those who had attained higher education. It is argued that low education level does not cause violence but it aggravates the frustration.

The reason for more violence among those who have higher education, may be that women with high education may not endorse the traditional role relationship and this may be considered as threat to the dominant position by their husbands. However, education can provide people with alternatives for resolving family disagreements. It is, therefore, expected that with the help of education individual learns different mechanisms to resolve the conflict in the conjugal relationships.

The educational background of the victim wives indicates that those who have low educational attainment or higher educational attainment had over representation as compared with those who had moderate level of education. There is a progressive decrease in the percentage of the victims from illiterate educational category up to graduation with the exception of those who had higher education. This curvilinear distribution of victims of violence indicates that women who have no education or have higher educational attainment are more prone to physical violence by their husbands.

The women with low education designate their complete dependency because with low educational background they will not be able to have economic independence or would be engaged in occupations with low economic returns and low prestige. In the case of those who have higher education they may be in better position to gain economic independence and with the higher education they may start questioning the dominant position of their husbands. Such a threat is not tolerated by the husbands and they use physical violence as their ultimate resource to maintain their dominant position in the family.

Occupation is an important indicator of a person's position in society. It is believed that the higher the education one has, the higher the occupation one holds and the higher the prestige he gets in society. Conversely, the lower the occupation, the lower will be the economic returns and as a consequence thereof, there are likely to be higher frustrations and greater marital conflicts.

Many studies indicate that persons engaged in occupations of lower prestige are more likely to resort to physical violence against their wives to give vent to their economic stresses. It is also argued that women who stay at home and are not engaged in paid work outside their homes are at somewhat greater risk of being physically abused than those engaged in paid work. This is probably because housewives are perceived to contribute less to family subsistence and are consequently valued less than women who are engaged in paid work outside the home. Wife beating is far less common in societies in which women have independent economic and social resources, perhaps because these resources are valuable enough to make a husband think twice before acting in ways that might force his wife to terminate the marriage.

In the sample there are only 65 women respondents who were found to be engaged in paid work. Out of these 47.69 per cent were victims of physical violence of their husbands. On the other hand, out of those not engaged in paid work outside their homes, only 26.67 per cent were physically abused by their husbands. The results of the present study support the findings of Homung *et al.* who, in one representative sample, found housewives had a lower risk of violence than working wives.

The reason housewives are abused less than working wives is because keeping in view their economic dependency they may have "Learned helplessness" with the result they have developed tolerance of such violence and do not share with outsiders that they are being abused or they would endorse the traditional gender roles and would not question the authority of their husbands. Hence, they do not provoke their husbands to use physical violence to maintain their dominant position in the conjugal relationship.

On the other hand, the working wives may not accept the dominant position of the husband in family decision making and raise questions about asymmetrical conjugal relations. Such a situation may prompt the husband to use physical force to retain his dominant position.The general contention that working gives economic Independence to women, hence, they would be relatively free dependence to be correct in the present from abuse is also not found to study on the other hand, it is the working women who are than the non-working women. The association abused more, status and her physical abuse will between wives' working which these become more clear if the type of occupation in which women are engaged in, is taken into consideration.

As the number of respondents under the working category were limited to 65 cases only, their occupations were grouped under three categories, i.e., occupations with low prestige, medium prestige and high prestige. The data reveal that the percentage of the victims goes on decreasing from low occupational prestige category to higher prestige category. In short, there was inverse relationship between occupational prestige and physical violence, i.e., the lower the prestige of paid work, the greater was the violence against wives. The results indicate that it is not the working status per se which provides women freedom from physical violence of their husbands but it is the nature of the occupation and associated prestige and economic returns which facilitate women to be free from physical abuse.

The Concept of Social class

The concept of social class has been defined by several sociologists. They have, however, given emphasis to different attributes. One salient feature of different definitions is that members of a class group have common style of living and value orientation. Wolfgang and Ferracuti in their study of subculture of violence have even divided a class into subclasses depending upon value orientation of the members. Similarly, a number of scholars have tried to find out association between class background and family violence. One set of studies maintains a positive association between lower class and wife battering. Whereas some researchers do not endorse their findings and they have contended that wife battering transgresses the boundaries of class.

An attempt has been made to find out association between class background and wife beating. The class background of the respondents has been worked out based on education, occupation and income of the husbands of the respondents because a majority of the women respondents were not found to be working and hence, had no independent income of their own. While selecting the sample their living arrangement was taken into consideration and 50 cases from each house type were included in the sample, which were redistributed into different social classes. The class background of the respondent was also divided into lower, working, middle and high for the purpose of finding out differential behaviour pattern, i.e., wife abuse in different classes.

The data indicate that in contrast to 19.23 per cent victims of physical violence in the upper class, there were 51 .85 per cent victims in the lower class. There is a progressive decrease in the percentages of victims of physical violence from the lower through the middle to the upper class. Similarly, among the non-victims the higher per cent (80.77) belong to the upper class. In short, women belonging to the lower class were at a higher risk of being physically abused by their husbands. The results of the study indicate inverse relationship between class background and wife battering.

These findings support the contention of those researchers who found that women belonging to the lower class were at a higher risk of physical violence which was attributed to their way of life. The use and approval of physical violence in the lower class has been attributed to what Lewis calls, the culture of poverty. The concept implies that the poor people have a distinct subculture. Due to common experiences they have developed certain attitudes and behaviour pattern which have been transmitted from parents to children. These include the casual resort to physical violence, an inability to plan for the future, seeking of immediate gratification, weak impulse control and fatalistic attitude towards the future. Davis while describing the class linked, violence contends that physical violence in the lower class families is normal, socially approved and socially, in-culcated type of behaviour. Similarly, Whitehurst while making a distinction between the middle and the lower class families with regard to control over violence, maintained that violence-responses were much more built into lower class subculture as a means to achieve some goals to assert independence and masculinity.

The members of the lower class are subject to a lot of economic pressures and strains and they cannot show their resentment and frustration, against those who are highly placed and hence they give vent to their frustrations at the slightest provocation by beating their wives on whom they can exert their power. On the other hand, members of the middle and upper classes have more resources and can keep their violence private and additionally, because of the sensitivity of the issue and embarrassment, the victims are not likely to admit its existence in their conjugal relationship.

Individual's social status is determined by his ascriptive and acquired attributes. In the Indian society ascriptive attributes, like caste, determine not only his social milieu as castes are hierarchically placed but also his opportunities to acquire new attributes. Although an individual is now theoretically permitted to achieve any position and support any ideology yet caste plays an important role in influencing his behaviour pattern. Keeping in view the importance of caste in the Indian society, it will be worthwhile to find out an association between caste and wife battering.

The distribution of the victims of physical violence according to their caste background indicates that respondents belonging to the lower castes group and those who have not specified their caste were more victims in contrast to the respondents belonging to the higher castes. Among the twice-born, the respondents belonging to trading castes were at a higher risk in contrast to Khatris and Aroras. Similarly, among the non-victims the higher percentages of respondents were found among the twice-born.

The higher frequency of physical violence present among the members of the lower castes may be attributed to their lower class background. Similarly, among those cases who have not specified their caste, most of them belonged to Muslim and Christian religion and these respondents were having lower socio-economic status. The association between caste background and physical violence would remain incomplete unless their economic status is also considered. Preceding analysis has indicated that members belonging to the lower class were more likely to resort to physical violence for the resolution of conjugal conflicts.

Religion is an important institution which instills a particular philosophy of life in an individual. His outlook towards himself and others as well as his behaviour pattern are likely to be influenced by his religious belief system. Is wife abuse a characteristic of a particular religious group? To find out an answer to the question religious background of the respondents was considered. No clear-cut association was found between religious background and physical violence against wives. Among the two main religious groups present in Chandigarh, there was no marked difference in the percentage of victims.

In case of Muslims and Christians 50 per cent of the respondents belonging to these religious groups were the victims of husband's violence. This again may be attributed to the low economic status of the respondents. The results of the present study do not establish any association between religion and wife battering.

The family as a social institution lays down norms and values to regulate the behaviour of the members of the social group. Family as a social group is structured in such a manner that one member, usually the husband, assumes the dominant position and the other members take up subordinate positions.

The family provides a social setting where husband and wife play complementary roles. One of the conditions which maximises the cooperative elements in the family is the similarity of social values and ideologies which promotes not only cohesiveness and harmony but also helps in the proper functioning of the group. In the patriarchal traditional societies, like India, sex role expectations favour male dominance in the family. Traditional ideology promotes and serves to justify male dominance as well as helps in cultivating a belief system among the husbands and wives as to how they should behave in the marital relationship.

Motivated by traditional ideology, division of labour in the family was worked out into a male provider and a female to focus more narrowly on the domestic realm. Such a task specialization and differential evaluatior. helped men not only to have greater control over economic resources but also a greater access to power in the family. The power structure in the family is maintained through the actions of the members involved in the relationships. Those at the top of the power structure behave in dominant ways and they do not hesitate to use coercive methods to retain their dominant position.

Attempts have been made to find out association between traditionality and wife abuse. A number of studies have concluded that men who were more traditional in their attitudes towards women were more likely to become wife abusers. Some importance is also given to sex role orientation of the victims. Walker is of opinion that non-traditional wives if paired with traditional husbands are at higher risk of being abused. An attempt has been made in the present study to find out correlation between wives' traditional orientation and their being victims of abuse.

Traditional sex role orientation of the respondents was worked out based on the responses to eight statements. The level of traditionality was further divided into three: High, Medium and Low, to find out association between level of traditionality and wife battering. It is assumed that respondents who have low level of traditional role orientation are at higher risk of physical violence than those at high level of traditionality because wives with low level of traditional orientation are more likely to question asymmetrical power relations in the family.

In contrast to 22.86 per cent of the wives showing high level of traditional sex role orientation, 40.32 per cent wives indicating low level of traditionality were the victims of physical violence by their husbands. Similarly, among the non-victims, their percentages go on increasing from low level of traditionality to high level of traditionality. In short, it can be concluded that wives with non-traditional sex role orientation are at higher risk of being physically abused. The reason for wives showing less traditional sex role orientation being victims of physical violence may be attributed to their attempt in questioning the traditional power structure in the family. The husbands in such situation are likely to use physical force as the last resort to maintain their dominant position.

The norms and values relating to intra-family violence indicate cultural contradiction. On the one hand, there is a myth of family non-violence which reflects cultural norms for the family as a group characterised by love and harmony. On the other hand, there seems to be social norms which imply right of the family members to strike each other. The legitimation of violence in the family is explicit and mandatory—as in the case of rights and obligations of the parent to use a necessary and appropriate level of physical force to adequately train and control a child.

Violent wives as well as violent husbands express more approval of violence than do non-violent husbands and wives. Levinson in his cross cultural study on family violence came to the conclusion that wife beating was more common and frequent in societies in which adults solved conflicts by resorting to physical violence, indicating attitude in favour of violence.

The cultural norms and values permitting and sometimes encouraging husband to beat wife actually reflect hierarchical and male dominant type of society like India. The right to use force exists, to provide the ultimate support for the existing power structure of the family in which the wife assumes a subordinate position.

Respondents' values in favour or against use of violence in the family were obtained from their reactions to 12 statements. Their scores were divided into three categories depicting low, medium and high scores. This exercise was done with an assumption that the respondents with high score on values in favour of violence in the family would be at a higher risk of being victims than those with low score. The data did not depict any clear-cut association.

On the other hand, it was noted that those respondents who had medium score on values favouring use of violence to resolve family conflict were more victims in contrast to those who had high or low score. The reason for lack of association may be attributed to the fact that there is a lot of gap between values and actual behaviour pattern. Secondly, the values were taken of the wives rather than the husbands who were the perpetrators of physical violence against their wives.

The respondents might be holding values against the use of violence but had no control over the values and behaviour pattern of their husbands.

The above discussion on social variables highlights certain salient features which contribute to husbands' physical violence against wives. Lower caste background, low and high educational attainment, lower working status, lower social class background and low level of traditionality were found to be contributing factors for husbands' physical violence against wives. However, no association was found between religious background and value system of the respondents and their being victims and non-victims of physical violence.

Dependency is a state, both physical and mental, depicting assistance from a person or persons for continuing living in the community. The human child has to depend upon his parents for his growth, development and social recognition. The Indian society has placed women in a state of dependency as a daughter on her father, as a sister on her brother, as a wife on her husband and lastly as a mother on her son. Further, sexual division of labour and gender roles accentuate these differences.

Additionally, patriarchal social norms not only grant control of family resources and property to men but also provide dominant position to them. To maintain their dominant position, the husbands are likely to use coercive methods including physical violence against their wives. Sometimes physical violence is used as a means to an end and at other times as an end in itself. Dependency is also treated as a cause of physical violence in the conjugal relationships. Researches have utilized this explanation in two ways. In case, a wife is completely dependent, both physically and socially, her husband exploits her dependency and uses violence at whim to reinforce his dominant position in the conjugal relationship. A few scholars are also of opinion that when a husband is dependent upon his wife he resorts to physical violence as a last resort against his wife as he is afraid of losing his spouse or a person on whom he can exert his dominant position. Hence, dependency of husband over his wife is also treated as a cause of wife abuse.

As the present study is limited to wife abuse, the analysis is limited to wife's perception regarding the conditions which make her dependent upon her husband and how this state of dependency results into her being abused. To find out association between wife's dependency and her abuse, dependency has been divided into objective and subjective. It does not, however, mean that we can draw watertight compartments between the two. In certain cases objective dependency may lead to subjective dependency, whereas in other cases even though there is no objective dependency yet the individual remains subjectively dependent upon her spouse. It can, however, be assumed that a wife who experiences both objective and subjective dependency is at higher risk of being abused in contrast to those who have only objective or only subjective dependency.

For the purpose of analysis wife's objective dependency stands for conditions like not working, i.e., being economically dependent upon husband; not having any property in her name; not receiving any financial assistance from her family of orientation; inability to live alone; inability to do shopping alone, and inability to go outside the city alone.

Further, level of objective dependency may vary from case to case hence, objective dependency was further divided into three levels: low, medium and high. The wives who are objectively dependent upon their husbands are at higher risk of being abused because it would be difficult for these women to come out of the abusive relationship as they do not have the resources to live alone. Their objective dependency is also known to their spouses who may fully exploit the situation knowing fully well that their wives would not be able to leave them. It is further envisaged that wives who have high level of objective dependency are at greater risk of being abused.

Wives with high level of objective dependency are physically abused more in contrast to those who have low level of objective dependency. This is evident in the percentages of the victims at different levels of dependency. Similarly, the percentage of non-victims goes on decreasing to high level. There were 33 respondents who had high level of objective dependency, out of which 60.61 per cent were not the victims of physical violence.

The results of the study support the contention of a few scholars who are of opinion that high level of women's marital dependency is not associated with wife abuse because husbands of dependent wives can maintain their dominant positions without resorting to violence as their wives are in no position to question their dominance. Although no cause and effect relationship can be established between dependency and wife abuse yet the data show an indicative trend that wives who have high level of objective dependency are abused more as compared to those who have low level of objective dependency.

A few scholars contend that objective dependency of the wife per se does not result into her abuse but is mediated by her tolerance. One may, however, raise the question why she develops this tolerance to abuse? One reason may be that she remains subjectively dependent upon her husband because her social reality has not been constructed outside the marital relationship. In Indian society marriage is a must for every woman, unless she adopts a life of celibacy. Remaining unmarried or living a life of a divorcee is looked down upon.

Hence, whether a wife is objectively dependent upon her husband or not she remains subjectively dependent. It is not, however, true in the case of husbands.

Remarriage after divorce or separation is easily available to a man than a woman. Such a discriminatory practice perpetuate subjective dependency in the wives.

Subjective dependency in the present study stands for, not leaving the husband even under adverse circumstances; divorce not considered good; perception that married women even if abused enjoy higher status than divorced; lack of support from kin; greater commitment and more devotion to marital relationship. It is also expected that wives are likely to have different levels of subjective dependency. Depending upon their scores they are divided into three categories: low, medium and high. It is expected that wives having higher level of subjective dependency will be at higher risk of being physically abused in contrast to those having lower level of subjective dependency.

In contrast to 23-94 per cent wives having low subjective dependency more than 42 percent of the wives with high level of dependency are the victims of physical violence of their husbands. There was a steady increase in the percentage of abused wives from low level of subjective dependency through medium level to high level of subjective dependency. Taking into account 38 cases having high level of subjective dependency it was noted that more than 42 per cent were the victims of husbands' physical violence and approximately 58 per cent were free from being physically abused.

Although, no positive correlation could be established between subjective dependency of wife and her being victim of physical abuse yet the high percentage of victims having high level of subjective dependency designate a partial association between subjective dependency and her being battered. The reason for high percentage of such victims can be attributed to wife's commitment to marriage and her inability to use alternative mechanisms to get out of the abusive relationships. Such a situation forces her to cultivate tolerance and continue living in the abusive relationship.

Similarly, the husband uses coercive methods to assert his dominant position in the familial network of relationship because he is confident that his violent behaviour would not be challenged and he can attain the desired goal, that is, subduing his wife. The results of the present study on subjective dependency and wife abuse partially support the findings of other researchers.

Subjective dependency in certain cases may be treated as a consequence of objective dependency. In other cases subjective dependency may not be the outcome of objective dependency. It was for this reason that these two facets of dependency were treated separately, however, to find out the impact of dependency on wife abuse both objective and subjective dependencies have to be combined. In other words, to find out the validity of dependency framework to explicate wife abuse, both the facets of dependency are combined to find out their combined effect on physical violence.

The total dependency scores of the respondents have been arranged into three categories—low, medium and high. The data indicate that wives with higher level of dependency are at higher risk of being abused in contrast to those with lower level of dependency. In contrast to 27.42 per cent of wives with low level of dependency more were the victims of husbands' physical violence. The percentage of non-victims goes on decreasing from lower level of dependency to higher level.

5

Copying Behaviour

There were major social factors associated with the problem of wife abuse they have advocated different coping mechanisms for the solution of the problem. Different researchers have given attention to develop programmes for the wife batterers, such as individual therapy marital and family therapy psychoeducational or psycho-therapeutic group approach; Anger control technique cognitive behaviour strategies and coordinated programmes involving group treatment and community intervention.

In addition to research on batterers treatment programmes, researches have also suggested treatment techniques for the victims. Andersen *et al.* argue that separation of the abused wife from her husband is an important factor for the treatment of abuse and ultimately for her survival and yet when she leaves her husband, she exposes herself to an ever increasing risk of violence.

Thus a wife must not leave her husband until she has the resources to stay away either permanently or long enough to facilitate significant change in the husbands behaviour. Gondolf and Fisher argue that it is the woman's separation that is the prime motivator for a man's attending counselling in the first place, once batterer "gets her back" he is much more likely to drop out of counselling and batter again.

Although different researchers in the United States have started working on the solution of wife abuse, yet they are unable to reach at a consensus because most of them are naive. There is high drop out rates in such programmes. After such programmes their battering ceases but psychological abuse heightens. Stordeur and Stille argue that patriarchal society will not change overnight and that men in society who are reaping the rewards of violence will resist relinquishing their domination, men who attempt to give up their violence will be faced with covert and overt pressures from other men to come back in fine with the attitude of masculine superiority.

The procedures advocated by these researchers may not be applicable to the Indian cultural situation. First, because the available knowledge regarding violence against wife is only anecdotal but there is also no consensus on the definitions of wife abuse. Additionally, no national sample survey has been conducted in India to find out the extent and the severity of the problem. Under these circumstances efforts should be made to assess the nature and the extent and the severity the problem as well as to identify the factors associated with wife abuse.

Further, coping involves three sets of behaviour pattern. First, reactions to violent relationship; secondly, procedures adopted to deal with abusive relationship and thirdly, to develop mechanisms for countering violent behaviour pattern or getting freedom from abusive relationship. Because of above noted reasons this chapter is restricted to only the reactions of the victims to different forms of violence as well as the steps they take to deal with the situation. Husband's violence against wife is not a continuous process but revolves around relative peace and violence. There would be certain periods when the partners exhibit complete sympathy, understanding and love for each other

On other occasions the relationship would be marred with violence. Most of the women who are victims of their husbands violence are of the view that conflicting situation in their intimate relationship is transitory. It is perhaps with this false hope that they continue living in the abusive relationship.

The perceptions of abuse by victims are likely to be different depending upon their training, life situation and availability or non-availability of alternatives. They, in turn, are likely to have ramifications on their reactions to their abusive situation. Further, their reactions are likely to be coloured by the presence or absence of other members in the household. In case, the conjugal violence takes place in the absence of other members of the family or outsiders, the victims are likely to react differently as compared with those victims who are abused in the presence of others.

Victims who are abused in the presence of others are more likely to feel humiliated as they may develop a feeling of having been let down in the eyes of others. The victims are likely to react sharply even to the, mildest form of abuse in case such abuse takes place in the presence of children and in-laws. In case of children, the victims may feel that their limited area of authority over children has been eroded. On the other hand, if the abuse takes place before the in-laws and outsiders, the battered women are likely to feel that they have been let down in the estimation of their in-laws and outsiders. Such victims are more likely to develop a feeling of helplessness. Before taking into account the victims' reactions to their abuse it is therefore essential to know, in whose presence their abuse had taken place.

Out of 187 cases of victims of violence, only 24 victims informed that their abuse took place in the absence of other members of the family or outsiders. It is only in these cases where violence can be labelled as a "private matter" between husband and wife. In a majority of cases their abuse took place in the presence of their children. Such a situation is likely to create a sense of powerlessness among the victims. Further it would have negative effect on the children.

A number of researchers are of an opinion that children who are brought up in violent families are more likely to become violent parents. It was only in 25 cases where women were abused by their husbands in the presence of outsiders. Such a situation is likely to create greater humiliation and shame for the victims. Approximately one-fourth of the victims were abused in the presence of their in-laws. Their abuse may be attributed not only to interference in the conjugal relationship by the in-laws but also depicts stronger ties with family of orientation of the husband than his family of procreation.

As the respondents were allowed multiple choices it was noticed that a number of victims told that they were abused in the presence of other members of the family as well as outsiders. These are the victims who are more likely to be depressed as the charm of their married life starts fading away.

Studies conducted on wife abuse and victims- reactions report a high incidence of depression among the victims. Wife abuse has been claimed to produce reactions among the victims such as "paralyzing terror", "terrifying intimidation", "shame and degradation" and "humiliation and isolation". A number of clinical studies report a high incidence of depression and anxiety.

The literature on psychological problems of battered women consistently report depression, anxiety and somatic problems. The samples of the battered women in these studies are exclusively the samples of women who come forward and seek help, hence are not the representative samples of the abused wives.

It is quite probable that there may be psychologically troubled and more anxious abused wives who have not sought such help. Keeping in view the methodological shortcomings and the small size of the sample and lack of comparison group, it becomes difficult to draw any generalization with regard to reactions of the abused women. Further, it is not known whether they have been abused on single occasion or repeatedly.

Additionally, psychological distress experienced by battered women was initially thought to be responsible for their battering. Recently researchers have proposed that depression, anxiety and somatic disorders reported by battered women are the consequences of their being abused rather than a cause.

Based on Second National Family Violence Survey in the United States, Gelles and Harrop examined the effects of violence against women as per the information provided by 3002 female respondents. Women who reported experiencing violence also reported higher level of depression, anxiety and somatic disorders. Such a situation has prompted these battered women to contemplate suicide and a higher percentage of them had reportedly made suicidal attempts in comparison to non-battered women.

The battered women may also develop a feeling of helplessness as they may find themselves unable to check the violent behaviour of their husbands as well as they find that social definitions are unsupportive in helping them to come out of the abusive relationship. The abused women often suffer from, what Walker calls "Learned helplessness", in that the victims come to the conclusion that no relationship exists between their actions and the outcomes. After trying and failing to prevent the abuse of their husbands they give up.

In addition, learned helplessness is more likely, when the victims of abuse attribute the abuse to internal, stable and global causes. There is, however, another side to this learned helplessness. The helplessness on the part of the victims is created by their perpetrators of violence. It is in this context that Kipnis opines that battering males may induce guilt in their victims by blaming them for the abuse, until they come to blame themselves.

Blaming the victims is frequently used to justify use of coercive power. Further, the battering men arouse fear in the victims by frightening them with threat of abandonment and of physical violence and by actual physical violence of varying severity. Additionally, the victims are forced to develop a feeling of powerlessness and helplessness because they find that social support system would not come to their rescue, hence they continue to suffer humiliations in silence with the hope that things may improve.

There would be a few cases who may not accept a victim's role and as a consequence of being abused by their spouses, they may develop a feeling of hatred and may also become vengeful. Keeping in view the cultural ethos and status of women in India, where a wife is expected to treat her husband as God (*Pati Parmeshwar*) few victims of such abuse may develop a feeling of hatred against their husbands.

In the present study an attempt was made to find out the reactions of the victims to their abuse. It was expected that most of the victims would give their reactions which would be self-directed rather than directed against the perpetrators of violence, i.e., their husbands. Keeping in view the reactions of the victims of different types of violence in the conjugal relationship it was noted that a majority of the cases had developed a feeling of depression. The results of the present study support the findings of Gelles and Straus and Gelles and

Harrop that high level of depression was a consequence of their being abused by their husbands.

Further, a number of respondents assumed the responsibility of provoking their husbands to be violent and hence, started blaming themselves for their abuse. These cases developed a feeling of guilt in them and indirectly endorsed the contention of their abusers that they had "asked for it. A number of researchers have also come to this, conclusion in their studies in which the victims assumed the responsibility of provoking their husbands to be violent a and suffered from the feeling of guilt. Additionally, a few respondents became afraid after having been abused by their husbands. These were the cases who have been threatened of dire consequences by their husbands if they did not act according to their dictates. As a consequence of their abuse they became very fearful and hence, their conjugal relationship was marked with fear rather than mutual love and understanding.

As expected, a few victims blamed their husbands for their violent acts. There were only 11 cases who developed 117 hatred against their husbands because of their violent behaviour pattern against them and three cases as an outcome of their being abused developed animosity and hostility to such an extent that they became vengeful and would like to take up some action against their perpetrators of violence. It can, thus be assumed that these cases who have developed hatred and enmity against their abusive spouses are likely to seek intervention from the formal agencies so that they could teach a lesson to their abusers.

The above description regarding the reactions of the victims helps in concluding that in spite of being abused by the husbands, the women in India suffer in silence and do not develop a feeling of hatred against their spouses. It does not, however, mean that they have not reacted to their abuse but their reactions were self-directed rather than directed against the abusers.

The strategy an individual adopts depends upon ones perception of the abusive situation. The analysis of the reactions of the victims to their violence indicated two types of reactions. One, self-directed and the second as 'other directed'. However, keeping in view one's training, socialization, life situations and the possibility of getting help from kin and others, one would act accordingly. It is further, envisaged that marital relationship is marked both by mutual sympathy and conflict. When two persons interact there may be a number of issues on which they think alike as well as have difference of opinion.

Keeping in view the quality as well as the permanency of relationship, some incidents of dispute between the partners or sporadic incidents of conflict or violence may be accepted by the partners as part and parcel of their intimate relationship. As stated earlier conjugal relationship is not marked with continuous conflicts and fights but there are occasions when such conflicts stop and partners have cordial relationships. Hence, the conjugal relationship revolves around love and conflict and there is a tendency on their part to overlook certain sporadic incidents of disputes.

The basic assumption of exchange theory that human interaction is guided by the pursuit of reward and avoidance of punishment is not applicable to the husband wife relationship particularly in the Indian society. The following writers Homans and Blau, Gelles believe that an individual who provides a reward to another thereby places him or her in debt, so that the second individual must furnish benefits to the first in return. The interaction will continue if rewards come equally to both the parties, if not, it will be broken off. However, intrafamilial relations, particularly, husband-wife relationship, cannot be broken off easily. As a consequence, when a partner perceives injustice or is abused, the individual may become angry but keeping in view, the social definitions and societal reactions a person may think twice before initiating any step which would permanently break off the relationship.

Each victim of abuse is likely to work out her own strategies to deal with abusive situation in the conjugal relationship. It is only when violence becomes recurrent and individual strategies fail to bring about change in the violent behaviour pattern of the spouse, the victim may feel quite helpless. It is this helplessness on the part of the victim which would force her to seek some assistance from other persons. Frieze *et al.* found that members of the wife's family are more likely to be sought out help to end battering than any other informal help source.

Among the formal agencies police were likely to be approached than other formal sources. Almost similar conclusions were drawn by Pagelow with regard to use of formal sources. Based on indepth interviews of the victims Bowker came to know about different techniques used by the women, to get their husbands to stop battering. These techniques were clustered into three types:

a. personal strategies, including talking, promising, threatening, hiding, passive defense, aggressive defense and avoidance;

b. use of informal help sources, including family members, in-laws, neighbours, friends and shelters; and

c. formal help sources, including the police, social service agencies, lawyers and district attorneys.

It is expected that the victims would first use informal help sources before seeking formal help in case she is not able to check the violent behaviour of their husbands. Further, the help from the informal sources would not imply asking them to intervene but by sharing one's experiences with them and seeking their advice for dealing with the abusive relationship. It was in this context that the victims were asked, whether they shared their abusive experiences with their relatives and close friends?

It is interesting to note that a majority of the victims did not share their abusive marital relationship experiences even with their relatives and close friends but preferred to rely upon their own strategies to deal with the abusive situation. It needs an independent study to find out the reasons as to why these cases have not shared their experiences with their informal sources for seeking their advice to tackle the abusive situation as well as the reasons why they are continuing to stay in the abusive relationship. As the scope of the present study was limited to finding out the coping behaviour pattern of the victims, the description would be limited to only those cases who have sought informal and formal help to deal with the situation.

Out of 187 victims of violence, only 50 cases shared their experiences with their informal help sources, i.e., kin and close friends. Out of these 50 cases, 36 cases were the victims of physical violence of their husbands and 6 victims were adopting "passive" and "aggressive-defence" mechanisms. In the remaining 14 cases, they were free from physical violence but were the victims of verbal and psychological violence of their husbands.

When the victims own strategies to deal with violent situation fail, they are likely to approach their informal group to seek advice to face the situation.

As the victims themselves have failed, they seek their advice with the hope that by acting on their advice, they will be better equipped to change the behaviour pattern of their husbands so that they could have cordial relations with their spouses. Whenever there is a conflict between husband and wife and this conflict is brought to the notice of informal group of the conjugal unit, there would be certain persons who would show sympathy to the victims and others may take the side of the husbands.

Depending upon the nature of the abuse, the reactions of the informal group are likely to vary. Further, some members of the informal group may advise the victims to patch up for the purpose of saving their marriage whereas others may simply lend lip-service but would not give any concrete advice. Still others, are likely to advise the victims either to seek help from formal agencies or to break off the abusive relationship.

Data reveal that in a majority of the cases, the members of the informal group advised the victims to patch up with their spouses. Indirectly these members valued their continuation in the conjugal relations and advised them to reconcile to the situation for the purpose saving their marriage.

As in the case of the victims, their informal group also endorsed the traditional values, wherein it is the wife who is expected to yield irrespective of the fact whether she is at fault or not just in opposition to this, 10 victims were advised to seek help from formal agencies and in 8 cases the members of informal groups even advised for breaking off marital relationships. In addition to these, there were 15 cases where the victims found the attitudes of the members of their informal group not of much help because they showed indifference to their problem.

After seeking the advise of the members of the informal group the victims are not likely to translate the advise into practice irrationally and immediately. They would re-evaluate their situation and would work out their own strategies to deal with the situation. To the marital partners the richest payoff of well managed conflict comes with yielding after a fight. Any intimate relationship implies some readiness to yield one's own self-interest when it clashes with that of a partner. Give and take relationship between husband and wife also implies bending one's own will to the wishes of the other. Yielding, no doubt, involves loss of self-respect but those who value the relationship yielding is a small price so long as it leads to cessation of the conflict and an improvement in the quality of the relationship.

Given the lower status of women in our society, as well as the stigmatized position of the single woman, the victims are likely to take the initiative of patching up the differences because they do not like to break off the relationship permanently. It does not, however, mean that it is only the women who move first in the direction of reconciliation. In the conjugal relationship both the partners are likely to patch up if they value the relationship. The husband, the perpetrator may also realize his mistake and may become very apologetic over his behaviour pattern. It is, therefore, expected that both the partners would take the initiative for reconciliation, however, more wives than the husbands are likely to take the first step. The data indicate that in a majority of the cases both the partners take the initiative to patch up, i.e., sometimes the husband reconciles first and at other times, it is the wife who takes the initiative for reconciliation. Either husband or wife here means that whosoever realizes his or her mistakes first, takes the initiative for reconciliation.

Secondly, more wives than the husbands take the first step for reconciliation. Further, out of 33 husbands who tried to reconcile first after the quarrel, 78.79 per cent were also the initiators of the quarrel whereas in cases of 44 wives who tried to reconcile first, only 59 per cent had started the quarrel, but less percentage of husbands had tried to reconcile. On the other hand, less number of wives had started the quarrel but a higher percentages of them had taken the steps for reconciliation. The results reinforce the dominant position of husbands in the conjugal relationship.

In spite of reconciliatory approach of the wives to put an end to the conjugal quarrel, it might erupt again and again and might force them to seek help from some formal agencies. Their decision to involve formal agencies in the intimate relationships is not an abrupt or a spontaneous response to one isolated violent act on the part of their spouses. Their decision is an outcome of recurrent violent behaviour of the spouses as well as based on negative experiences over a period of time. It has been argued that the battered women are in a kind of "social trap" in which an immediate pay off obscures the violent events that precede it.

In this process the relationship alternates unpredictably from periods of violence to periods of relative peace, thereby creating hope that things could be made to be alright if the women can just keep things running smoothly. However, when the situation escalates and goes beyond their control only then, they would venture to seek the help from the outside sources. It, however, does not mean that all the victims of their husbands' violence would seek intervention from formal sources after having failed to control the abusive behaviour pattern of their husbands.

A number of victims may be ignorant about the type of the formal help available or they have developed "learned helplessness" and reconciled to their fate or they may be afraid that such intervention instead of helping them may enhance the severity of abuse against them. This is an area which needs an independent study, particularly in Indian setting where research on conjugal violence is very much limited. After having failed in their personal strategies to deal with violent situation they seek help from the informal groups. In case such help also does not yield any result and violent situation persists as a natural consequence thereof, they may seek help from the formal agencies. It is, however, expected that few victims of husbands violence will seek intervention from formal agencies. It is in this context the victims were asked, "Had they sought help from the formal agencies for resolving the violent situation?" It is surprising to note that out of 187 cases of husbands violence only 16 victims had sought help from outside formal agencies. Nine victims sought the intervention of influential persons who could have some control over their husbands and seven victims sought the help of women organizations like Punjab Istri Sabha.

However, when such intervention failed to yield the desired results two victims had sought help from the legal counsellors and one case sought help from Crime Against Women Cell of the Police Department.

It would be in the fitness of the thing to explain the background of such victims who have sought help from the formal agencies. Out of 16 such cases, 14 were the victims of their husbands' physical violence and among these 14 cases there were 5 victims who had also used 'defensive violence' against their violent husbands. The remaining two cases were the victims of other form of violence. It is surprising to note that out of 67 victims of battering, only 14 battered women have sought help from-the formal agencies.

The results of this study do not support the contention of Gelles that the greater the severity of battering, the more likely the victim would seek intervention from formal agencies. As to why the remaining cases have not sought such help can be the subject matter for another independent study. As the present study has been restricted to only those cases who sought help from the formal agencies, the subsequent analysis will be restricted to only those 16 cases.

With regard to the educational background of the victims who sought help from formal agencies, it was found that either those respondents who were less educated or had high educational qualifications sought such help. Out of 16 cases, 9 had graduated and above. On the other hand, 6 cases who were either illiterate or had education up to middle level sought such assistance. Although it is difficult to draw any generalization based on 16 cases yet it is safe to conclude that women who are highly educate or had lower level of education seek assistance from the formal agencies and women, who belonged to middle category. With regard to the working status of the victims who had sought intervention from the formal agencies, no clear cut trend was noticeable. Out of 16 cases, 5 were those who were not engaged in any paid work outside the household. In addition there were 3 cases who had lower occupational status. In contrast to these, 8 victims were engaged in occupations of medium prestige. In other words, the victims having higher educational attainment but engaged in medium prestige occupations are more likely to seek help from formal agencies.

The class background of their spouses was also checked and no distinction was found with regard to their class affiliation. These 16 cases were equally distributed in an the four social classes, however, with the exception of the victims of upperclass, the cases belonging to other three classes were the victims of physical violence of their husband and in the upper class out of four cases, only two were the victims of physical violence and remaining two cases were the victims of other forms of violence. In short, no clear cut association was found between the class background and seeking help from formal agencies.

With regard to the type of help advanced by these formal agencies, it was noted that in 6 cases the women organizations provided them social or moral support implying thereby, listening to their problems sympathetically and assuring them that their injustices would be vacated. In five other cases, help in the shape of counselling was extended. The women organization as well as the influential persons had a meeting with their husbands, and family of orientation of both the spouses.

In these cases attempts were made to seek the assistance of the kin of both the partners for settling the dispute between the conjugal unit. One victim was helped in filing a divorce case against her husband. There were four victims who informed that these formal sources neither came to their rescue nor gave them any constructive advice.

To what an extent the intervention of the formal sources was helpful to the victims? In other words were the victims able to have congenial relationship subsequent to intervention from the formal sources? Out of 16 cases, 5 victims gave the reply in affirmative. These victims contended that after the intervention from the formal agencies, their abuse at the hands of the husbands had stopped. However, out of these 5 cases one had already sought divorce and 4 have been provided legal separation. As all these five cases were not staying with their abusive partners, they got freedom from daily quarrels and abuse.

In the remaining 11 cases even after the intervention of the formal agencies their abuse has not stopped. Despite their efforts at the personal level, informal level and intervention from the formal sources their abuse continues and in the absence of other alternatives they are continuing to stay in the abusive relationship. In short, it can be concluded that intervention even by the formal agencies has not helped the victims to get freedom from violence of their spouses. They can be relieved of the abusive situation only when they leave their perpetrators. In case they become aware that leaving the abusive spouse is the best mechanism to get rid of violence but when they continue to stay with the abusive partner and suffer, one may raise the question, why do they stay with them?

A number of studies have been conducted to find out answer to this question. Legal writer Elizabeth Truninger lists seven factors that help to explain why women do not break off relationships with abusive husbands. These are : (a) the women have negative self-concepts, (b) they believe their husbands will reform, (c) there is economic hardship, (d) they have children who need a father's economic support, (e) they doubt they can get along alone, (f) they believe divorcees are stigmatized, and (g) it is difficult for women with children to get work. Strube and Barbour argued that the more committed a woman is to the relationship the harder it is to justify psychologically that leaving is the best decision.

Similar ideas have been reported by other research who argue that economic and psychological dependency, social stigma, presence of small children, lack of alternative support system and embarrassment to admit that she has stayed in such a bad situation for so long, force her to remain in violent relationship. However, another group of researchers explains their stay in terms of cost and benefit. They feel that women have invested too much in the shape of time, effort and emotional involvement that they can't think of leaving the relationship.

Marriage in India is not a social contract. It is not contracted to seek personal happiness from the marital relationships. Marriage is considered as a social and religious obligation. This is more true in case of Indian women whose destiny in life has been marriage and motherhood. The Indian women right from their childhood are trained to be submissive, expected to develop patience and courage to face different odds in life but not to seek separation from their spouses. Although legally she is allowed to seek divorce because of the atrocities of her husband, yet social definitions, values and norms have not undergone appropriate changes to create congenial situation for her to go for divorce if circumstances so demand.

Consequently, divorce for women is still stigmatized. Under these circumstances, it is not easy for her to terminate the marital relationship even though it is abusive. Additionally, she may be economically, psychologically and socially dependent upon her husband or she had made so much emotional investment in her marital relationship and children that she would continue to suffer rather than go for the last resort, i.e., separation or divorce.

To get a clearer picture the remaining 11 cases were asked the obvious question, why do they continue to stay in the abusive relationship? These respondents indicated different compulsions and gave a number of reasons which force them to continue staying in the abusive relationship, e.g., for the sake of children, for the sake of family reputation, with the hope that things will improve one day and that they could not think of alternative way of living.

6

Marriage Systems

In most cases, it is the elderly ladies of the families concerned who take the lead in the matter of marriage. They consider it their foremost duty to suggest marriage proposals for marriageable girls and boys. Other members of the family also keep on the lookout for suitable by young people. The grand parents particularly, taken the greatest care to keep themselves well-informed about suitable boys and girls.

When the elderly ladies of the two parties meet at some function or other the opportunity is available of the discuss the possibility of an alliance. As it is a family matter and previously contemplated, both parties give authority an elderly lady who settles a date for a talk between the families. This generally happens when the lead is taken by the elder people of the family.

Another procedure is through interested friends and relatives, especially when a suitable match is not available amongst near-relations. Friends and relatives often suggest the name to the guardians concerned and the process of investigation and settlements starts. In this way common friends and relatives are useful in the process of selection.

The third procedure is by ascertaining a suitable match through servants, fruit and sweet vendors, barber's wife and the like who move among several families and are able to render service to various families.

Thus, in Oriental countries the process of selection rests mainly with the guardians, their friends, and relatives and well wishers. In Western countries the procedure is quite deferent as the selection of mates is to a great extent mutual and direct. Girls as well as boys move freely in society and have opportunities to come into contact with and to get closely acquainted with each other. Co-education, professions and social gatherings, etc., afford favourable occasions. There is no question of the guardians taking the consent of the young people, but it is the young people themselves who inform their guardians of having settled a betrothal.

In present society, though the old role of the parents still prevails under the influence of Western education more and more, it is considered proper to take the consent of friends and cousins. This practice is becoming common.

The initiation of a marriage proposal as such is a very important item for it opens the way to negotiation and settlement. The main initiation starts, no doubt, with the guardians concerned but there are other people also connected with it e.g., relatives, friends and intermediaries.

The initiation of a marriage in Western countries is different from ours, as they settle the marriage directly and the initiation is also direct. In India the initiation starts from the side of the girl, amongst the Hindus, but amongst the muslims it always start from the side of the boys. Thus among the Shias also the marriage proposal is initiated by the guardians of the boy, either through correspondence or personal interview. The right to initiate a marriage by the mates themselves has been sanctioned any Islam. But in India, it has become a social custom that usually the boys and girls do not initiate the proposals on their own. It is customary even now for the guardians to initiate the marriage proposals. There is, however no had and fast rule in the religion as to which party should initiate the proposal, though generally the guardian of the boy take the lead in this respect and it is open to the guardian of the girl to accept of reject the proposal. In some cases it has also been observed that the proposal is not made directly by the guardians but through intermediaries. A marriage proposal from the girls side is considered to be humiliating or indecent and therefore is always avoided.

But a change is perceptible in this connection. (During the last decade it has been the tendency of some of the educated and enlightened Shia guardians to take the consent of the mates before the initiation of marriage proposal). Respondents' education and sex and the degree to which they favoured initiation of marriage proposals by boys and girls themselves have been examined in this connection.

Negotiation starts after initiation through intermediaries and friends, and when concurrence has been reached in settlement, they become more and more defined and details are discussed and a day fixed for final settlement. As already pointed out earlier, it is the bridegroom's party that takes the initiative and makes the proposal for the marriage, but owing to the impact of Hindu culture and customs and the migration of a large number of suitable Shia young men to outside India, sometimes the bride's party takes the initiative and makes the proposal for the marriage. Thus, the custom as it originally existed has undergone a change owing to the circumstances mentioned above.

As in initiation, so in negotiations, elderly ladies, mutual friends and close relatives play prominent role. Apart from them, a unique personality known as Mushatta was accustomed to play a great role in the marriage negotiations. A Mushatta is a working woman visiting well-to-do families to help young girls to complete their toilet, etc. Because of their close associations and unchallenged access to different families and mixing with them, they used to gain close and deep knowledge of the status of the different families, the character of the individuals and their behaviour. Such Mushattas are practically few now, but in the past amongst the erstwhile Muslim Estates and Zamindaries, they played a great role. They were, however, paid liberal sums as rewards for their services. The following table shows the role played by different people in the marriage negotiations.

On the details of the procedure in negotiations, it is worth mentioning that in some cases the guardians of the bride have been known to ask guardians of the bridegroom to transfer some immovable property such as a house, etc., in the name of bride, so that she becomes the owner of some immovable property from her husband's side. Another condition which is also imposed in some cases is that the husband should pay Rs. 50 or Rs. 100 (Whatever amount is settled between the parties) as expenses of the pan dan (betel case) to the wife every month. This has nothing to do with other domestic expenses.

Another interesting feature in connection with the procedure of the negotiation for a marriage is that, in some cases, the guardians of a bridegroom, if he is well-established in life, demand costly presents in the shape of movable or immovable property from those guardians of the bride. This may be either an old relic of the past or may be due to the impact of Hindu customs. Though not widely prevalent amongst the Shias, yet some of the guardians of educated and employed youths have an eye on such a custom.

A somewhat similar tendency which is gaining strength among rich guardians of the girl is the concept of Ghar

Damadoo the intention being to keep the daughter and the 'son-in-law' in the guardian's own house after the marriage. In recent years this practice has become common specially in wealthy Shia families and where the bride happens to be the 'only' daughter.

In some cases an important issue which is generally settled at the time of the guardian is in a position to give such an assurance by reason of the high position or status he may be holding. It has been observed that in several cases such promises had not been fulfilled by the guardians of the girl after marriage and differences had arisen between the two parties sometimes after the marriage. It has also been observed that in certain cases matrimonial alliances are settled on a mutual basis, a boy of one family marrying a girl of the other and a boy from the latter family marrying a girl from the former.

Generally, Shias consider the negotiation complete after the ceremony of Istikhara. According to them, it is taking the consent of God for concluding a particular matter. Generally, the Mujtahid (Religious Head) obtain the consent of God with the help of a Tasbih (Rosary) and when the Istikhara is wajib (super affirmative) it is considered that the marriage between the parties should be finally settled.

The mother of the boy or some other near woman relative (if the mother is dead), accompanied by her female friends and relations, pays a visit to the house of the girl with sweets and Imam Zamin to see the girl immediately after Istikhara. The guardians of the girl accept the sweets and entertain them with refreshments. In most cases the girl is adorned and the women members of the mother of the boy ties the Imam Zamin round the upper portion of the bride's right arm (a silver or gold coin wrapped in a silken cloth). This ceremony is called the Imam Zamin ceremony.

In some of the Shia families there is also the betrothal or mangni ceremony. In this ceremony, the female members of the boy's family visit the house of the girl, taking with them sweets, fruits and vegetables (according to the status of the boy's or girl's family). In some families even five to ten maunds of sweets are taken. The sweets are distributed among the relatives and friends of the girl's family. In return sweets, fruits and vegetables are sent to the boy's house and there also sweets are distributed among the relatives and friends of the boy's family.

In some families at the Mangni ceremony, gold or silver rings are also exchanged. After this ceremony the marriage proposal is supposed to be finally settled.

Generally at the time of Imam Zamin or Mangni, the date for the marriage is settled by the guardians of the couple. Among the Shias, marriages mostly take place in the months of Rajah, Shaban, after the tenth of Id-ul-Zuha and the second half of Rabi-ul-Awwal. Moharrum is considered as an inauspicious occasion for marriage because of the tragedy of Karbala which took place in this month.

Amongst the Shias the 'mourning period', is observed for 2 months and 8 days i.e., from the 1st. Moharrum upto the 8th of Rabi-ul-Awwal, the day when the female members of the family of the Holy prophet reached Madina after the tragedy of Karbala. Usually marriages do not take place in the month of Ramzan also, because people fast during this month. There are a very few cases in which marriage proposals were broken down after the ceremony of Istikhara.

Parents are solely responsible for the settlement of the marriage in the Shia community. They initiate the marriage proposals, and negotiate them on their initiate. They inquire about family status, character and other necessary particulars from the other party, and when wholly satisfied, give their final consent. It is obvious, therefore that parents or guardians still play a prominent role in the settlement of the marriages of their wards. Even in the case of a love marriage, the parents or guardians do exercise a sort of cheek on the youth. As has been observed earlier, the deference between the Western system and the Indian system and the Indian system is that in the West the partners themselves seek partners, while in India, including the Shia community, it is the parents who take the lead in the marriage negotiations.

Another remarkable deference is that in the West a union of hearts takes place before the union of hands. India, generally, a union of hands takes place before the union of hearts. The relationship between the educational background of the respondents and their views on the question of giving full liberty to boys and girls in the selection of their life partners has been studied in one table. In the other, the relationship between the cities in which the respondents resided and their views has been studied.

The institution of marriage is a sacred contract between two people which has been practiced since times immemorial. Dr. L.M. Singhvi has defined it in these terms, "Marriage is an ancient institution validated by individual needs and social utility, sanctified by scriptural approval and fortified by manifold norms and injunctions. As an institution, it has survived in the midst of many changes." Some have dubbed marriage as a futuristic institution in an archaic age. "In our society everything has become so commercialised, that even marriage has become so. It is also a case where ostentatious living has become more important than human beings".

It is well to remind ourselves from time to time that marriage protects women from themselves, as well as from men and raises the status of both sexes in their intimate relation with each other. Ideas change with the times. The mosaic law prescribed penalty of death on both parties when a married woman committed adultery. The old Roman law punished adultery on the part of the wife, but not on the part of the husband; and although a father has the right to kill both his daughter and her accomplice if she was taken in adultery either in his house or her husband's. A husband has no such right as to his wife in any case.

Sexual activity is essentially a physical response to a mental stimulus which may affect different persons in different way, and one person may be attracted by a feature or quality to which his neighbours is indifferent. In fact, sexual offences, are more liable to be misjudged by prejudice and ignorance, perhaps than the majority of criminals and bias is almost inevitable if their conduct is reviewed solely in the light of narrow person experience and the tastes and distastes of the assesser. Sexual offenders are generally regarded as individuals who engage in certain illegal sexul activities. The medical conception is wider and includes cases of theft, burglary, etc., if the offence has for its purpose the immediate of delayed gratification of normal or abnormal sexuality.

Marriage has also been defined as a mutual commitment to make a home where member of the family will share common problems and have mental space of each other.

A married woman's condition is as bad as a person in quarantine. In the year 1984, was passed Family Courts Act 1984 which provides for the establishment of family courts with a view to promote conciliation in and secure speedy settlement of, disputes relating to marriage and family affairs. The Act envisages that those judges shall be responsible or bringing about conciliation who are:

"committed to the need to protect and preserve the institution of marriage and to promote the welfare of children and lawyers will not be ordinarily allowed and the proceedings shall be in camera and once an agreement is reached between the parties, there will be no appeal."

Unfortunately, even today women are, taught to bear up with very humiliation, beating, molestation and even being burnt but not to speak but become the slaves of the family otherwise she will be put in jeopardy. And thus the women become very vulnerable to violence within the four walls of her house away from public gaze. The most unfortunate part is that when a woman goes to the police station to lodged a complaint, she is quite often told not to bring family matters in the police or police themselves try to reconcile the husband and wife and by that thus all evidence is destroyed.

Child marriage is beyond doubt having pernicious effects on the physique of Indians. It is by no means an ancient institution in India. Macdonell and Keith and Sir Herbert Risley and other scholars who have studied the question all agree that the Hindus of the rest Hindu India married not as children but as adults. It seems safe to say that child marriage was not common in India before the Musalman invasion. How and when exactly this evil system became prevalent may be uncertain, but there can be no doubt that it is today eating into the vitals of the nation.

However, it is one thing to admit child marriage to be one of the factors responsible for the material and spiritual ills of present-day India and quite another to make its existence a pretext for ignoring the still more important factors. Give dog a bad name and hang it is a recognised maxim in political propaganda and Miss Mayo's observation on early marriage in India do not ignore it.

Child marriage was prevalent among several of the people that produced great civilization in antiquity. The Greeks who still inspire the models in harmonious development of the whole man as well as of the physical man, married very early.

The Romans who made good soldiers and administrators married as children. So also did the Hebrews. In England down to the time of the Stuarts child marriage was common.

If child marriage were enough to make a nation effete, the Greeks and the Romans and the Hebrews would not have left such a lasting impression on history. The fact is that a devastating factor like child marriage is seldom allowed by Society to go altogether without counterbalancing safeguards. In India this safeguard is provided in many of the child-marrying castes by postponing the consummation of marriage till a considerable period after the marriage ceremony. Marriage thus becomes a sort of betrothal and child betrothal. Not all Hindus marry too early.

The lower castes for the most part marry comparatively late. Among the higher castes also the system is not without safeguards in most parts. This fact of safeguards has been observed by all competent observers, among them being Sir Herbert Risley and Sir Edward Gait, both of whom had ample experience in the matter in their official capacity as Census Commissioners. Observed Risley and Gait in the Census Report of 1901:

"No one has seen a Punjab regiment man past, or has watched the sturdy Jat women lift the heavy water-jars at the village well is likely to have any misgivings as to the effect of their marriage system on the physique of the race". Sir Denzil Ibbertson pointed out earlier in his Report of the Punjab Census that the Rajputs in the Punjab marry when about 16 years old and begin to co-habit immediately, the jat on the other hand marry between 5 and 6 years generally—but the bride does not go to the groom's house for several years with the result that for practical purposes the Jats begin married life sometimes even later than the Rajputs do.

For the Hindus, marriage is a sacrament an event expected to bring joy, glory and fulfilment to the man and his wife. However, the marriage ceremony, with its elaborate rituals, Sanskrit chants, flowers and music has mystified the true nature of the institution.

Since the Hindu marriage is not a contract (unlike the Muslim Marriage) there is no religious (or legal) requirement that the two people, getting married must consent, even formally, to living together as husband and wife. It has been held by the Madras and Allahabad high courts that "under the Hindu Law, marriage of lunatic or an idiot or an impotent person is valid unless invalidated on the ground that the capacity for performance of the essential ceremony of marriage is lacking in the bridegroom." And thus for hundreds of years men and women (in fact, little girls and boys) were forced into marriage which was based on neither love nor respect for each other. Hindu marriage was based solely on the need of the family to perpetuate itself through the male line. If we trace the legal history of the institution of Hindu marriage, we will see that it is a history of how, though a long and painful struggle, Hindu marriage is becoming a contract between two consenting adults instead of being a sacrament imposed on unwilling men and women. It was specially cruel for women who had no other life other than the one confined within the four walls of their marital home.

We must remember that there was no such things as the Hindu marriage, because there was no consolidated community called the Hindus. People were divided into castes, sub-castes and sects, each with different sets of customs and usages which determined the rights and obligation's of men and women within the family. These customs were very different from each other. Among the lower castes, women, like their menfolk and equal rights to divorce and often they had rights to immovable property. The lower castes did not have many inhuman practices like sati or enforced widowhood. This was party because they did not have property and so they were not obsessed with preserving family lineages. However, whatever the customs or rituals, there was one common feature to all type of Hindu marriage—they were based on inequality between men and women. This inequality was expressed by the emphasis of double standard of morality, one for the man and another for the woman.

The hypocrisy of religious practices was exposed by courageous social reformers like Pandit Ramabai who wrote "... there were two things on which all those books, the Dharma Shastras, the sacred epics, cpics, the puranas and the modern poets (the popular preachers of the present day and orthodox high-caste men) were agreed, that women of high and low caste, as a class, were bad, rather very bad, worse than demons, as unholy as untruth and that they cloud not get moksha as men. The only hope of their getting this much desired liberation form karma and its results, that is countless millions of births and deaths and untold suffering was the worship of their husbands."

It was the efforts of the social reformers like Raja Ram Mohan Roy, Ishwarchandra Vidyasagar and Ranade that the British were compelled to ban sati in 1829 and widow remarriage became legal in 1956. The first widow remarriage was celebrated in Calcutta on 7th December, 1856 between Shrischand Vidyaratna and Kalimati Debi, Vidyasagar attended it. The weaves of Shantipur move a special sari with a song for the occasion move into the border.

In 1870 female infanticide was outlawed: two years later inter-caste marriage became legal and in 1874 the widow got life interest in her husband's property. At every stage there was opposition. Tilak opposed the Age of Consent Act of 1891 which raised the age of consummation of Marriage from 10 years to 12 for girls and Bankim Chandra opposed the legislative interference into the bararic practice of polygamy among Kulin Brahmins who married little girls for fat dowries. The stiffest opposition came from the propertied classes.

One petition against widow marriage was signed by 37,000 persons under the leadership of a local Raja and the Pundits of Nadia (in Bengal). One case in 1907 decided by the Allahabad Court shows how even the courts took double standards of morality as natural and applied them without though to the discrimination it implied. The case concerned one Musammat Samundra Kaur was married to Trilok Tiwari. She had left him long ago and became a prostitute. On her death there was a dispute about who her legal heir would be. The court held:

"It is true that an unchaste wife cannot inherit property but that is because under the Mitakshara law it is only a chaste wife who can inherit to husband or obtain maintenance. By her degradation, a woman does not cease to be a Hindu unless she becomes a convert to some other religion, and therefore the rule of succession to her property would be the ordinary rule of Hindu law."

So a "unchaste" woman has no right to her husband's property but he can inherit hers, even if it is acquired by the fruits of her unchastity! In 1937, Hindu Women's Rights to Property Act was passed and in 1941 a committee was set up under the chairmanship of B.N. Rau to look the question of possible condification of Hindu law.

This was a stupendous task. Each caste and sect had its own customary law and the British had encouraged this as part of their divide and rule policy. Whether it was the Travancore Ezhawas, Nambudiri Brahmins, Jats of Punjab, Kulins of Bengal or the Nairs of Kerala, each had their own laws condified by the British. And the condification had resulted in the stagnation of customs with no possibility of their development. Then came independence. One of the first major issues debated in the Constituent Assembly was the Hindu Code Bill drafted on the basis of B.N.Rau Committee's recommendations. This Bill sought to give more rights to Hindu women. It was hotly debated on the eve of election and dropped. It is significant that a leader of the Scheduled Castes and independent India's first Law Minister, Baba Saheb Ambedkar, resigned over the issue.

Hindu Marriage Act made marriage with a lunatic, epileptic or a child, void. This was the first step towards recognising the fact that the marriage ought to be based on mutual consent between the man and the woman. It was only in 1976 that the provision for divorce by mutual consent was incorporated and in 1978 the minimum age for marriage under Hindu Law raised to 18 for women and 21 for men. Daughters got equal rights to their father's property, and dowry was prohibited by an Act of 1961 which was made more stringent in 1985. Despite these changes in the law, Hindu marriage continues to be based on inequality and injustice. Legally, a Hindu woman cannot be a member of the coparcenary and consequently she cannot be the Karta or ask a partition. She still does not get any share in the ancestral property (Kerala is the only state in India which has abolished the institution of Hindu Undivided Family). The father is considered to be the natural guardian of the children and the Hindu woman has no right to decide where the matrimonial home will be her adode after marriage or to take up a career which may keep her away from her husband.

In reality the position of the Hindu woman is even worse, little girls continue to be married off even puberty; the social sanction makes it virtually impossible for widows to think of remarriage; there are several incidents of sati to remind us of the recent past. In other words, under Hindu Law the woman's first primary duty is to her husband.

Prohibition of widow remarriage is also one of those evil customs which cannot be justified. The lot of the Hindu widow is bad indeed, but the wild statements made about the morality of the Hindu widows can only be described as products of an evil mind. In general Hindu widow lead a life of sacrifice and service. Their morality stands on a higher pedestal than Miss Mayo's mind can conceive of. In making her sweeping statements she has only her ignorance of the real conditions and her readiness to generalise on very meagre data.

Firstly, the prohibition against widow remarriage is not universal. The vast majority of Hindus remarry their widows as a rule. This is the practice in all classes considered pastoral or military. This is also the practice among what are known as the low castes. "At the bottom of society, as understood by the average Hindu, we find a large group of castes and tribes practcising adult marriage and widow marriage. The restrictions are generally confined to people of higher castes whose number can in no case exceed 30 per cent of the total Hindu population". Secondly, the rules prescribed for widow's life are not the same in all provinces or among all castes. I have never seen a Hindu widow's head shaved anywhere in the N.W.F. Province or the Punjab or the UP or Rajputana.

"The position and life of the Indian widow varies of course, with the personality of the woman and with the family in which her lot is cast. From writers like Dobois one would judge that she is always on object heartless persecution, a sad and unwilling drudge, while sister Nivedita and her school would have one suppose that the Hindu widow is ever loved and fondly cared for and that she becomes a nun given over to good works, which spring spontaneously from her sorrow-crowned character. Both views are doubtless true in their limited way, and neither should be accepted without modification from the other. Certainly the widow's lot is a sad one at said, that for the widow sadness it better than joy. And doubtless these widows who acquiesce in this judgment and give themselves upwillingly to a lie of utter self-abnegation and service shine at the end as gold purifies by fire....The widowed mother of the head of he house has a position not only of respect and affection, but of authority and power. Younger widows, of course, have no such authority, but they have nearly as much work, and if the service be for the young woman who has no ambition noneless, and for the young woman who has no ambition to be a martyr or a nun the fate of widowhood in India is very heard indeed".

"On the whole, the Indian home is a very narrow and limited place, but it may be a very sweet and holy place as well; and it has produced a type of woman who knows how to love and how to suffer and be faithful and lose herself in those she loves: a type that has great limitations, by which is not without a certain lofty beauty, even through at the antipodes from that of the modern militant suffragette."

Fourthly, the Hindu widow if she is a mother is simply worshipped, perhaps nowhere in the world, says Mr. Pratt, is there more profound reverence for the mother than in India.

"The wife becomes regent," says Sister Nivedita, "when a man dies during the minority of his son; and even if the latter be already of age, his ownership of an estate if an estate is by no means free complete during the lifetime of his mother.

The whole world would cry shame if he acted without her occasional advice, and indeed, the Indian woman's reputation for business capacity is like the French that it is commonly said of encumbered property that it needs a widow's nursing." Dr. G.W. Leitner, first Principal of the Lahore Government College, who studied the Punjab life during the last quarter of the last century very intimately, wrote thus of the lofty conception of marriage and of the state of widows among the Hindus.

The sorrow of a poor widow is said enough in all countries to deserve sympathy, but it is minimised in India by the following considerations:

1. The widows of Muhammadans, of Sikhs, of most of the hill tribes, and of nearly all the lower Hindu castes to marry, and the widows of jats are bound to marry their deceased husband's brother for the protection of the inheritance.

2. The widows who have grown up sons or whose age entitles them to have a voice in the management of the household, practically, and in numerous cases admittedly, rule it.

3. There, therefore only remains a comparatively small number of widows in the higher and middle Hindu castes, and among them only those are to be pitied who are poor or who have unfeeling or no relatives a rare circumstance.

4. The misfortune of these, however, is alleviated:

   (a) by the ideal of the sacredness of the marriage tie; the hope of rejoining the husband and being made worthy of his regard in proportion to her, generally self-inflicted privations, such as sleeping on the floor instead of on a charpoy. It is here where religion strengthens and raises the character of a noble-minded Hindu widow;

   (b) the social consideration which is given to a widow who by her acts shows her underlying grief for her deceased husband;

(c) the sympathy of her own family to which she, in many instances, returns;

(d) the generally liberal provision for life that has been made for her on the 13 the day, which relieves her, at any rate, from the most gnawing cares and allows her to address herself to the education of her children, if any.

"An Inmate of her husband's home at the time of his death, the widow, although she has no legal claim for protection, may be retained there on the terms above described or she may be turned adrift. Then she must live by prostitution, into which she seldom falls. And her dingy, ragged figure, her bristly, shaven head, even though its stubble be white over the haggard face of unhappy age, is often to be seen in temple crowds or in the streets of pilgrimage cities, where sometimes niggard piety doles her a handful or rice." Miss Mayo only shows her ignorance of Hindu Law when she says'a widow has no legal claim for protection. A widow has the first lien on a deceased Hindu's estate for her maintenance and housing. This had to be arranged according to the social position of her deceased husbands.

Like many other communities of the world, Shias too give preference or priority to certain of their kin while settling marriage. Due to some socio-cultural factors "Cousins" occupy a significant place in the matrimonial alliances of the Shias and hence they evolved "cross cousin" and "Parallel cousin" marriages, which are still popular among them. The most probable reason for these sort of matrimonial alliances is that siblings among them yearn for remaining close to each other and hence they want their children to intermarry and give the demonstration of "sibling solidarity."

Two main forms of marriage can be identified on present standards, (1) where the arrangement and settlement of the marriage are entirely in the hands of parents and guardians, (2) where the selection of the partner is entirely the business of the young couple.

As arrange by parents, the selection of a marriage partner is based on social and economic considerations, including the status of the family, their standing and relationship which may be helpful in the bridegroom's advancement in life. They also keep under consideration their (the couple's) compatibility of temperaments and feelings. In all countries of the Orient, China, India, Japan, Korea and the Philippines, as in ancient society, arrangement for marriage is controlled by the parents. On the other hand, marriages arranged by the couples themselves proceed on an entirely different footing. They make their choice on the basis of companionship formed by marital experiences, compatibility of temperament, personality, needs and common interests and ideals. Such factors for mate selection are common in Western countries.

In India the criteria of selection of marriage partners, as pointed out by Professor Kapadia, may be understood from the following extract in which he says : "The question of selection in marriage may be considered from three points of view, namely, the field of selection, the party to selection and the criteria of selection. The field of selection is restricted in two ways. Among some tribes and communities there is a preferential code, enjoining marriage with a particular relative as more desirable, or at times even obligatory. There are, likewise, certain restrictions prohibiting marriage with certain relatives or between certain groups as such marriages are considered in incestuous or undesirable.

There are further restrictions of an endogamous character enjoining marital union within the bounds of a certain group. The Hindus have both endogamous and exogamous rules limiting the selection of a mate. The Hindu community is divided into a number of castes which are endogamous groups; in practice, the caste is again divided into a number of sub-castes, each of which is further sub-divided into a number of sections".

While selecting a partner the main consideration of the father is to see that the selected partner does not suffer from any disease or defamation. What stands out as a prominent consideration is that the spouse must come from a family which is well-known for its adherence to the cultural traditions of the community. Thus, the family is an important factor in the selection of a spouse.

"Now-a-days the idea is to ascertain that the family is not quarrelsome, has no history of persons suffering from incurable diseases and is held high in social estimation for is standard of living, material as well as cultural". In the old days the choice was left to the father and a partner in marriage had little voice in settling it, and marriage did not very often prove unhappy because the parents were fastidious in selecting the spouse from proper families and the social ideals of marriage and joint family organisation offered little change for clash of interests or ideology.

Muslims as such have no limitation in the field of selection of mates and are divided into four Qaums, viz., Syeds, Sheikhs, Moghuls and Pathans. There is no religious restriction in connection with marriage amongst the different Qaums though Islam has no doubt prohibited marriage between certain categories of women and men. On the one hand, there are the Indian ideas about caste, its various forms, divisions and sub-divisions and on the other is the Islamic universality of equality and spirit of anti-restriction. The Shias, being Muslims, ought to be free from caste bias but though they may have no caste they have Qaums determined on a racial basis. So, indirectly and sub-consciously, Hindu ideals have somehow crept into their minds also.

In selecting mates, the Syeds are held in the highest esteem. Although the Syeds themselves prefer a settlement within their own Qaums, especially in the case of the daughter, there are examples where they have chosen non-Syed girls for their sons. Generally each Qaum likes to be married within his or her own circle but inter-Qaum marriages may be witnessed among non-Syeds. Shias mostly give first preference to cousins because of the following considerations : (1) pride of lineage and notions of purity of blood, (2) family solidarity, (3) the prospect of the Jahaz or dowry given to the daughter at the time of marriage remaining in the same family.

Of the above, the most significant is the family consideration. It may be split into (1) consideration pertaining to the bridegroom and (2) consideration pertaining to the bride. Among the qualifications of the bridegroom, apart from the family status, are education, employment, income, health, behaviour, temperament, inclination, social and economic status, relations and sphere of influence. As far as the merits of the bride are concerned, she must be beautiful, of good character and conduct, and also possess perfect mental and physical health. She must be well-trained in household management and such accomplishments such as needle-work, knitting, etc. Amiability, sensibility, consideration, sympathy, attracti-veness, good behaviour are also considered necessary elements.

Marriages between Shia men and Sunni women and *vice versa* were common about 50 years ago in Uttar Pradesh. But such marriages are not prevalent amongst the two sects at present with the exception of love marriages. Islam does not permit inter-religious marriages. Shias dislike marriages with any other Islamic sect. Shia and Sunni marriages used to take place previously, but in the last 50 years or so the relations between both sects have become strained due to certain controversies. So far as converted Shia girls are concerned, some Shias are of the opinion that they may be taken in marriage provided they are ready to follow Shia tenets. In spite of this liberal view such marriages are very rare.

Chief Criteria in Mate Selection

A. *Family factors:* The shias are very particular about the family. The guardians generally do not like to marry outside the family or in a family of lower status.

B. *Personal factors*: Among the Shias, factors that affect a person's choice in marriage are personality, health and temperament, likes and dislikes, attitudes and tendencies. The main consideration before the father or the guardian, however, is that the selected spouse does not suffer from any disease or deformity.

C. *Inter-personal factors*: As described earlier, generally the marriages among the Shias are solemnised with the cousins. Both of them are supposed to know each other since childhood. Such marriages are expected to be helpful in establishing better relations between the mates. A marriage so based on mutual understanding may be described as a sort of "love marriage" because both parties have known each other from childhood.

Jahaz (dowry) is not a major consideration in the selection of a partner. Chastity and morality are regarded as the highest virtues and essential qualifications for a girl. Some parents regard the bride as a gift, to be given to the bridegroom and, therefore, exercise absolute independence in the selection of the mate. Under the notion of marriage as a gift there is little scope for girls' rights in the selection of the partner. Therefore, the father or the guardian is the whole and sole authority in giving this gift to a person whom he considers deserving and fit.

In Indian society, country to the Western one, occasions of contact between unmarried young men and women are rare. Social life does not provide such opportunities as the girls are always under strict vigilance. In India, due perhaps to the impact of Hindu culture on Islam, social stratification amongst the Muslims is also conspicuous. Generally, all the four Qaums among the Shias prefer to marry, not only in their own Qaum, but specially within their families or blood relations. No doubt, some Moghuls, Sheikhs and Pathans give preference to marrying their daughters to Syeds, but the syeds are not at all inclined to accept the sons of these Qaums.

Generally the non-Syed Shias are shy of marrying the daughter of Syeds because the syeds are considered to be higher in status than the non-Syeds. Another reason why the Syeds do not want to give their daughters to non-Syeds is that the issue of such a marriage would naturally belong to the Qaum of their husbands and hence, the continuation of the Siadat (the continuance of the Syed-line would end with the daughter, while if she is married to a Syed the lineage will not end. It has also been observed that some Syeds marry their sons to the daughters of non-Syeds but very rarely and only when they are not able to find a suitable match for their sons in their own *Qaum*.

If the status of women has to be raised and they are to be given their full role in social and economic development, it is essential that their age at marriage should be high enough. Though the legal age of marriage for females is 18 years, a large majority of them in India are married at a much lower age. What is the age at marriage of females in India and what are the regional variations in this respect.

To look at this issue, we have to turn to the census data, data on the age at marriage has been collected in the Indian censuses from 1971. A direct question on the age at marriage has been canvassed both in 1971 and 1981 census. While the 1971 data was presented at district level also, which has made it easier to identify the areas where priority action is required. In this article, we have looked at the data on the female age at marriage collected during the 1981 census.

From these data, the mean age, at marriage of currently married women in India (excluding Assam where census was not taken) in 1981 was 16.7 only. In many of the states, the mean age was much lower. The lowest mean age at marriage was 15.5 years for Madhya Pradesh, closely followed by Rajasthan 15.7 years, Bihar 15.9 years. Andhra Pradesh 16.0 years, Uttar Pradesh 16.2 years and West Bengal 16.3 years. In the rural areas, the mean age at marriage was 16.5, but what is more surprising to note it that even in the urban areas, the mean age at marriage was 17.6 only lower than the legal limit laid down under the law.

Bihar, Madhya Pradesh and Rajasthan were the three states where the mean age at marriage for females was less than 16 years, while in Andhra Pradesh, Uttar Pradesh, Haryana, Maharashtra, West Bengal, Karnataka, Orissa and Tripura, the mean age at marriage was 16 or more but less than 17 years. Of the major states, Kerala, Tamil Nadu, Gujarat and Punjab were the only four states in which the mean age of marriage for females was more than 18 years. Besides these four states, the other smaller states/UTs in which the means age was 18 years or more were Manipur, Meghalaya, Nagaland, Sikkim, Arunachal Pradesh, Dadra and Nagar Haveli, Goa, Doman and Diu, Chandigarh, Delhi and Pondicherry.

Out of the 402 districts in 1981 (excluding Assam), in 35 districts the mean age at marriage for females was below 15 and in 79 districts, it was between 15 and 16 years. That is, in as many as 114 districts of the country, the mean age at marriage for the females was less than 16 in 1981. In another

101 districts, the mean age at marriage was more than 16 but less than 17, while in 79 districts, it was more than 17 but less than 18. In 108 districts only, the mean age at marriage of female was more than the statutory limit of 18 years.

Looking at the various states, the mean age at marriage was less than 16 years in 33 out of 45 districts of Madhya Pradesh, 15 out of 26 districts of Rajasthan, 18 out of 31 districts of Bihar, 20 out of 56 districts in Uttar Pradesh, 11 out of 23 districts in Andhra Pradesh and 7 out of 16 districts of West Bengal. The country can easily be divided into a few regions with similar levels of female age at marriage. The most prominent group of regions is a group of 92 districts spread over the states of Rajasthan (15), Madhya Pradesh (33), Uttar Pradesh (20), Bihar (18) and West Bengal (6) wherein the mean age at marriage of currently married females is below 16 years.

Another group of contiguous districts with mean age at marriage below 16 years is seen in the South Central India, consisting of 11 districts of Andhra Pradesh, 5 districts of Maharashtra and 3 districts of Karnataka. Bordering the districts where the mean age at marriage is below 16 years, different groups of districts with mean age at marriage is between 16.0-16.9 years is seen. The largest of such groups consists of 30 districts spread over Madhya Pradesh (2).

Another prominent region with the mean age between 16 to 16.9 years is seen in the northern part over the states of Rajasthan, the hill districts of Uttar Pradesh, the southern districts of West Bengal, north-east Bihar and adjoining districts of Uttar Pradesh and north-east Bihar and border districts of West Bengal, also, the mean age at marriage is between 16.0-16.9 years. Districts with the mean age at marriage between 17.0-17.9 years from three major groups of contiguous districts; first one consisting of some districts of

Andhra Pradesh, Karnataka and Tamil Nadu; the second one is spread over Bihar, Andhra Pradesh, Madhya Pradesh and Orissa; and the third consisting of districts spread over Haryana, Himachal Pradesh and Uttar Pradesh. There is a group of contiguous districts spread over the states of Karnataka, Kerala and Tamil Nadu where the mean age at marriage is more than 18 years. Excepting the districts of Daman, Raigarh, Uttar Kannad and Malapuram, the mean age at marriage is more than 18 years in all the districts of the West Coast. Punjab forms another region where the mean age at marriage is more than 18 years. Also, in most of the districts in the north-eastern states (excluding Assam), the mean age at marriage is more than 18 years.

In 1971 the mean age at marriage was 15.7. That is, in the decade 1971-81, the mean age at marriage for females increased by one years only. A perceptible increase in the female age at marriage was noticed in Andhra Pradesh, Bihar, Gujarat, Haryana, Madhya Pradesh, Punjab and Rajasthan in 1971-81.

As the educational level of women increased, the mean age at marriage rose very sharply. In the rural areas, the mean age at marriage for illiterate women was 16.3, 17.1 for literate but below middle women, 17.8 for middle but below matric, 19.3 for matric but below graduate and 21.6 for graduate women. In the urban areas, the figures for the respective educational levels were 16.7, 17.4, 18.1. 19.3 and 21.9. This brings out two every significant facts: (a) for all women who were matric or above, the mean age at marriage was more than 19 years, both in the rural as well as in urban areas; and (b) even for women below matric but who had passed middle, mean age at marriage was more than 18 in the urban areas and close to 18 in the rural areas. However, it has also been observed that even in case of illiterate women, the mean age at marriage was as high as 20.6 in the rural areas of Nagaland and 20.2 in the urban areas of Mizoram.

We can examine this issue in another way also, by looking at a proportion of currently married females with age at marriage below 18 years. More than two-thirds (67.7% to be exact) of the women in India had age at marriage below 18 years. In Madhya Pradesh, 81.5% of the currently married women had age at marriage below 18 years; figures in case of other major states were Rajasthan (79.3), Bihar (77.3), Andhra Pradesh (77.1), West Bengal (75.5), Uttar Pradesh (73.8) and Haryana (70.3). In Mizoram, only 19.7% of the currently married females had their age at marriage below 18 years; Nagaland being a close second (24.5).

Kerala and Punjab were the only two major states where in this proportion was less than 40 per cent. The low age at marriage of females has a significant correlation with higher birth rate and higher child mortality. In most of the districts in which the female age at marriage is very low, the the crude birth rate was observed to be between 39-44 in 1981 and child mortality, in terms of number of deaths up to the age of two per 1000 live births, was estimated to be generally between 160 to more than 200. We have identified 48 districts in the country in which the proportion of married females in the age group of 15-19, the child mortality and the crude birth rate were very high. Of these 48 districts, 18 are in Madhya Pradesh,12 in Rajasthan and 18 in Uttar Pradesh, together constituting a population of 74 million.

These are the districts which deceive priority action in raising the female age at marriage. These districts are Bhind, Chhatarpur, Damoh, Datia, Guna, Gwalior, Hoshangabad, Morena, Panna, Raisen, Rajgarh, Rewa, Sagar, Satna, Shivpuri, Tikamgarh and Vidisha in Madhya Pradesh; Ajmer, Alwar, Bharatpur, Bundi, Chittaurgarh, Jaipur, Jhalawar, Kota, Pali,

Sawai Madhopur, Tonk and Udaipur; in Rajasthan; Allahabad, Banda, Basti, Budaun, Etah, Farukhabad, Gonda, Gorakhpur, Hardoi, Jaunpur, Lalitpur, Mainpuri, Pilibhit, Pratapgarh, Rai Bareili, Shajhanpur, Sitapur and Sultanpur in Uttar Pradesh.

From time immemorial certain ceremonies and rites have been associated with the institution of marriage and those rites and ceremonies have differed from society to society in different epochs. The religious or social practices attached to the institution of marriage are called ceremonies or rites. Among the Shias in India two distinct types of marriages are found to exist side by side. The first is the Sharai (strictly religious) from of marriage and the second is the Urfi customary form.

The "Sharai" Marriage

This type of marriage is completely in accordance with the principles of Islam regarding marriage. The Sharai marriage requires to Rusumat (ceremonies) as the Holy Prophet observed in the marriage of his own daughter Hazrat Fatima Zehra. In this form of marriage, only simple directions of religion are observed.

The nature of such a marriage is always simple and sober. The bride, bridegroom and the Mujtahid (religious teacher) are necessary. There may or may not be more persons at the time of the Nikah.

A welcome feature of the Sharai marriage is the comparatively small amount of Maher. Generally, Muslims think that it is better to pay the amount of Maher at the time of the marriage, but according to custom, in most cases, it is not paid at the time of Nikah. Among the Shias, relatively more Sharai than Urfi marriages take place.

The 'Urfi' Marriage (Customary Form)

The Urfi marriage is more common among the wealthy sections of the Shia community i.e., the Nawabs, wasi-qadars (Royal Pensioners) an ex-zamindars, etc. The Urfi marriage is celebrated among the Shias with elaborate ceremonies. Generally, many people accompany the marriage party, and a large number of people assemble at the bride's place also. There is provision for music, dance and fire-works as well. Usually the amount of Maher is in thousands or lakhs, which is not possible for a bridegroom to pay at any time in his life, and

After the advent of Muslims in India, the Sharai marriage acquired new forms in conformity with the regional and class differences of the country. Staunch followers of religion pronounce these customs as innovations and deviations from the tenets of religion, destroying its austerity. They go even so far as to consider it a heresay against Divine faith. Customs are a product of social activity and are to be considered as such, irrespective of what they ought to be. We are rather concerned with what they actually are and how they have come to be what they are.

The main religious ingredients have never changed. It is the local colouring as a cirumsurrounding fringe that has changed without affecting the main procedure. The Urfi marriage contains all the requisite elements of marriages and in addition something more. The chief functions along with the simple Sharai Marriage Ceremony, though not incumbent are for public advertisement of the marriage. The gathering of relations and friends in an assembly and the marriage feast in a Sharai marriage prove this fact, and when we consider the social background of the Urfi marriage customs, we find the same trend working as the purpose of each one of these customs and ceremonies is to proclaim the marriage publicly.

The various ceremonies and processions to and from the bridal house preliminary to the actual wedding i.e., the Baraat serve the same purpose. Again, the ceremonies that follow the wedding are similarly motivated. These ceremonies may be divided into two sections.

1. Those that have a wide public range and are associated with processions, music, bands and fire-works. They are mainly for the public, although the near relatives and friends take part in them.

2. Those that are celebrated only by near relatives or very intimate friends. They are generally held in the form of Chalas (feasts given to the married couple by near relatives) after the marriage for an intimate get-together of the near relations. Each one of these relations invites the bridal pair, and entertains them; gifts are also presented to the married couple. These may be costly ornaments and apparels, and close intimacy with the new relations in thus established. The historical development of such customs is the impact of Hindu culture on Muslim civilisation.

Shia marriage customs, however, vary according to the financial status of the individuals in society, but the significance to these customs remains. For example, the attire of the bridegroom and bride makes them conspicuous compared to others. In olden times, these dresses were similar to the court garments. But such garments no longer need to be worn and these dresses are not worn by any one after the marriage is over and become useless except as a family relic. The flower veil or Sehra is put on to make the bridegroom prominent. Similarly, the Sohag Pura, which is really a toilet combination, has now been replaced by a modern toilet box and make-up recipes.

Some of these customs may be traced to the old Indian Rajput culture when brides were acquired through warfare. The mimic fight with flowery sticks, the battering vollies of vegetables and fruits in Chauthi, and the general custom of taking the bridegroom on horse back or on an elephant goes back to this martial practice. Again the Baraatis of the bridegroom's side are not given any eatables, meals or drink before the marriage.

These latter-day customs should only be critically examined from sociological standpoint and should not be pedantically pronounced as irreligious. Strictly speaking, the so-called religious people who declare anything they dislike to be irreligious have to consider that even normal cloths, food and even vociferation and language change with a change of the environment and history. Thus, changes in customs are a necessary and natural product to social environment and are not to be denounced in so far as they do not affect the main characteristics.

Widow Remarriage

Widows are equally entitled to remarriage, for the verse of Holy Quran about the marriage of girls applies to widows as well as to virgins. Islam does not approve of any the right which is also to be found also have been given the right which is also to be found in the Holy Prophet's traditions.

The Holy Prophet advised every sort of alliance for the multiplication of Muslims and wished his followers to allow procreation to the utmost limit. Thus, widows have full right to be remarried. In this way they can have a family of their own, enjoy in company of a supporting husband and beget children. This Islamic legal view is full of foresight for the strength of a religion depends upon the number of its followers and social expansion. Widows have rights of inheritance also, not only from parents but also from husbands. If a widow has no children, she is entitled to a fourth of her husband's property in cash and kind. If there are children she gets only one eighth. If the widow is the sole surviving heir of the deceased she takes the whole of the property. In this way a widow has strong rights over the property of her husband in proportion to her share or over the whole property as described above. She is free to remain celibate but it is better for her to remarry; in the later case she enjoys the full rights of a wife with the second husband. If she does not remarry, she enjoys the right of support in her paternal or conjugal family. She has full right to manage her property, either by herself directly or through relatives on whom she can confer powers to act on her behalf. She has full rights to sue in the courts and to file suits and conduct the procedure thereof.

The duties of a widow are also numerous. Her first duty is to observe Iddat which is a period of celibacy covering 4 months and 10 days. During this time she has to avoid marriage in memory of her dead husband. This period is generally recommended to be passed in the house of her husband. The main aim of Iddat is to ensure that she is not pregnant through her first husband and if she is pregnant, this period is extended upto the delivery of the baby if it exceeds four months and 10 days. Iddat thus provides a safeguard against any ambiguity about the paternity of a child she is about to bear.

Also during this period she has full opportunity to study the attitude and behaviour of her supporters for finding out the extent to which she is welcome in the family, she thus gets time to ponder over the future course of life in the light of her changed circumstances. During this period she has to lead a simple and unsophisticated life, keeping with the mourning for her husband. She is expected to remain in the house throughout the period without even visiting her relatives. She has also to look after the well-being of her children and the preservation of their father's property till they are mature. If it is a newly born child, she has to nurse it. If the child is grown up she to bring it up with due care. She is the regent of her children but has no personal right (over their inherited property, except in so far as she requires it for their maintenance. Even if she marries, her duty towards her previous children to remains the same.

So fat as her social obligations are concerned she may either be a dependent of her paternal family or that of her husband. As a natural consequence of the support she gets, she has to live as a cooperating member in any of these families. If she supports and maintains herself, having sufficient property, her first care should be her children, for besides being a mother, she has also to bestow the protection and care of a father.

In short, a widow was to a great extent independent rights. She is the master of her own property, either inherited from her parents or from her husband or acquired by her own efforts. She has full obligations in respect of her issues of support and care. Even in the presence of the father, the rights of the mother are three-fold. After the death of the father, she is the sole monarch of all these rights. She is not an encumbrance on any body and lives as a free, chaster member of the society.

She is entitled to a second marriage if she so desires. In the eyes of religion, she is as good as any other in law or by religious observances. She has ample social rights also and has a well-marked position in society. Widowhood, according to Islam, does not cast any ominous shade over her destiny. In this sense she is as pure and dignified as any married or unmarried woman.

The influence of Hindu culture is clearly visible on the social status of Shia widows, because it is due to Hindu influence that widows do not enjoy the same unqualified respect and good humour of society, although the Islamic view is otherwise, so far as their status is concerned.

The verse of the Holy Quran which makes it obligatory for girls to marry applies equally to virgins as well as to widows. It turns as follows: "Marry your children, as well as the virtuous among your slaves, whether male or female; if they are poor, God will turn them into rich by His generosity, and God has an extensive knowledge (of very thing)." This verse which composes a duty is binding generally on all Muslims and especially on guardians and masters (of slaves). It applies equally well to the unmarried, whether virgin or widow. There is also a promise that people should not be deterred from discharging this duty from any apprehension of their poverty, for God takes the responsibility upon Himself of making them rich.

Marriage in reality is a means of procreation and multiplication of the species and hence is naturally incumbent. To keep away any sex from procreation is biologically wrong and that is why the marriage of widows should be as desirable as that of virgins. In a sense, the marriage of widow is considered more necessary for she has enjoyed life, and would therefore remain miserable all the more. A widow is either childless or has children. If she is childless she must be encouraged, according to Islamic principles, so that she may have a flourishing family of her own. If she has children, she will be able to support them better after remarriage. Thus, widows can be classified according to their age into three categories:

1. Those of very age, victims of early marriage, who if not remarried, would have their whole life wasted by remaining either celibate or by becoming a blot on the

on her supporters and guardians and would be a check on her turning to wrong ways. It is known from figures collected on prostitution that a number of them belonging to all castes and creeds are from the ranks of widows. Even though the number may be small, yet had widow remarriage taken place extensively a large number of the prostitutes may not have taken to that trade. It may be said therefore that in present-day society, widow remarriage is a necessity and any conservation ideas ingrained by force of custom should be dispelled. The conservatism of custom, however, still the ground in various gaums of Muslims and specially among the Syeds, who have always valued pride of family honour. But in other gaums and even in some Syed families the spell is breaking in the face of economic difficulties.

Changes in the social environment and outlook of Hindu have also taken place. Among new influence may be cited the expansion of modern scientific education and critical estimates and judgment of sociological principles which are the basic foundations of all social customs. Among Hindus as well as among Muslims, widow remarriage associations have been formed and are working actively. In this order of ideas, Muslims could revert to their original position as far as widow remarriage is concerned.

Widow remarriage has been one of the most important and burning questions which Indian as well as Shia society have been facing for a long time. Widow remarriage in India was regarded undesirable by Hindu India and the impact of Hindu culture on Muslims had influenced the Muslims also. It was a cumbrous blessing. Considered a dishonour for the family as well as for the woman concerned, and a blot on the house where she was married, no one cared to marry a widow. Though Islam, which recommends procreation, is against celibacy; the social element has been more powerful than the religious in the light of the Indian concept that a woman can love only one person and only once and for all. In a sense it was an example of the elevation of their moral and social standards.

The custom of sacrifice of the widow at the funeral of her husband (Sati) was common since ancient times. "The custom began to become gradually popular from 400 A.D." There were, however, social thinkers who were opposed altogether to this custom during that time. However, owing to the social recognition which the custom had received they were ineffective. The custom was most popular among the fighting classes Rajputs, Marhatas, etc. During the period ranging from 700-110 A.D. it was quite common in north India and more in Kashmir. "Muslim rulers as a general rule did not like the customs". In the 22nd year of his reign Akbar translated his opposition to the custom into action by appointing inspectors to see that no force was used to compel widows to burn themselves against their will. Many Muslim administrators had made it a rule that no widow should be allowed to mount the funeral pyre without the permission of the local government officer.

Though the custom was prohibited in British India in 1829 A.D. it continued upto 1861 A. D. in the princely states of Rajputana.

A most significant factor which helped in increasing the number of widows was the practice of child marriage. Generally, women with children did not prefer to marry again. Many widows had a genuine love for the departed soul and therefore were not in favour of remarriage. It was only with the advent of Western education during the second quarter of the last century that some social workers raised their voice against the then existing social evil of perpetuation of widowhood.

Ishwarchandra Vidyasagar was most prominent and was responsible for the passing of the Widow Remarriage Act of 1956. Many social thinkers have now come forward in support of daughters and the daughters' issues raised economic problems. After the change in Hindu outlook, the Muslims also began to alter their opinion and widow remarriage, though still not considered desirable, was not altogether considered a social evil, but a sort of blessing. The Syeds, like the Hindu Brahmins continued to hold the ground staunchly against remarriage, though other gaums began to relax their opinion and favourable marriage for a young widow was not deferred. This opened the door to the social emancipation of the widow, who ceased to be an inauspicious member of society.

The present Shia society has to consider this problem against its changing economic conditions. The number of guardians who can afford to maintain their daughters in their widowhood is decreasing as the number of widowed daughters increases. A natural solution to this problem is not only marriage of the marriageable girls but also marriage of widows who would prove a blessing to both families. In this way, the daughter would lessen the burdens on their families and become useful and experienced members of other families. The effect of modern education and Western civilization has also done a great deal in giving girls a reasonable outlook on life and such girls are not generally opposed to remarriage. They are now free of old conservatism and full of new freedom of thought and liberal views.

7

Custodial Justice to Women

Accordingly, custodial justice to women has been one of the thrust areas of the activities of the Commission since its inception. The visits to the jails revealed extremely unsatisfactory conditions under which women prisoners live. While the visiting members conveyed to the concerned authorities their general observations about the living condition of women and made specific suggestions about certain hard cases, it was felt that a study should be undertaken to assess the existing conditions in the jails throughout the country.

Observations and Suggestions made by Members Inspecting the Jails

(i) Adequate arrangements for vocational training should be made for women inmates in jail and a programme prepared for rehabilitation of released prisoners. To take an example the visiting Members came across the case of life convict in Assam who was to be released shortly but was very appre-hensive of her future since the thought that her husband and society might not accept her. She wanted to acquire some professional skill to be economically independent. She had aptitude for nursing. At the suggestion of the Member she was given training in midwifery and was ultimately able to make her by into the profession.

(ii) Courts should ensure that female prisoners are handed over to *bona fide* guardians after release so that they may not fall into the hands of imposter guardians who may force them into immoral trafficking as hand come to light in many cases.

(iii) Mentally ill women should be kept separate from the other women prisoners.

(iv) Certain women prisoners had been kept in custody on the ground of being lunatic despite the fact that they were not actually lunatics. There should therefore, bean objective medical examination of such cases.

(v) The women's wing of Tihar jail was found to be overcrowded by more than four times its capacity. Construction of additional accommodation was suggested to ameliorate the condition of women inmates. It was noted that the women inmates were encouraged to engage themselves in the training of various vocations. Also, a de-addition centre had been set up by the jail authorities. However revamping of the training programme was suggested so that the inmates were enabled to produce marketable goods and make an earning for themselves for future security.

(vi) In the Jail, Delhi there was a case of a smart girl who had secured the job of a police A.S.I. by impersonation but she was a Karate expert. It was suggested to the Jail authorities to engage her in some fruitful activity like imparting physical training to other come prisoners. A similar approach is necessary in alike cases.

(vii) In certain prisons, some women inmates were found to suffer from T.B. It was suggested that they should be suggested that they should be segregated from the others and also given proper medical treatment.

(viii) In the Central Jail at Bombay the Tata Institute of Social Science was conducting some useful services for the jail inmates in collaboration with the Bombay Police such as literacy classes, creches for children vocational training counselling, legal guidance, placement on release, etc. This was considered as a good example to be followed.

(ix) The authorities at Sabarmati Central Jail, Ahmedabad expressed the view that the vocational training facilities for male prisoners could not be extended to female inmates as their number was too small. It was suggested that in such cases women inmates could be congregated in one or two suitable jails for making such facilities available or, alternatively provided with such other work as gardening cooking, etc. and wages paid for the same.

(x) In several jails, regular visits by doctors are not made but they are called only when needed. Also no facilities for lady doctors or nurses exist for women prisoners. It was suggested to the concerned jail authorities that it is desirable that women prisoners are treated only by women doctors, unless the prisoners opt otherwise. However, medical examination should be provided as a matter of routine.

(xi) In the jails visited in Madhya Pradesh, it was found that most of the prisoners were tribals and had their own cultural traditions. The crimes committed by them were not pre-planned and had altogether different background. Therefore, instead of convicting them straightaway under the provisions of Criminal Procedure Code, a lenient view should be taken in the context of their socio-economic environment. It was as suggested that suitable training should be given to Adivasi women prisoners in bidi making sericultre and other related industries to which they are traditionally accustomed.

(xii) Women prisoners convicted under TADA were generally found to be young school and college going girls. It was suggested that they should be provided with facilities to continue their studies and persistently motivated to return to the mainstream of life.

Existing Conditions in Jails

The personal visits of Members to the jails convinced the Commission that there was a serious shortfall in the delivery of services to women who are in custody in jails. The Commission therefore decided to issue a Questionnaire to all the States and Union Territories calling for data/information in respect of facilities available to women inmates with regard to diet accommodation medical aid sanitation education vocational training legal aid, recreational opportunities provisions for children accompanying prisoners, visitorial facilities ventilation of grievances, etc.

The information received from all over the country is being processed in the Commission and an analysis thereof will be presented before the Export Committee with a view to formulating recommendations bearing on the conditions of women in custody and norms therefor.

The commission also thought it fit that some immediate suggestions should be preferred it the Ministry of Home affairs, Government of India, for adoption in order to secure custodial justice for women behind the bars. While drawing up these suggestions consideration was given also to the aspect of gender justice in the relam of criminal law a administration after taking a stock of the recommendations made by various Commissions and Committees on the subject, notable among which is the Report of the National Expert Committee on Women prisoners headed by justice Krishna Iyer as well as that of All India Committee for Jail Reforms and also various findings of the Supreme Court of India on the subject.

The suggestions were want for immediate imple-mentation as these are supposed not to entail any substantial strain on the governmental exchequer and are implementable as a short term measure. These are given below.

(1) Women shall not be arrested between sun-set and sun-rise and shall not be arrested expect in the presence of women. This will necessitate amendment of section 46 Cr. P.C. 1973.

(2) In all cases of bailable offences bail on her bond shall be granted forthwith by the police themselves. As far as possible in non-bailable cases also, bail should be granted unless special circumstances warrant a different course, in which case, the arrested woman shall be remanded to judicial custody with utmost expedition.

(3) On arrest the police should immediately obtain from the arrestee the name a relative or friend to whom the intimation of her arrest should be promptly given.

(4) If consideration of arrestee's own safety and freedom from ensnarement by anti-social elements demand detention in public institutions bail shall be refused to the women in her own interest unless she is specifically states her willingness to be thus released even after being altered to the above consideration.

(5) The person of a women shall not be searched except by a women authorised by law, and in a manner strictly in accordance with the requirement of decency. Whether in

custody or in transit, the arrested woman must always be guarded by a women police or female surrogate. Wile resorting a relative may be permitted to accompany the female arrestee.

(6) Whenever a women is to be examined by the police or other investigative agency as a witness it should be done only at her residence; nor should she be summoned to the police or investigative station unless she expresses her preference to be examined at the station.

(7) No female prisoner shall be subjected to any form of corporal punishment or use of handcuffs fetters or isolation as a form of disciplining.

(8) When women are examined in court as accused or as witnesses, sue courtesy and decency shall be shown. If circumstances so demand in the interest of modesty and privacy of a women the trial may be held in camera or the women may be examined on commission through women advocates.

Exclusive Custody for Women:

(1) There should be police stations exclusive for women and exclusive lockups under the control of women police. This will necessitate amendment of prison Act and police Act. Separated space for female arrestees in every police lockup and complete segregation of women prisoners in jail and other custody should be maintained.

(2) Where such facility is not available, a female arrestee may be lodged in a special home or institution designated under any law for the time being in force to receive women. At no time shall a women arrestee be left unguarded by a women guard or surrogate.

In all places of police custody, basic amenities such as living space, water, toilet, food medical examination and care, and provisions to meet the special needs of women shall be provided.

(3) As far as possible each state should have at least one or more separate jail for women.

(4) There should be separate custodial facilities for convicts and undertrial women. Separate institutions or reception centres where undertrial and remanded women may be kept, should be set up in larger cities district headquarters, and in female-crime-endemic areas. Where convicts and undertrials are currently housed in one institution they must kept apart in separate wings until independent facilities are set up.

Visitorial Provision in Custody:

(1) Additional provision should be made in the existing legislation conferring visitorial rights on recognised institutions or individuals institutional and individual accountability for lapses and exesses should also be provided for.

(2) Information on women in custody should be made available to recognised social organisations and individuals on request. Persons and institutions accredited as visitors should be allowed as of right free access to police stations and records.

(3) Visiting Committees to jails should be constituted in consultation with professional bodies and university department of laws, criminologists, social workers and social scientists from the neighbouring area. Visitors should be nominated on the bases of merit public spiritedness activist record and actual time likely to be made available to the visitorial function.

A women DIG should be appointed at state headquarters preferably from the prison service to specifically look after the work relating to women prisoners and women prison staff.

Autonomous Prisons for Women

Women superintendents of separate prisons for women (currently six in number) should be made fully autonomous in functioning.

Prisoners Councils

Prisoners Councils or Bandi Sabhas should be set up in all prisons to help airing prisoners grievances and difficulties.

Socio-legal Counselling

(1) Socio-legal counselling cells should be set up in every prison for women inmates.

(2) In exceptional circumstances when a women arrestee is taken to a police lock-up the police should immediately give intimation to the nearest Legal Aid Committee or recognized legal service or body which must render all necessary legal services at State expense.

(3) Magistrates shall inform women when first produced of their right to legal aid at state expense and direct the provision of necessary services. They shall also explain the nature and scope of the proceedings against her and her rights in it.

(4) Legal aid and counselling through professional bodies assisted by para-legal and social workers should be institutionalised in respect of every prison and custodial institution.

Law schools and schools of social work should be encouraged and permitted to render socio-legal counselling service to the inmates.

(5) In the disposition of women offenders courts should mandatory call for and give due regard to the probation officers report and to the report of medical/psychiatric examination. Where probation officers are not available probation investigation should be entrusted to recognized and accredited institutions and individuals.

Released Prisoners Aid Society

(1) Released Prisoners Aid Societies should operate in every district to provide a single-window assistance towards rehabilitation and mainstreaming of the released women prisoners.

(2) Before a female prisoner is released her relatives should be informed and where no relative exists or shows up the released prisoner should be sent to her destination with a female escort.

(3) Appropriate assistance should be rendered to every female prisoner on release whether during or after completion of sentence. For this purpose a centre for assisting released prisoners should be set up to service a cluster of prisons and custodial institutions on an area-wise basis. Even without the centre the prison authorities should take necessary steps to arrange the rehabilitation of the released prisoner either through the family the relief centre or a voluntary organisation.

(4) Aftercare and short-stay homes for women prisoners may be established in every state to serve those prisoners who are homeless or rejected by their families.

Children Accompanying Women in Police Custody/Jail Custody:

(1) When arresting a women, proper arrangements for the protection and care of her accompanying children should be the responsibility of the state. Children who need to be custodialized jointly with their mothers should enjoy rights justly needed, while in custody in terms of food, living space, health, clothing and visitation.

(2) In the disposition of women to custody or otherwise, the magistrate must enquire and direct that suitable for the welfare of their children be made in a manner that protects the rights of children. While sentencing women to imprisonment or any form of custodialisation suitable orders should be made for the custody and welfare of their children.

(3) Expectant mothers in custody should be shown special consideration by way of medical and nutritional care, education in child rearing and mother craft.

Women's Assistance Police Unit

(1) Women's Assistance Police Unit contacting cadre of men and women police with specific task of crime prevention work and assistance to women should be set up in each district.

(2) In endemic female crime areas, or wherever otherwise desirable exclusive police station or booths and counters within police stations, shall be set up to deal with women needing protection of or coming in conflict with law. Such booths and police stations should be managed by an integrated cadre of men and women police specially trained and sensitized to deal with women.

On 3rd February, 1993, the Commission organised in New Delhi a conference of Inspectors General of Prisons from all over the country with a view to obtaining their views on the diverse issues relating to custodial justice as well as gender justice in the realm of criminal law administration.

The Conference discussed at length a host of issues arising out of the topic of custodial justice to women as well as gender justice in the realm of criminal law administration. It was felt that the issues deserve a more thorough probe in the light of desirability as well as implement ability of the various suggestions emerging out of the Conference.

Moreover, the suggestions were also desired to be screened and reviewed by the Expert Committee on Custodial justice in order that light may be shed from all angles of views and a consensus arrived at. Accordingly a sub-committee of eight persons out of the participants of the Conference was appointed to inter-act with the Expert Committee on Custodial justice to women on all the significant suggestions and in particular about the suggested amendments to the laws in force in the realm. This culminated in formulation of recommendations by the Commission for amendment of the code of Criminal Procedure.

8

Women and Law

One of the directive principles of state policy prescribes that the state should direct its policy towards securing equal pay for equal work for both men and women. Although the directive principles are fundamental in the governance of the country and are to be applied in enacting legislation, they are not judicially enforceable. In this context, one of the provisions of the Constitution is of special significance. After having laid down that the state shall not discriminate against any citizen on grounds of sex, among other things, it provides that nothing in this article shall prevent the state from making any special provision for women and children. So there is a Constitutional provision in India permitting the state to discriminate in favour of women, if such discrimination is found necessary.

Child marriage, especially of the female infant, was common; widow marriage was prohibited, even if she succeeded in escaping from the funeral pyre of her deceased husband where she was expected to be burnt alive; a divorce was generally looked down upon and her remarriage was socially disapproved. If some of these attitudes still persist it is not because legislation has lagged behind, but because law has not succeeded in playing its role of social engineering and changing certain deeply rooted social attitudes. During the last two decades a number of laws were adopted with a view to ensuring equality of status and opportunity for women. But it appears that in practice this equality eludes the Indian woman's grasp.

In what follows an attempt is made to examine some of the more important legislation enacted by the Central legislature in India to ameliorate certain unhappy conditions in which women, particularly Hindu women, found themselves. Occasionally, there is talk about ameliorating the conditions of Muslim women, but political consideration stand in the way of doing anything substantial towards that end. Muslim personal laws are considered to be part of the religion of Islam and government generally considers it necessary not to interfere directly in matters regarded as religious.

With a view to preventing child marriages, especially the giving away of infant girls in marriage, the Child Marriage Restraint Act was passed in 1929 declaring it an offence for a man to marry a girl under fifteen years of age. Any person who performs a marriage where the bridegroom is below 18 years or the bride below 15 years commits an offence, as also parents or guardians of the bridegroom or the bride.

This socially motivated legislation has been made relatively ineffective by stating that a marriage celebrated in violation of the stipulation regarding age would nevertheless be valid. The same restrictions regarding marriageable age are found in the Hindu Marriage Act, 1955. There is a Dowry Prohibition Act also in the Indian statute book which prohibits the giving or taking or dowry. But this again is ineffective in practice mainly because any dowry given may be construed as "presents" which are not prohibited by law if made at the time of marriage. In the case of both these statutes the teeth of the legislation are practically blunted both by loopholes within the law and by the resistance of social structures and attitudes to change. Certain conservative section of the community regard child marriage a good, if not a proper, thing and would prefer to pay a fine rather than keep their infant sons and daughters unmarried. A large number of young men and their parents consider dowry a legitimate stepping stone to higher rungs in the social ladder, and possibly a passport to domestic comfort if not happiness.

Two years before the adoption of the Hindu Marriage Act, which *inter alia* provided of or divorce, the Special Marriage Act, 1954 was enacted. There is a provision in the Special Marriage Act for obtaining a decree of divorce by mutual consent, provided the parties have lived separately for a year and three years have elapsed since the date of marriage. Apart from the common grounds on which either party to the marriage may obtain dissolution of a marriage performed or registered under the Act, the wife may sue the husband for divorce on the ground that he has committed rape, sodomy or bestiality. Persons married under the Act with the result that they would now be governed by its provisions.

Those who marry under the Act or whose marriages are registered under it are, in matters of inheritance, governed by the Indian Succession Act, 1925. When a man to whom the Indian Succession Act applies dies leaving a widow and lineal descendants, the widow is entitled to one third of the property of the deceased and the lineal descendants to two-thirds. Under the Act, in the case of Christians, a widow in the absence of lineal descendants will get the entire property of the husband provided its value does not exceed Rs. 5,000. If it does, she will receive Rs. 5,000 and a share in what remains along with the kindred of the deceased according to the specific rules laid down in the Act. Some persons, especially women, prefer to be married under the Special Marriage Act because of its beneficial provisions regarding divorce and intestate succession. We shall advert to this later.

It may be said in general that the right of a wife to obtain a divorce in India is much more restricted than that of the husband under customary law; however, in certain Hindu communities, as also among most tribal groups, it is possible for the husband and the wife to obtain divorce without resource course to court.

They are only required to follow some customary practice, like making a declaration before the elders of the community or the headman of the tribe that they no longer desire their marital relationship to continue. It is well known that among Muslims, while the husband can unilaterally and without assigning any reason divorce his wife by pronouncing talaq (that is by uttering the words, "I divorce you") three times, the wife has to get a judicial pronouncement of divorce on specified grounds.

It is, however, possible for the wife to have the power of divorce delegated too her by the husband at the time of entering into the marriage contract. For instance, it may be stipulated that if he takes a second wife, she should have the option of repudiating her marriage. Such delegation is, however, uncommon. Considering the fact that the constitution makes provision for equality of the sexes, it may be desirable to give judicial recognition to fasaq by means of which a Muslim wife may unilaterally repudiate her marriage. An opportunity for such recognition was lost when the Kerala High Court in 1975 ruled that the right of Muslim women to obtain divorce is exclusively governed by the Dissolution of Muslim Marriages Act, 1939 and that it is not permissible to go beyond it.

The divorce provisions of the Hindu Marriage Act, 1955 maintain equality of the sexes in the matter of grounds for divorce. The Act applies to Hindus, Buddhists, Jains and Sikhs. In the provisions of the Indian Divorce Act which applies to Christians there is some discrimination between the sexes in the matter of grounds for divorce. A single isolated act of adultery on the part of the wife is a valid ground for granting a divorce on the petition of the husband but, if a wife has to be successful in her petition for divorce, she has generally to prove against her husband not only adultery, but also an additional ground such as desertion or cruelty.

Commission or rape, sodomy or bestiality by the husband can also be ground for obtaining a decree of divorce. This Act was modeled after English enactments for matrimonial reliefs adopted about the middle of the last century. Over a hundred years later the United kingdom prescribed by legislation a single valid ground for divorce, that is, irretrievable breakdown of marriage.

If in 1869 the idea was that Indian Christians would do well to follow in the footsteps of the British in obtaining matrimonial reliefs, is there any valid reason to assume that they should be governed by rules different from those applicable to the British after the passage of a century. If irretrievable breakdown of marriage is made the only ground for judicial declaration of divorce applicable to all communities and religious groups in India there will be equality of treatment not only between men and women but also between various religious groups.

Perhaps one has to wait for the adoption of a uniform civil code for such unification of laws. In the meantime the Indian Divorce Act could be amended making grounds for divorce identical for both men and women, preferably adopting the provision regarding irretrievable breakdown of marriage as the sole ground of divorce as laid down in the (British) Divorce Referm Act. 1969.

During the pendency of a suit under the Indian Divorce Act, a wife may apply for alimony and the court may grant an amount not exceeding one-fifth of the husband's average net income. While passing a decree for divorce or judicial separation, the court may order the husband to pay a lump sum or make periodical payments for life to the wife, taking into account her fortune, the means of the husband and the conduct of the parties.

There are similar provisions for the benefit of the wife in the Parsi Marriage and Divorce Act, 1936. The spirit of equality envisaged in the Constitution finds clear expression in the Hindu Marriage Act, 1955. It makes provision for the grant of expenses of matrimonial suits and a monthly allowance for the support of either spouse during the pendency of legal proceedings, provided the spouse applying for the expenses and allowances has not sufficient income to support himself or herself.

The Act also has a provision for making an order for permanent alimony or maintenance in favour of either of the spouses. On remarriage the spouse loses his or her right to maintenance. Further, if the recipient of the alimony is the wife, she is required to remain chaste; if maintenance is granted to the husband, he is enjoined from having sexual relations with any other woman.

In spite of the provisions for divorce contained in the Act of 1955, it is not often that recourse is had to them : this is because Hindu social values in general are opposed to the concept of divorce. As Kapadia puts it, "the principle of divorce is alien to the social pattern" with the result that "the norm accepted by law has not been accepted in practice". Whereas prior to 1955, divorce was considered absolute anathema by women of the higher castes, after the passing of the Act it is the women of the upper classes and higher castes as well as the rich and educated in urban areas who petition the courts for divorce. Probably, the illiterate women in the rural areas do not even know that there are legal provisions for divorce apart from those enshrined in the customary law of certain communities or tribes.

Marriage under the Special Marriage Act has the effect of making the provisions of the Indian Succession Act applicable to the parties. These provisions were more beneficial to women, be they Hindus, Muslims Indian Christians of Pondicherry or Indian Christians in those areas of Kerala which formerly comprised the princely states of Travancore and Cochin, provided they were not governed by matrilineal custom. Before the adoption of the Hindu succession Act in 1956, when a woman succeeded to the divided property of a deceased Hindu male, she took only a limited interest. A woman was denied legal capacity to be a coparcener in a Hindu joint family.

The Hindu Succession Act, 1956 which applies to Hindus, Buddhists, Jains and Sikhs determines the their on the basis of consanguinity or affinity without any discrimination on the ground of sex. It gives a woman full ownership in the property inherited or acquired by her. The widow, the mother and the daughter now not only inherit property along with the son but also take an equal share with him. A Parsi woman takes only half the share that her brother gets in their father's property. A similar half share is the lot of Muslim women as well. Though the Indian Succession Act is generally applicable to Christians there are various regions in the country where the Act is not applied.

There are also certain Christian Communities to which it not made applicable. Certain tribal Christian communities and those who follow matriliny are outside the purview of the Act. As the Act is not extended to the Union Territory of

Pondicherry, Indian Christians in the territory are governed by traditional Hindu law (that is, Hindu law as it was in force in the region before certain changes were effected by the Indian Parliament in 1955 and 1956) in the matter of inheritance with all the disadvantages and disabilities which that law imposed on women.

In the erstwhile princely states of Travancore and Cochin, there are in operation local enactment relating to succession among Christians which appear to discriminate against women. Under the Travancore Christian Succession Regulation, 1916 the share of the widow in the estate of the husband is a life interest, terminable on her death or remarriage, except where she gets the whole estate in the absence of certain specified relatives of her deceased husband.

Under the Cochin Christian Succession Act, 1921 the widow gets share equal to two-thirds of the share of a son if the deceased is survived by a son or lineal descendants of a son. The Travancore Regulation seems to discriminate against daughters who can take only one-fourth of the value of the share of a son or Rs. 5,000 whichever is less. The Regulation does not apply to the small body of Indian Christians in the taluk of Neyyattinkara of the erstwhile princely state who follow *marumakkathayam* (matrilineal descent).

The Roman Catholic Christians of the Latin rite and certain non-Catholic Christens living in a few southern taluks of Travancore follow their customary usage, and among them male and female heirs of an intestate share equally in his property. Under the Travancore Regulation, the maternal relatives are excluded from succeeding to the intestate if there are paternal relatives surviving him, whereas in the Cochin Act no maternal relatives are included among the heirs.

The areas where these two enactments are still in force are remarkable for a high female literacy rate and a large number of highly educated women. Nevertheless the fact remains that these women, if they happen to be Christians to whom these enactments apply, have a right to only a quarter of the share of a brother in the property of their deceased father. Would these educated women and their literate sisters think of reverting to matriliny which was once prevalent in these areas? At the moment they do not appear to be eager to effect any change.

The Hindu Minority and guardianship Act, 1956 also bestowed a few additional rights on Hindu women. It provides that though the father may appoint by will a guardian for his minor children, any such appointment will not take effect during the lifetime of the mother if she survives the father. It will take effect only on her death, provided she has not appointed a guardian by her own will. A Hindu mother is entitled to act as the natural guardian of her minor children if the father ceases to be a Hindu or renounces the world by becoming a hermit or ascetic. The Hindu widow and the Hindu mother, entitled to act as natural guardians of their minor children, are empowered under the Act to appoint guardians for them by will.

In 1956 substantial changes were effected in the law of adoption applicable to Hindus. The Hindu Adoption and Maintenance Act, 1956 has invested the Hindu woman with certain rights of adoption which she had not enjoyed before. Previously an adoption could only be to a male but, under the Act, a woman is competent to adopt to herself a son or a daughter.

Again, under the Act, a married man cannot, except under certain special circumstances, make an adoption without the consent of his wife. Under the earlier law her consent was immaterial but under the present law, her consent is unnecessary only when she has renounced the world or has ceased to be Hindu or has been judicially declared to be of unsound mind. A Hindu woman who is not of unsound mind and who is not a minor is now competent to adopt a son as well as a daughter, provided she is a spinster, divorcee, or widow or one whose husband has finally renounced the world or has ceased to be a Hindu or has been judicially declared to be of unsound mind. In general, during coverture it is only the husband who can adopt. If the woman wants to adopt a son, she should not have a Hindu son, son's son or son's son's son living at the time of the adopted should be younger to her by at least twenty one years.

If she intends adopting a daughter, an essential condition is hat she should have no Hindu daughter or son's daughter living at the time of the adoption. Corresponding requirements have also to be observed by the man who wishes to adopt a son or daughter.

The wife has a right to maintenance for life. She may not forfeit this right even if she lives separately from her husband on certain specific grounds such as the husband's cruelty, desertion, keeping a concubine or having another wife, his suffering from a virulent form of leprosy, his conversion to another religion or any other cause justifying her living separately. She, however, forfeits her right to maintenance if she is unchaste or ceases to be a Hindu.

The Factories Act, 1948 empowers state governments to prohibit employment of women in dangerous operations. A few enactments lay down the general rule that women should not be permitted to work between 7 p.m and 6 a.m., but this rule is relaxable in certain circumstances. Provisions for maternity benefits for women have been incorporated in the Employees State Insurance Act, 1948 and a number of state enactments. While maternity benefit in coal mines is governed by the Maternity Benefit Act, 1961 women workers in factories and plantations are entitled to maternity leave according to the maternity benefit enactments of different states. Both the Factories Act, 1948 and the Plantations Labour Act, 1951 make it obligatory for factories an plantation employing not less than fifty women to provide creches. In spite of these statutory benefits and the constitutional directive regarding equal pay for equal work, women agricultural labourers generally get 10 to 60 per cent less in wages than men for the same work. It is not infrequent that, when the husband becomes a "bonded labourer" for the landlord or the labour contractor, the wife also becomes similarly "bonded" with the not unusual result that she is made vulnerable exploitation including trafficking for immoral purposes.

Only 13 Per cent of Indian women, according to the 1971 Census, may be regarded as workers, i.e, those who are engaged in some form of economic activity. About 80 per cent of these working women are engaged in agriculture. Only 12 per cent of the total employees in central and state administrative services and public sector undertakings are women. This may not be unrelated to their education or lack of it.

Only 18 per cent of India women are literate. Though one of the directive principles of the Constitution requires the state to provide free and compulsory education for all children under 14 years of age the directive is generally followed with callous disregard of its spirits and its significance for the country. Coupled with the general apathy to women's education, this indifference to put in practice a constitutional directive results in greater social and economic deprivation for girls than for boys.

At the primary school level while 97 out of 100 boys attend school, the corresponding figure for girls is 62. Further, out of 100 girls who enter the first grade only 26 go up to the fifth grade. It is only about 2 per cent of women who are able to benefit by the opportunities provided for higher education. In 1971-72, 36 girls only were under instruction at various levels of education compared to a hundred boys. If in 1971 about 18 per cent of women were literate this may appear to compare well with only 8 per cent literacy for women on the eve of independence in 1947, but an increase of 10 per cent in the not too short span of about three decades is hardly something that should make us complacent.

There are certain other types of social legislation which seek to protect interests an benefits that are of special concern to women. The Suppression of Immoral Traffic in Women and Girls Act. 1956. As its title indicates, is intended to protect helpless women and girls from a typical mode of exploitation not altogether unknown in the country. The same year saw the enactment of another piece of social legislation: the Women's and Children's institutions (Licensing) Act, 1956. This was later on superseded by the Orphanages and Other Charitable Homes (Supervision and Control) Act, 1960.

The object of the enactment was to regulate the activities of these institutions and to prescribe a proper standard to which the treatment and the training of the inmates should conform. Such a measure was found necessary because, while there are many good and properly managed charitable institutions, there are many others run with the objective of exploitation as their main and sustaining inspiration.

The Medical Termination of Pregnancy Act, 1971 may also be mentioned in the context of social legislation relative to women. The enactment seeks, among other things, to protect women's interests. It has a few provisions which, it is clear, were enacted with the sufferings of women in the legislator's mind. It provides that a pregnancy may be terminated where the length of the pregnancy does not exceed twenty weeks, if two medical practitioners are of the opinion that the continuance of the practitioners are of the opinion that the continuance of the pregnancy would involve a risk to the life of the pregnant woman or of grave injury to her physical or mental health. Two explanations are offered in the enactment itself of what constitutes grave injury to the mental health of the pregnant woman. The first explanation reads: when any pregnancy is alleged by the pregnant woman to have been caused by rape, the anguish caused by such pregnancy shall be presumed to constitute a grave injury to the mental health of the pregnant woman.

In this case the "anguish" is perhaps palpable. The second explanation is more intriguing in that "anguish" is given an extended application. It states:

Where a pregnancy occurs as a result of failure of any device or method used by any married woman or her husband for the purpose of limiting the number of children, the anguish caused by such unwanted pregnancy may be presumed to constitute a grave injury to the mental health of the pregnant woman. Though the promotional slant of the government's family planning programme may be perceptible in this explanation, it is evident that Parliament cannot be blamed for any lack of solicitude for the largest minority in the country.

This solicitude may be even more evident in another provision of the Act which stipulates that in determining whether the continuance of a pregnancy would involve grave risk to the health of a pregnant woman, account may be taken of her actual or reasonably foreseeable environment. This enactment has been hailed as "a major landmark in India's social legislation", and "a far-reaching measure assuring the women of India freedom from undesirable and unwanted pregnancies.

From a study of the ameliorative legal provisions relating to women and the actual situation in which they find themselves, it is clear that something more than legislation is required. Perhaps that first thing to be attempted is to make women aware of their rights, however this is done. It is also necessary to change the attitudes of both men and women, of society in general, to social objectives sought to be achieved by legislation. A radical change in the attitudes of women induced by an awareness of their rights which are constitutionally guaranteed and legally protected will be the first step in the complex process of transforming the social structure so that women may enjoy full equality with men in every sphere of life.

Convention on the elimination of all forms of disrimination against women

The states parties to the present Convention,

Noting that the Charter of the United Nations reaffirms faith in fundamental human rights, in the dignity and worth of the human person and in the equal rights of men and women,

Noting that the Universal Declaration of Human Rights affirms the principle of the inadmissibility of discrimination and proclaims that all human beings are born free and equal in dignity and rights and that everyone is entitled to all the rights and freedoms set forth therein, without distinction of any kind including distinction based on sex,

Noting that the States Parties to the International Covenants of Human Rights have the obligation to ensure the equal rights of men and women to enjoy all economic, social cultural, civil and political rights,

Considering the international conventions concluded under the auspices of the United Nations and the specialized agencies promoting equality of rights of men and women,

Noting also the resolutions, declarations and recommendations adopted by the United Nations and the specialized agencies promoting equality of rights of men and women,

Concerned, however, that despite these various instruments extensive discrimination against women continues to exist,

Recalling that discrimination against women violates the principles of equality of rights and respect for human dignity, is an obstacle to the participation of women, on equal terms with men, in the political, social, economic and cultural life of their countries, hampers the growth of the prosperity of society and the family and makes more difficult the full development of the potentialities of women in the service of their countries and of humanity,

Concerned that in situations of poverty women have the least access to food, health, education, training and opportunities for employment and other needs,

Convinced that the establishment of the new international economic order based on equity and justice will contribute significantly towards the promotion of equality between men and women,

Emphasizing that the eradication of apartheid, all forms of racism, racial discrimination, colonialism, neo-colonialism, aggression, foreign occupation and domination and interference in the internal affairs of States is essential to the full enjoyment of the rights of men and women,

Affirming that the strengthening of international peace and security, the relaxation of international tension, mutual co-operation among all States irrespective of their social and economic systems, general and complete dis-armament, in particular nuclear disarmament under strict and effective international control the affirmation of the principles of justice, equality and mutual benefit in relations among countries and the realization of the right of peoples under alien and colonial domination and foreign occupation to self-determination and independence, as well as respect for national sovereignty and territorial integrity, will promote social progress and development and as a consequence will contribute to the attainment of full equality between men and women,

Convinced that the full and complete development of a country, the welfare of the world and the cause of peace require the maximum participation of women of equal terms with men in all fields,

Bearing in mind the great contribution of women to the welfare of the family and to the development of society, so far not fully recognized, the social significance of maternity and the role of both parents in the family and in the upbringing of children, and aware that the role of women in procreation should not be a basis for discrimination but that the upbringing of children requires a sharing of responsibility between men and women and society as a whole,

Aware that a change in the traditional role of men as well as the role of women in society and in the family is needed to achieve full equality between men and women,

Determined to implement the principles set forth in the Declaration on the Elimination of Discrimination against Women and, for that purpose, to adopt the measures required for the elimination of such discrimination in all its forms and manifestations,

Have agreed on the following :

Article I

For the purposes of the present Convention, the term

"discrimination against women" shall mean any distinction, exclusion or restriction made on the basis of sex which has the effect or purpose of impairing or nullifying the recognition, enjoyment or exercise by women, irrespective of their marital status, on a basis of equality of men and women, of human rights and fundamental freedoms in the political, economic, social, cultural, civil or any other field.

Article 2 States Parties condemn discrimination against women in all its forms, agree to pursue by all appropriate means and without delay a policy of eliminating discrimination against women and, to this end, undertake:

(a) To embody the principle of the equality of men and women in their national constitutions or other appropriate legislation if not yet incorporated therein and to ensure, through law and other appropriate means, the practical realization of this principle;

(b) To adopt appropriate legislative and other measures, including sanctions where appropriate, prohibiting all discrimination against women;

(c) To establish legal protection of the rights of women on an equal basis with men and to ensure through competent national tribunals and other public institutions the effective protection of women against any act of discrimination;

(d) To refrain from engaging in any act or practice of discrimination against women and to ensure that public authorities and institutions shall act in conformity with this obligation;

(e) To take all appropriate measures to eliminate discrimination against women by any person, organization or enterprise;

(f) To take all appropriate measures, including legislation, to modify or abolish existing laws, regulations, customs and practices which constitute discrimination against women;

(g) To repeal all national penal provisions which constitute discrimination against women.

Article 3: States Parties shall take in all fields, in particular in the political, social, economic and cultural fields, all appropriate measures, including legislation, to ensure the full development and advancement of women, for the purpose of guaranteeing them the exercise and enjoyment of human rights and fundamental freedoms on a basis of equality with men.

Article 4

1. Adoption by States Parties of temporary special measures aimed at accelerating de facts equality between men and women shall not be considered discrimination as defined in the present Convention, but shall in no way entail as a consequence the maintenance of unequal or separate standards; these measures shall be discontinued when the objectives of equality of opportunity and treatment have been achieved.

2. Adoption by States Parties of special measures, including those measures contained in the present Convention, aimed at protecting maternity shall not be considered discriminatory.

Article 5: States Parties shall take all appropriate measures:

(a) To modify the social and cultural patterns of conduct of men and women, with a view to achieving the elimination of prejudices and customary and all other practices which are based on the idea of the inferiority or the superiority of either of the sexes or on sterectyped roles for men and women;

(b) To ensure that family education includes a proper understanding of maternity as a social function and the recognition of the common responsibility of men and women in the upbringing and development of their children, it being understood that the interest of the children is the primordial consideration in all cases.

Article 6: States Parties shall take all appropriate measures, including legislation, to suppress all forms of traffic in women and exploitation of prostitution of women.

Article 7: States Parties shall take all appropriate measures to eliminate discrimination against women in the political and public life of the country and, in particular, shall ensure to women, on equal terms with men, the right:

(a) To vote in all elections and public referenda and to be eligible for election to all publicly elected bodies;

(b) To participate in the formulation of government policy and the implementation thereof and to hold public office and perform all public functions at all levels of government;

(c) To participate in non-governmental organizations and associations concerned with the public and political life of the country.

Article 8: States Parties shall take all appropriate measures to ensure to women, on equal terms with men and without any discrimination, the opportunity to represent their Governments at the international level and to participate in the work of international organizations.

Article 9

1. States Parties shall grant women equal rights with men to acquire, change or retain their nationality. They shall ensure in particular that neither marriage to an alien nor

change of nationality by the husband during marriage shall automatically change the nationality of the wife, render her stateless or force upon her the nationality of the husband.

2. States Parties shall grant women equal rights with men with respect to the nationality of their children.

Article 10 States Parties shall take all appropriate measures to eliminate discrimination against women in order to ensure to them equal rights with men in the field of education and in particular to ensure, on a basis of equality of men and women

(a) The same conditions for career and vocational guidance, for access to studies and for the achievement of diplomas in educational establishments of all categories in rural as well as in urban areas; this equality shall be ensured in pre-school, general, technical, professional and higher technical education, as well as in all types of vocational training;

(b) Access to the same curricula, the same examinations, teaching staff with qualifications of the same standard and school premises and equipment of the same quality;

(c) The elimination of any stereotyped concept of the roles of men and women at all levels and in all forms of education by encouraging coeducation and other types of education which will help to achieve this aim and, in particular, by the revision of textbooks and school programmes and the adaptation of teaching methods;

(d) The same opportunities to benefit from scholarships and other study grants;

(e) The same opportunities for access to programmes of continuing education, including adult and functional literacy programmes, particularly those aimed at reducing, at the earliest possible time, any gap in education existing between men and women;

(f) The reduction of female student drop-out rates and the organization of programmes for girls and women who have left school prematurely;

(g) The same opportunities to participate actively in sports and physical education;

(h) Access to specific educational information to help to ensure the health and well-being of families, including information and advice on family planning.

Article 11 1. States Parties shall take all appropriate measures to eliminate discrimination against women in the field of employment in order to ensure, on a basis of equality of men and women, the same rights, in particular;

(a) The right to work at an right of all human beings.

(b) The right to the same employment opportunities, including the application of the same criteria for selection in matters of employment;

(c) The right to free choice of profession and employment, the right to promotion, job security and all benefits and conditions of service and the right to receive vocational training and retraining, including apprenticeships, advanced vocational training and recurrent training;

(d) The right to equal remuneration, including benefits, and to equal treatment in respect of work of equal value, as well as equality of treatment in the evaluation of the quality of work;

(e) The right to social security, particularly in cases of retirement, unemployment, sickness, invalidity and old age and other incapacity to work, as well as right to paid leave;

(f) The right to protection of health and to safety in working conditions, including the safeguarding of the function of reproduction.

2. In order to prevent discrimination against women on the grounds of marriage or maternity and to ensure their effective right to work, States Parties shall take appropriate measures:

(a) To prohibit, subject to the imposition of sanctions, dismissal on the grounds of pregnancy or of maternity leave and discrimination in dismissals on the basis of marital status;

(b) To introduce maternity leave with pay or with comparable social benefits without loss of former employment, seniority or social allowances;

(c) To encourage the provision of the necessary supporting social services to enable parents to combine family obligations with work responsibilities and participation in public life, in particular through promoting the establishment and development of a network of child-care facilities;

(d) To provide special protection to women during pregnancy in types of work proved to be harmful to them.

3. Protective legislation relating to matters covered in this article shall be reviewed periodically in the light of scientific and technological knowledge and shall be revised, repealed or extended as necessary.

Article 12

1. States Parties shall take all appropriate measures to eliminate discrimination against women in the field of health care in order to ensure, on a basis of equality of men and women, access to health care services, including those related to family planning.

2. Notwithstanding the provisions of paragraph 1 of this article, States Parties shall ensure to women appropriate services in connection with pregnancy, confinement and the post-natal period, granting free services where necessary, as well as adequate nutrition during pregnancy and lactation.

Article 13 States Parties shall take all appropriate measures to eliminate discrimination against women in other areas of economic and social life in order to ensure, on a basis of equality of men and women, the same rights, in particular:

(a) The right to family benefits;

(b) The right to bank loans, mortgages and other forms of financial credit;

(c) The right to participate in recreational activities, sports and all aspects of cultural life.

Article 14

1. States Parties shall take into account the particular problems faced by rural women and the significant roles which rural women play in the economic survival of their families, including their work in the nonmonetized sectors of the economy, and shall take all appropriate measures to ensure the application of the provisions of the present Convention to women in rural areas.

2. States Parties shall take all appropriate measures to eliminate discrimination against women in rural areas in order to ensure, on a basis of equality of men and women, that they participate in and benefit from rural development and, in particular, shall ensure to such women the right:

(a) To participate in the elaboration and implementation of development planning at all levels;

(b) To have access to adequate health care facilities, including information, counselling and services in family planning;

(c) To benefit directly from social security programmes;

(d) To obtain all types of training and education, formal and non-formal, including that relating to functional literacy, as well as, inter alia, the benefit of all community and extension services, in order to increase their technical proficiency;

(e) To organize self-help groups and co-operatives in order to obtain equal access to economic opportunities through employment or self-employment;

(f) To participate in all community activities;

(g) To have access to agricultural credit and loans, marketing facilities, appropriate technology and equal treatment in land and agrarian reform as well as in land resettlement schemes;

(h) To enjoy adequate living conditions, particularly in relation to housing, sanitation, electricity and water supply, transport and communications.

Article 15

1. States Parties shall accord to women equality with men before the law.

2. States Parties shall accord to women, in civil matters, a legal capacity identical to that of men and the same opportunities to exercise that capacity. In particular, they shall give women equal rights to conclude contracts and to administer property and shall treat them equally in all stages of procedure in courts and tribunals.

3. States Parties agree that all contracts and all other private instruments of any kind with a legal effect which is

directed at restricting the legal capacity of women shall be deemed null and void.

4. States Parties shall accord to men and women the same rights with regard to the law relating to the movement of persons and the freedom to choose their residence and domicile.

Article 16

1. States Parties shall take all appropriate measures to eliminate discrimination against women in all matters relating to marriage and family relations and in particular shall ensure, on a basis of equality of men and women:

(a) The same right to enter into marriage;

(b) The same right freely to choose a spouse and to enter into marriage only with their free and full consent;

(c) The same rights and responsibilities during marriage and at its dissolution;

(d) The same rights and responsibilities as parents, irrespective of their marital status, in matters relating to their children; in all cases the interests of the children shall be paramount;

(e) The same rights to decide freely and responsibly on the number and spacing of their children and to have access to the information, education and means to enable them to exercise these rights;

(f) The same rights and responsibilities with regard to guardianship, wardship, trusteeship and adoption of children, or similar institutions where these concepts exist in national legislation; in all cases the interests of the children shall be paramount;

(g) The same personal rights as husband and wife, including the right to choose a family name, a profession and an occupation;

(h) The same rights for both spouses in respect of the ownership, acquisition, management, administration, enjoyment and disposition of property, whether free of charge or for a valuable consideration.

2. The betrothal and the marriage of a child shall have no legal effect, and all necessary action, including legislation, shall be taken to specify a minimum age for marriage and to make the registration of marriages in an official registry compulsory.

Article 17

1. For the purpose of considering the progress made in the implementation of the present Convention, there shall be established a Committee on the Elimination of Discrimination against Women (hereinafter referred to as the Committee) consisting, at the time of entry into force of the Convention, of eighteen and, after ratification of or accession to the Convention by the thirty-fifth State Party, of twenty-three experts of high moral standing and competence in the field covered by the Convention. The experts shall be elected by States Parties from among their nationals and shall serve in their personal capacity, consideration being given to equitable geographical distribution and to the representation of the different forms of civilization as well as the principal legal systems.

2. The members of the Committee shall be elected by secret ballot from a list of persons nominated by States Parties. Each Party may nominate one person from among its own nationals.

3. The initial election shall be held six months after the date of the entry into force of the present Convention. At least three months before the date of each election the Secretary-General of the United Nations shall address a letter to the States Parties inviting them to submit their

nominations within two months. The Secretary-General shall prepare a list in alphabetical order of all persons thus nominated, indicating the States Parties which have nominated them, and shall submit it to the States Parties.

4. Elections of the members of the Committee shall be held at a meeting of States Parties convened by the Secretary-General at United Nations Headquarters. At that meeting, for which two thirds of the States Parties shall constitute a quorum, the persons elected to the Committee shall be those nominees who obtain the largest number of votes and an absolute majority of the votes of the representatives of States Parties present and voting.

5. The members of the Committee shall be elected for a term of four years. However, the terms of nine of the members elected at the first election shall expire at the end of two years; immediately after the first election the names of these nine members shall be chosen by lot by the Chairman of the Committee.

6. The election of the five additional members of the Committee shall be held in accordance with the provisions of paragraphs 2,3 and 4 of this article, following the thirty-fifth ratification or accession. The terms of two of the additional members elected on this occasion shall expire at the end of two years, the names of these two members having been chosen by lot by the Chairman of the Committee.

7. For the filling of casual vacancies, the State Party whose expert has ceased to function as a member of the Committee shall appoint another expert from among its nationals, subject to the approval of the Committee.

8. The members of the Committee shall, with the approval of the General Assembly, receive emoluments from United

Nations resources on such terms and conditions as the Assembly may decide, having regard to the importance of the Committee's responsibilities.

9. The Secretary-General of the United Nations shall provide the necessary staff and facilities for the effective performance of the functions of the Committee under the present Convention.

Article 18

1. States Parties undertake to submit to the Secretary-General of the United Nations, for consideration by the Committee, a report on the legislative, judicial, administrative or other measures which they have adopted to give effect to the provisions of the present Convention and on the progress made in this respect:

(a) Within one year after the entry into force for the State concerned;

(b) Thereafter at least every four years and further whenever the Committee so requests.

2. Reports may indicate factors and difficulties affecting the degree of fulfilment of obligations under the present Convention.

Article 19

1. The Committee shall adopt its own rules of procedure.

2. The Committee shall elect its officers for a term of two years.

Article 20

1. The Committee shall normally meet for a period of not more than two weeks annually in order to consider the reports submitted in accordance with article 18 of the present Convention.

2. The meetings of the Committee shall normally be held at United Nations Headquarters or at any other convenient place as determined by the Committee.

Article 21

1. The Committee shall, through the Economic and Social Council, report annually to the General Assembly of the United Nations on its activities and may make suggestions and general recommendations based on the examination of reports and information received from the States Parties. Such suggestions and general recommendations shall be included in the report of the Committee together with comments, if any, from States Parties.

2. The Secretary-General of the United Nations shall transmit the reports of the Committee to the Commission on the Status of Women for its information.

Article 22

The specialized agencies shall be entitled to be represented at the consideration of the implementation of such provisions of the present Convention as fall within the scope of their activities. The committee may invite the specialized agencies to submit reports on the implementation of the Convention in areas falling within the scope of their activities.

Article 23 Nothing in the present Convention shall affect any provisions that are more conducive to the achievement of equality between men and women which may be contained:

(a) In the legislation of a State Party; or

(b) In any other international convention, treaty or agreement in force for that State.

Article 24 States Parties undertake to auopt all necessary measures at the national level aimed at achieving the full realization of the rights recognized in the present Convention.

Article 25

1. The present Convention shall be open for signature by all States.
2. The Secretary-General of the United Nations is designated as the depositary of the present Convention.
3. The present Convention is subject to ratification. Instruments of ratification shall be deposited with the Secretary-General of the United Nations.
4. The present Convention shall be open to accession by all States. Accession shall be effected by the deposit of an instrument of accession with the Secretary-General of the United Nations.

Article 26

1. A request for the revision of the present Convention may be made at any time by any State Party by means of a notification in writing addressed to the Secretary-General of the United Nations.
2. The General Assembly of the United Nations shall decide upon the steps, if any, to be taken in respect of such a request.

Article 27

1. The present Convention shall enter into force on the thirtieth day after the deposit with the Secretary-General of the United Nations of the twentieth instrument of ratification or accession.
2. For each State ratifying the present Convention or acceding to it after the deposit of the twentieth instrument of ratification or accession, the Convention shall enter into force on the thirtieth day after the date of the deposit of its own instrument of ratification or accession.

Article 28

1. The Secretary-General of the United Nations shall receive and circulate to all States the text of reservations made by States at the time of ratification or accession.

2. A reservation incompatible with the object and purpose of the present Convention shall not be permitted.

3. Reservations may be withdrawn at any time by notification to this effect addressed to the Secretary-General of the United Nations, who shall then inform all States thereof. Such notification shall take effect on the date on which it is received.

Article 29

1. Any dispute between two or more States Parties concerning the interpretation or application of the present Convention which is not settled by negotiation shall, at the request of one of them, be submitted to arbitration. If within six months from the date of the request for arbitration the parties are unable to agree on the organization of the arbitration, any one of those parties may refer the dispute to the International Court of Justice by request in conformity with the statute of the Court.

2. Each State Party may at the time of signature or ratification of the present Convention or accession thereto declare that it does not consider itself bound by paragraph 1 of this article. The other States Parties shall not be bound by that paragraph with respect to any State Party which has made such a reservation.

3. Any State Party which has made a reservation in accordance with paragraph 2 of this article may at any time withdraw that reservation by notification to the Secretary-General of the United Nations.

Article 30 The present Convention, the Arabic, Chinese, English, French, Russian and Spanish texts of which are equally authentic, shall be deposited with the Secretary-General of the United Nations.

In Witness Whereof the undersigned, duly authorized, have signed the present Convention.

Declaration on the Elimination of Discrimination against Women

The General Assembly,

Considering that the peoples of the United Nations have, in the Charter, reaffirmed their faith in fundamental human rights, in the dignity and worth of the human person and in the equal rights of men and women,

Considering that the Universal Declaration on Human Rights assarts the principle of non-discrimination and proclaims that all human beings are born free and equal in dignity and rights and that everyone is entitled to all the rights and freedoms set forth therein without distinction of any kind, including any distinction as to sex,

Taking into account the resolutions, declarations, conventions and recommendations of the United Nations and the specialized agencies designed to eliminate all forms of discrimination and to promote equal rights for men and women,

Concerned that, despite the Charter of the United Nations, the Universal Declaration of Human Rights, the International Covenants on Human Rights and other instruments of the United Nations and the specialized agencies and despite the progress made in the matter of equality of rights, there continues to exist considerable discrimination against women,

Considering that discrimination against women is incompatible with human dignity and with the welfare of the family and of society, prevents their participation, on equal terms with men, in the political, social, economic and cultural life of their countries and is an obstacle to the full development of the potentialities of women in the service of their countries and of humanity,

Bearing in mind the great contribution made by women to social, political, economic and cultural life and the part they play in the family and particularly in the rearing of children,

Convinced that the full and complete development of a country, the welfare of the world and the cause of peace require the maximum participation of women as well as men in all fields,

Considering that it is necessary to ensure the universal recognition in law and in fact of the principle of equality of men and women,

Solemnly proclaims this declaration:

Article 1 Discrimination against women, denying or limiting as it does their equality of rights with men, is fundamentally unjust and constitutes an offence against human dignity.

Article 2 All appropriate measures shall be taken to abolish existing laws, customs, regulations and practices which are discriminatory against women, and to establish adequate legal protection for equal rights of men and women, in particular :

(a) The principle of equality of rights shall be embodied in the constitution or otherwise guaranteed by law;

(b) The international instruments of the United Nations and the specialized agencies relating to the elimination of discrimination against women shall be ratified or acceded to and fully implemented as soon as practicable.

Article 3 All appropriate measures shall be taken to educate public opinion and to direct national aspirations towards the eradication of prejudice and the abolition of customary and all other practices which are based on the idea of the inferiority of women.

Article 4 All appropriate measures shall be taken to ensure to women on equal terms with men, without any discrimination:

(a) The right to vote in all elections and be eligible for election to all publicly elected bodies;

(b) The right to vote in all public referenda;

(c) The right to hold public office and to exercise all public functions.

Such rights shall be guaranteed by legislation.

Article 5 Women shall have the same rights as men to acquire, change or retain their nationality. Marriage to an alien shall not automatically affect the nationality of the wife either by rendering her stateless or by forcing upon her the nationality of her husband.

Article 6

1. Without prejudice to the safeguarding of the unity and the harmony of the family, which remains the basic unit of any society, all appropriate measures, particularly legislative measures, shall be taken to ensure to women, married, or unmarried, equal rights with men in field of civil law, and in particular:

(a) The right to acquire, administer, enjoy, dispose of and inherit property, including property acquired during marriage;

(b) The right to equality in legal capacity and the exercise thereof;

(c) The same rights as men and with regard to the law on the movement of persons.

2. All appropriate measures shall be taken to ensure the principle of equality of status of the husband and wife, and in particular:

(a) Women shall have the same right as men to free choice of a spouse and to enter into marriage only with their free and full consent;

(b) Women shall have equal rights with men during marriage and at its dissolution. In all cases the interest of the children shall be paramount;

(c) Parents shall have equal rights and duties in matters relating to their children. In all cases the interest of the children shall be paramount.

3. Child marriage and the betrothal of young girls before puberty shall be prohibited, and effective action, including legislation, shall be taken to specify a minimum age for marriage and to make the registration of marriages in an official registry compulsory.

Article 7 All provisions of penal codes which constitute discrimination against women shall be repealed.

Article 8 All appropriate measures, including legislation, shall be taken to combat all forms of traffic in women and exploitation of prostitution of women.

Article 9 All appropriate measures shall be taken to ensure to girls and women, married or unmarried, equal rights with men in education at all levels, and in particular:

(a) Equal conditions of access to, and study in, educational institutions of all types, including universities and vocational, technical and professional schools;

(b) The same choice of curricula, the same examinations, teaching staff with qualifications of the same standard, and school premises and equipment of the same quality, whether the institutions are co-educational or not;

(c) Equal opportunities to benefit from scholarships and other study grants;

(d) Equal opportunities for access to programmes of continuing education, including adult literacy programmes;

(e) Access to educational information to help in ensuring the health and well-being of families.

Article 10

1. All appropriate measures shall be taken to ensure to women, married or unmarried, equal rights with men in the field of economic and social life, and in particular:

(a) The right, without discrimination on grounds of marital status or any other grounds, to receive vocational training, to work, to free choice of profession and employment, and to professional and vocational advancement;

(b) The right to equal remuneration with men and to equality of treatment in respect of work of equal value;

(c) The right to leave with pay, retirement privileges and provision for security in respect of unemployments, sickness, old age or other incapacity to work;

(d) The right to receive family allowances on equal terms with men.

2. In order to prevent discrimination against women on account of marriage or maternity and to ensure their effective right to work, measures shall be taken to prevent their

dismissal in the event of marriage or maternity and to provide paid maternity leave, with the guarantee of returning to former employment, and to provide the necessary social services, including child-care facilities.

Recommendation on consent to marriage, minimum age for marriage and registration of marriages

The General Assembly, Recognizing that the family group should be strengthened because it is the basic unit of every society, and that men and women of full age have the right to marry and to found a family, that they are entitled to equal rights as to marriage and that marriage shall be entered into only with the free and full consent of the intending spouses, in accordance with the provisions of article 16 of the Universal Declaration of Human Rights,

Recalling its resolution 843(IX) of 17 December 1954,

Recalling further article 2 of the Supplementary Convention on the Abolition of Slavery, the Slave Trade, and Institutions and Practices Similar to Slavery of 1956, which makes certain provisions concerning the age of marriage, consent to marriage and registration of marriages,

Recalling also that Article 13, paragraph 1b, of the Charter of the United Nations provides that the General Assembly shall make recommendations for the purpose of assisting in the realization of human rights and fundamental freedoms for all without distinction as to race, sex, language or religion,

Recalling likewise that, under Article 64 of the Charter, the Economic and Social Council may make arrangements with the Members of the United Nations to obtain reports on the steps taken to give effect to its own recommendations and to recommendations on matters falling within its competence made by the General Assembly,

1. Recommends, that, where not already provided by existing legislative or other measures, each Member State should take the necessary steps, in accordance with its constitutional processes and its traditional and religious practices, to adopt such legislative or other measures as may be appropriate to give effect to the following principles:

Principle I

(a) No marriage shall be legally entered into without the full and free consent of both parties, such consent to be expressed by them in person, after due publicity and in the presence of the authority competent to solemnize the marriage and of witnesses, as prescribed by law,

(b) Marriage by proxy shall be permitted only when the competent authorities are satisfied that each party has, before a competent authority and in such manner as may be prescribed by law, fully and freely expressed consent before witnesses and not withdrawn such consent.

Principle II

Member States shall take legislative action to specify a minimum age for marriage, which in any case shall not be less than fifteen years of age; no marriage shall be legally entered into by any person under this age, except where a competent authority has granted a dispensation as to age, for serious reasons, in the interest of the intending spouses.

Principle III

All marriages shall be registered in an appropriate official register by the competent authority.

2. Recommends that each Member State should bring the Recommendations on Consent to Marriage, Minimum Age for Marriage and Registration of Marriages contained in the present resolution before the authorities competent to enact legislation or to take other action at the earliest practicable moment and, if possible, no later than eighteen months after the adoption of the Recommendation;

3. Recommends that Member States should inform the Secretary-General, as soon as possible after the action referred to in paragraph 2 above, of the measures taken under the present Recommendation to bring it before the competent authority or authorities, with particulars regarding the authority or authorities considered as competent;

4. Recommends further that Member States should report to the Secretary-General at the end of three years, and thereafter at intervals of five years, on their law and practice with regard to the matters dealt with in the present Recommendation, showing the extent to which effect has been given or is proposed to be given to the provisions of the Recommendation and such modifications as have been found or may be found necessary in adapting or applying it;

5. Requests the Secretary-General to prepare for the Commission on the Status of Women a document containing the reports received from Governments concerning methods of implementing the three basic principles of the present Recommendation;

6. Invites the Commission on the Status of Women to examine the reports received from Member States pursuant to the present Recommendation and to report thereon to the Economic and Social Council with such recommendations as it may deem fitting.

9

Changing Role of Women in India

There are many such urbanised villages within metropolitan Delhi-the one in which the present research is being undertaking has been gradually incorporated into the growing city over the past 40 years, the last remnants of land having been lost to agriculture about 12 years ago. The Rays or Raya or Rava Rajput caste was the dominant caste of this village. Because all but an insignificant account of the village land had formerly been under the ownership of members of this caste, they have profited greatly from the acquisition of its territory for urban construction.

While at present the financial status of the Raya families still resident in Rayapur varies widely (depending upon the amount of land originally owned and their success in keeping or augmenting the money paid in compensation), all of the local inhabitants of the caste are at least relatively well-off: all own their own homes and most have other real estate which they give on rent; all have the basic necessities of life and certain luxuries as well, while some are wealthy even by Indian urban standards.

The indigenous definition of old age (bur-happa) has been treated from the beginning as one of the empirical questions to be researched, and therefore it was decided not to establish any a prior chronological age as a cut-off point for delimiting the universe of study. Indeed, to do so would have been to come up against a serious difficulty in the wide-spread ignorance of precise chronological age, especially among the elderly. While various devices, such as the making of a time-events table, can be used to get at a fairly close approximation of chronological age in such situations, it was felt that for our purposes it was more appropriate to select for study those who consider themselves and are considered by others as "old". in the context of their own society, regardless of actual age.

While the self-perception and the perception of others as old obviously differs from one individual to another, and tends to depend to an important degree on such variable external sings of aging as tooth-loss and graying hair, the general consensus seems to place primary stress on life-cycle criteria. Thus the marriage of one's children-particularly of one's sons marks the beginning of old age in this society far more clearly than does the passing of a specified number of years. We have, therefore, included in our "aging" sample all persons with effectively married sons or adopted sons. In case of son-less or childless persons, we have included them on the basis of their contemporarily with those already in the sample. There are so few of these, almost of a clearly advanced age, that ambiguities about proper assignment to the sample have been negligible.

The women of the elderly sample are all either married or widowed-a significant number have been remarried after the death of a first husband, usually to his younger or elder brother. None of the women was born in Rayapur: because of the practice of village exogamy, all coal "wives" come from other village and those of this older group come for the most part from village in Meerut and Muzaffarnagar Districts in

Uttar Pradesh. A few were born in Raya Rajput villages located elsewhere in the Delhi area. While it sometimes happens in this region that a separated woman or a widow will return to live in her natal village, or that a man without sons will invite a daughter and her husband to remain with him in her natal village (as ghar jamai) there are no such cases within this caste in Rayapur among the elderly group.

The background of almost all of the women is rural before and after marriage-and in some cases, until fairly recently, they were actively engaged and child care, for in this caste it was (and still is in the rural areas) customary for women to work in the family fields, to cut fodder for cattle, to fetch water from the well for all the household needs, and so on.

Because of the fortuitous locations of Rayapur, these women now rather suddenly find themselves in a position to enjoy almost total leisure (if they so wish) and an urban middle class life-style, an some have such comforts in their homes as hot running water, gas stoves, refrigerators, air-coolers and Saturday night television. While they are almost universally illiterate, their younger daughters and their grand daughters are graduating from college, and they are observing and even fostering by their tolerance, new standards for the relationship of husbands and wives as they marry their sons and grandsons to educated girls of their caste from the other Delhi villages.

While similar changes are affecting the lives of millions of other older Indian women who at some point in their lives have migrated from a rural to an urban environment (and even in a lesser degree the lives of millions who remain in the also changing rural milieu), the situation of these Rayapur women, and of others in villages similarly "swallowed" by the relentless march of urbanism, is unique in many respects.

The old women of Rayapur live, with negligible exceptions, in "joint" households of three and sometimes four generations. The most frequent type of household includes an older married, couple, one or more married sons and their wives and children, and unmarried children of the older couple as well. Many such households also have additional members a widowed or separated daughter, a daughter's child or other young relative come to attend school in Delhi.

A few also include the elderly father or mother of the older couple, making a four generation family group. There are very few widows in the older sample no doubt partly because of the customs or widow remarriage. The bulk of the "older" women in the 55-65 age range (based on reported ages and other means of estimation) and there are very few over 70.

While the residential norm is thus for the aging woman to hold the position of mother-in-law and wife in a lineal extended household, there are some exceptions: those who have no sons or whose sons are young despite their own advancing age. A small number of married couples in this category live with adopted "sons" (usually a husband's brother's son or a daughters's son) or with their own unmarried young children. One couple in their late fifties lives alone with only a young granddaughter (a SoDa) their only son having died and his wife remarried out of the family.

A widow in her midseventies lives with her teenage granddaughter (DaDa), who has come to stay in Rayapur from her village home in order to look after her grandmother and attend high school. This woman never had a son and is on bad terms with her closest relatives in the village, her former co-wife and the latter's son, with whom she might otherwise reasonably expect to be able to make her home.

As the extended family residence pattern is the universally desired one by and for old people, it is not surprising that preparation for old age security begins early in terms of assuring that there will be such a family in which to live when the time comes. This preparation manifests itself first in the attempt to have at least one son. While in the literature on Indian society the need for a son in typically given a religious, other worldly rationale, for these villagers it is pre-eminently and most practically a matter off providing for someone to take care of one's needs in old age.

Childless couples, and those who have managed to produce only female, children begin at some point to consider the alternatives: remarriage, adoption (formal or informal), or the taking of a ghar jamai. While men sometimes take a second wife during the lifetime of the first in order to have a son, women may remarry only after the death of their husbands. Remarriage is almost routine in this caste if the woman is still in her child-bearing years and does not all ready have growing sons on whom she can begin to rely for support. Although the customs is justified in a number of ways one important reason given by the Rayas themselves is to ensure that the woman will not be destitute in old age.

Adoption is always of a male relative a daughter's son on the brother's son of adopted. The adoptee is usually a child, but there are instance of the adoption of boys in their late adolescence done with the explicit understanding that the arrangement is being made to ensure that there will be some one to "serve" the adopter (seva Karna) when the need arises. In some cases land or money is signed over to the adoptee at this time.

Widowed women rarely adopt, although widowed and unmarried men do so not infrequently. There are, however, some widowed women now living with adopted sons who were taken in during the lifetime of their late husbands. Taking ghar jamai seem to be a less attractive solution to the problem of care in old age, even though many women many be heard to maintain that "only a daughter can really serve her parents with all her heart. There is a certain awkwardness in the living arrangements of a couple with the wife's parents, not least or the live-in son-in-law himself who tends to be looked down upon by others as a young man with little to offer, reduced to living off his wife's family.

In other ways also the situation reverses or makes impossible of maintenance many of the accepted kinship role behaviour patterns. While there are least two cases of village sons who are living as ghar jamais elsewhere, there are no such cases among Rayas in the village, itself, although there are a few village "daughters" living with their employed husbands separate from those of their parents.

Whether an old couple or a widow a son of their own, or has made arrangements to adopt a substitute, it is expected (and almost always followed in practice), that this boy when married will live on in the family home with his new wife and subsequent children. No other alternative is even considered initially, except in the rare case of a family with several sons where one is asked to marry as ghar jama.

However, this arrangement does not always last definitely. When a man has had two wives, it is unusual for married sons of the first to live for long in a joint household with the second. And even in the case of a woman's own son, it often happens that after a number of years he and his wife will set up separate cooking arrangements and even cease contributing to the joint family budget (although he usually continues in joint ownership with his father and brother of any family property).

When a couple's sons are beginning to think about arranging their own children's marriages, it is common, at least nowadays, for a formal division of even this joint property to be undertaken, although for the "prestige" (izzat) of the family, it is still considered best to marry one's grandchildren while the family is still "together" (ikatte).

However, in spite of the desire and need for some degree of partition of the joint family over the years, one thing that is considered quite out of the question is to separate off the old couple-or a widowed parent-leaving them to fend for themselves in the brother has married. And if full partition among the brothers takes place while one or both parents is still living, arrangements will be made to have them live and eat with one of them. More rarely, all the bahus will feed them together or in turn.

Even in such circumstances, sons remain in the family home. It should be stressed that the number of sons in Rayapur who have actually moved out of the parental residence in course of a partial or complete partition of the joint family while either of their parents was still living is negligible. At most, some have moved by mutual agreement to another house owned by their family in the village. In fact, there has been very little movement out of the village by any men of this caste, with the exception of several families who have bought rural land elsewhere with the proceeds or their own land compensation and have left to farm it.

More typically, even these families maintain one or more of a set of brothers on the farm, while the main part of the family remains in Rayapur. Even leaving the parental home because of the demands of employment is extremely rare for young Rayapur couples.

Because Delhi as a large metropolitan city provides employment opportunities of all kinds and at all levels, and because few Rayapur boys have obtained the kind of high-level position of highly specialised advanced training that might make it difficult to insist on remaining in the city of the most favourable job opportunities are to be availed of, the kind of mobility that is becoming typical of much of the educated middle and upper classes in urban Indian has not yet affected Rayapur household structures appreciably.

It is evident that this lack of mobility is not accidental: parents consciously want to keep their sons at home and consider it a defeat and a cause of much unhappiness if the joint household dissolves during their lifetime-so much greater their distress if a son actually moves away from the village, Up to the present the very few cases of the latter have been the result of serve family dissension (either between the young couple and a parent or parents of between brothers and/or brothers wives).

Because of the view that such a breakup is something for the family to be ashamed, of they are usually presented to outsiders as cases in which the couple had to move because the son's place of work was on the other side of Delhi and it took long to commute, or because the young family was very large and the son's employer provided living family was very large and the son's employer provided living quarters free of charge, and so on.

It remains to be seen if this pattern of joint residence can be maintained in the next generation, for aside from the pressure of space which is already becoming severe in some homes, village young men are increasingly aiming higher than the B.A. or LL.B that only five years ago was a rare attainment for Raya boys, and a few are even making plans for postgraduate education a broad. But because of the persistence of the traditional residence pattern for the aged at present living in the urbanised village of Rayapur, we must still look at the elderly woman's life and earlier life-history within the framework of this type of house-hold structure.

Raya women tend to think about their own lives, and those of women in general, in terms of three main stages or periods, each having its own character and characteristics, its own appropriate set of activities, its own duties and rewards.

The first of these is childhood (bachpan), a time that form the perspective of the end of life is viewed as having been generally pleasant, carefree, without much responsibility and few demands for hard work or restraint of freedom. During this period a woman is felt to have received the only unqualified love and nurturance she will ever have, and the warm and pleasant associations of childhood, of life "in the mother's kingdom" (make raj me) colour a woman's perception of her natal home and village (pihar) forever afterwards.

Women in their sixties still look forward to frequent periodic visits "home", even when parents have long since died and other familiar faces are rapidly dropping out of sight as well. One of the most often heard laments in this are group concerns the inevitable loss of touch with the pihar as the years go on, and with few exceptions, these women do manage to make such a visit at least once very year or two. Similarly, Rayapur households receive periodic visits from elderly village "daughters" married 40 or more miles away.

For most of these women, childhood ended abruptly with the onset of puberty or shortly thereafter. Although there are a few examples of women of this age-group who married in their late teens, the majority were married before the age of 12 or 13 and went to take up married lie in their husband's households and villages (sasural) within two or three years. Some women claim to have been so young at the time of the wedding that they were unaware of what was going on. These, who may have been as young as 7 or 8 years old, did not, of course, join their husbands' households until they were physically mature, many yeas later.

The second major period of these women's lives (ironically referred to in contrast to the earlier period as "mother-in-law's kingdom" (sas ka raj) began for almost all in the position of junior member of a large joint farm family, where the contrast with the natal home in terms of workload ad the ability to move about and speak freely with households members and others was sharp and often traumatic. There was little time and less privacy in the first months and even years to develop a close relationship with the new husband ("those were 'simple' times", as one such woman put it), and frequent lengthy visits to their natal villages were a welcome respite from the physical and often emotionally trying atmosphere of the sasural.

The first pregnancy was eagerly awaited, and those who had difficulty conceiving or who aborted easily or whose first children died infancy report trying various measures, spiritual, magical and medical, to help them become pregnant or to ensure that their children would live beyond the perilous first year. Most did succeed in this, although some were never able to have a son, seen as so necessary for a worry-free old age.

They spent the succeeding years rearing their children (although in many instances this task was mainly pre-empted by their mother-in-law), and gradually, as in-laws died and brothers and cousins separated, succeeded to the position of senior woman of their own household, making the transition into old age with the marriage of sons and the coming of their wives and later of grandchildren—"the kingdom of the daughter-in-law (bahu ka raj).

Since the purpose of this research has been to look at old age in the context of the entire life-cycle, considerable attention has been given, in eliciting life-histories and in interviews, as well as in observing interaction and listening to spontaneous conversation involving the elderly, to obtaining an overview of their perception of the total life experience (in the present case, of the female experience), both in specific, personal, individual terms, and in the broad, generalised aspect. What emerges from the data is often contradictory—there seems to be a marked discrepancy between the largely pessimistic, discontented, and resigned verbal utterances about "woman's lot" and the sad fate of the aged, and the observed high level of good-humoured and extraordinarily active participation and interest in social, work and family activities.

Women's life has been described to us time after time as being "nothing but hard work, trouble, and pain from beginning to end". Our queries often receive such responses. "How can you ask about the best time of a woman's life? There is no good time." A typical answer to the enquiry "How are you?" (particularly if the greeter is another old lady) goes something like "I can only wish that God would take me right now, but I suppose I will somehow have to get through the days that are allotted to me, although I would rather be dead."

Detachment from worldly concerns is espoused as a necessary and desirable part of aging, while those who recommend it most vocally are on the go from dawn, to late at night managing the affairs of their family, visiting sick relatives, helping to arrange the marriages of neighbours, children attending wedding and funerals, buying clothes for festival presents for their married daughters, grinding two kilos of wheat by hand in the morning before breakfast, and fact of individual variability-which is considerable despite a high degree of cultural homogeneity and general similarity of life experiences among the women of this one caste in a single village-there remains a good deal to be sorted out from these apparently conflicting impressions.

We may try to do this by discussing these women's perception of the period of life in which they are presently living at three levels. First there is the level of ideals: how a woman's old age ought to be spent, how she should occupy herself and how she should be treated by others. Second, there is the way that these women perceive their old age, and the old age of other women they know, to be in actuality. Usually, the issue here degree to which their life as they see it approaches or deviates from the ideal. And third is the "objective" observer's view of their lives and her interpretation of it. This is made up partly from direct observation and questioning, and partly from clues provided by the women's own (or their members and relatives and neighbours) verbal reports of incidents in which they have been involved.

In ideal terms, old age is supposed to be a time of rest and leisure, a time when work responsibilities should cease, and one should be "served" by the sons the has raised for the purpose and by their wives. Elderly women describe a fortunate one among their peers as one whose bahu-bete ("daughters-in-law and sons") give them much "rest" (aram) and "service" (seva).

The stereotyped manner of praising a daughter-in-law is to say that she is hard-working and serves one well. The concept of seva is a broad one, an implied in it is not only the performance of all necessary tasks for the comfort of the older person, but love, consideration, thought-fulness, and devotion as well. However, this latter aspect is implicit rather than varbalised; when asked to explain the meaning of seva women almost always do so largely in terms of physical care : "I have very hard-working (bahut Kameri) and serving (seva karnevali) bahu. She gives me my meals, washes my clothes, prepares my bed at night. In all things, she serves me well."

Certain more personal services are also included in the concept of seva, such as scrubbing the older woman's bank when she bathes, combig and braiding her hair and most importantly and symbolically, massaging her legs at night and when she is ill or tired. Young women often relate how their sas makes them press her legs (pao dabvana) for hours at a stretch each night until they drop off to sleep from exhaustion, at which point the old woman is perversely brought back to wakefulness, demanding that the massaging continue. The older women, on the other hand, maintain that in their day they really served their mothers-in-law not like the bahus of today: "In those days when one of us massaged my sas's legs the others would be massaging her hands. But now! they claim that the custom is unfortunately dying that the old are no longer in a position to demand this kind of service, and they shrug off question about the practice in their own homes with a cynical laugh.

Seva also means care in time of illness. It is a common complaint among the old that members of the younger generation are not sufficiently sympathetic when an old person is not feeling well. "Here I have been coughing like this for so many days. I can't get my breath, yet no one has asked 'Mother, what is the matter?" keep my sorrows and sufferings to myself". Yet although modern medicine is widely accepted and utilised by persons of all ages it is rare four an elderly person to agree to go for a stay in the hospital, even in the case of serious illness. In fact, one might say that they are especially reluctant to go in case of serious illness, because of the fear of dying away from home and family. Therefore, it is not unusual for an old and helpless person to be nursed for months or even years by a daughter-in-law.

There is no thought given in this kind of situation to the hospital, even in the case of serious illness. In fact, one might say that they are especially reluctant to go in case of serious illness, because of the feat of dying away from home and family. Therefore, it is not unusual or an old an helpless person to be nursed for months or even years by a daughter-in-law. There is no thought given in this kind of situation to the possibility of hiring a nurse or other outsider to take over the less pleasant or physically exhausting tasks involved in caring for an invalid, even though for many of these families there are no financial constraints to their doing so. And I know of no instance in which an old person has been sent away to a hospital against his will, no matter how difficult the circumstances. Yet, despite the fact that no eat of being sent to die among strangers hangs over these women, they are unanimous in expressing the wish to die " while my hands and feet are still able".

The worst thing that can happen to someone, they say, is to become helpless in old age and to live on, a burden to others and to oneself. Indeed, whatever their private fears of death may be, they speak of it openly, cheerfully and with matter-of-factness. Typical is the statement of a healthy woman in her late fifties, a widow and mother of three sons, of whom the eldest is married: "I have sons, a daughter-in-law has come, there are son's children (pore-poti) and daughter's children (dhevte-dhevti). What more do I nee? I am ready to go at any time."

While the actual work involved in doing seva mainly falls upon a woman's daughter-in-law, the son himself tends to share the credit-and the blame-for the quality of its performance. Some women are of the opinion that it depends mainly upon the son whether his parents are well taken care of in old age, and there is a dominant tone of pessimism when they discuss this problem in general terms.

It seem to be felt that hard as one many try to ensure that one has as one may try to ensure that one has a son to provide for one in old age, and as much as one may do for him in bringing him up, nursing him through illnesses, educating him, and so on, it is in the end an unpredictable matter "how he will turn out". They explain that, "If the son is good, them everything will be fine. But there are very few sons like nowadays-at the most on in a hundred can be found who will really care for his parents in their old age. Some maintain that a really "good" son will make sure that his wife serves her in-laws well, but others fell that one's fate really lies in the hands of the stranger one has brought into the family. " The son may be good, but if his wife is off that kind she will turn his head (isko sikhaegi) against his parents, and then he will also neglect them.

There is a definite feeling that social change is having an adverse effect on the position of old people, and as evidence of this they point to the increasing tendency of young married men to separate from their parents shortly after marriage, Although this has not yet become an important trend within the village or in the caste as a whole, they see it as a real threat for the future, and claim that it is being learned from the Punjabis (a very visible out-group in the neighborhood to whom all unwelcome social deviance is credited), among whom it has become (according to them) the expected norm.

It is the minimum duty of a bahu to relieve her mother-in-law (sas) of such household jobs as cooking he meals an washing the utensils and clothes. It is said that "it doesn't look nice" (accha nahi lagta) to have an older woman cooking if there are on or more daughters-in-law in the house, and although some mothers-in-law continue to share the cooking if they have only one married son (usually in this case one woman will cook the morning meal, the other the evening meal), it is the more common and expected practice for her to cease cooking shortly after her son's marriage, except in emergencies such as the sickness or absence of the bahu. The appropriate feminine division of labour as described by Rayapur women has the mother-in-law doing the "outside work" (bahar ka Kam), while the bahu takes care of the work inside the house (ghar ka kam). This coincides with the traditional rural expectation that a young married woman should stay within the house as much as possible, and although young wives in Rayapur are by no means completely contained to the home (or when outside it to the chaperonage of their sas or other older woman) to the degree that these elderly women were in their youth, the standard is still recognised as legitimate and desirable, although perhaps not very practical of execution under present day circumstances.

There are many families in the village whose young married women leave the home only occasionally, and then only for such things as an excursion to the movies with their husbands (itself a serious departure from the kind of behaviour suitable for young married women in the youth and middle-age of the present-day elderly).

"Outside work" in this urbanised village includes shopping for staple provisions and vegetables and doing other errands involving contact with tradesmen and artisan specialists, such as the weavers to whom hand-spun cotton is entrusted each summer for weaving into blankets, or the cot-makers who may be called from time to renew the string webbing on the family cots. In all households some of these "outside jobs" may be taken care of by the men-either the old woman's husband or son-but a large part of this work, and particularly its organisation, is considered the province of the senior woman of the house.

Although financial arrangements vary greatly from one household to another, it is usual for the senior woman to keep back for their own and their wives' personal use (so that it does not mean total control over all purchases by family members), but it is nevertheless an important elements in her day-to-day managerial authority.

Care of animals is also in most families the province of older women. More than half of the households in which old people are present own at least one buffalo for milk and ghee and some own more than one and occasionally a cow as well. The symbolic significance of having one's milk own (ghar ka dudh) is probably as great as its contribution to the family diet. For the older generation, to have to purchase milk is one of the signs of times that is most to be deprecated. Although in the rural of this village, men took a large share in the care of milch animals, this task in most Rayapur households is now relegated mainly to women, and among them mainly to the old, of the young wives increasingly come to marriage unfamiliar with the intricacies of milking and the care and feeding of buffaloes. This job takes a great deal of a woman's time, and necessitates her being available in the home at almost all times.

A buffalo must be fed and watered three times a day, washed down at least once a day, milked twice a day (and the milk churned and ghee made) and her stall must be cleaned and the manure patted into dung cakes which are dried in the sun and later stacked and used for fuel. The latter job is one to which the older village women are so accustomed fro their earlier days-and the savings so accustomed when compared to the cost of wood, coal, or kerosene, not to mention bottled gas-that many who do not own an animal buy manure from one of the local dairies and make their own dung cakes.

Other household tasks that are typically taken care of by older women-although young women may also do them-are those which are fairly sedentary, such as spinning into thread the old cotton into the quilts before winter sets in and making such household staples in the appropriate seasons as pickles and hand-rolled noodles.

A major responsibility of the older women in most households is the care of young children, particularly toddlers. A grandmother will take charge of a young baby while its mother is busy with the cooking and washing, but when a baby is very small her contribution will usually be limited to holdings it and perhaps feeding it sugared water while its mother is otherwise occupied. Later, however and particularly after all of its care, having it sleep beside her at night, feeding it and taking it alone with her on errands or when she goes to visit neighbour or to any social or religious event. Grandmothers say "the interest is dearer then the capital" (mul se pyari byaj) to explain their fondness for their grandchildren, and their exceptional leniency and patience with the antics and whining of children whom they have hopelessly spoiled and to whom they allow liberties that they never permitted their own children.

It is not unusual for grandmothers in this way to attempt-and often succeed-in weaning a child's affection from his mother. But, young mothers. By and large, seem to accept the special relationship of grandmother and grandchild-perhaps partly because it relieves them of a significant burden of work-and are more apt to resent a mother-in-law who does not show special affection for their child or who shows favoritism to one of his cousins.

While the classical Indian four states of life (ashramas) are not clearly articulated in reference to the female life-cycle, either in the traditional literature or in the folk conception. Raya women do frequently use the classical terminology to refer to the second and major stage of life, that of the householder, grhastha. Ideally, they express the view that in old age a woman should leave grhastha, should detach herself from concern with the day-to-day running of the household.

To leave grhastha involves two aspects: first a readiness on the part of the bahu to take over the onerous household tasks formerly performed by the sas (with the indifferent assistance of her daughters), and second, a readiness on the part of the older woman to give up her managerial role and her feeling that she along is responsible for and capable of managing household affairs. These two rarely coincide. While the former is generally more or less accomplished within a week or two of the new daughter-in law's arrival, the latter is typically a very gradual process of withdrawal that may take may years and may never be completed before the senior woman's death. The symbolic act of "handing over the keys" to the daughter-in-law is often chided-and chide one another-for being "too much bound up in grhastha", it is actually rare in this community for any the work of the household and its organisation until she is either mentally or physically quite incapable of doing so.

It has long been a tradition in Indian society-and in other societies as well-to regard religious activities as particularly appropriate to the aged. To spend one's declining years in contemplation, to prepare oneself for the imminent departure from this world by devoting oneself to the purification of the inner self and the worship of a God for whom one had perhaps too little time to spare in one's younger days, is regarded not only as a virtue i itself but also as the better part of wisdom as the time of reckoning draws near, Consistent with this ideal, who note that the religiosity of the elderly woman in Rayapur is markedly greater than that of their younger relatives and neighbours, if we measure this in terms of proportion of time spent in solitary and group worship.

The majority of elderly women rise between four and five in the morning (often before their daughters-in-law awaken, contrary to the traditional rural pattern) and after going to the toilet and bathing spend one-half to one hour in prayer. Some go each morning to one of the village temples, others sit in front of their household shrine and "take Go's name", either alone or in the company of their husbands or other family members. Only after this do they take any refreshment. The other major form of religious participation is group hymn (bhajan) singing. There are regular weekly sessions at one of the village temples, organised by a women's satsang group. The leader of this group is a Punjabi woman who lives outside the village, but almost all of the regular members are Raya women and on any given occasion more than half of those in attendance are over 50 years of age.

There is a regular active core of such older woman with a few middle-aged and young women, most of the latter being women of nuclear households. The bahus of the older women rarely of ever attend. In addition to this regular human meeting, there are others held irregularly in private homes in the village, usually to celebrate some happy family event such as a child's birthday. A woman who enjoys such gatherings can easily spend several afternoons a week singing religious songs with her peers and exchanging gossip in the intervals.

When queried, very few of the older women admit to having had a serious concern with religion inn their youth, and in general they attribute their present preoccupation with such activities to their newly acquired leisure and to its appropriateness to their present stage of life. "When did I have time for it before? they say, or " Now that it is my time of rest I can do this".

There are a number of older women who have attached themselves as disciples of a guru whose main ashram is in a city several hundred miles away, but who spends much of the year in Delhi. He comes for several weeks each year to the village itself, where he is hosted by one of the wealthiest local Raya families.

Despite the popularity of religious pursuits among older Raya woman, there are a significant number in the sample who seldom or never gather to sing bhajans (except perhaps when they are invited to a private human-singing in the home of a close relative or neighbour). One such woman put it this way: "I don't have time for such things-I have to take care of my buffalo. Taking care of animals is a kind of worship (puja) too, you know."

One manifestation of the perception of old age as a time of detachment from the concerns of early adulthood is the tendency among again married persons to voluntarily and deliberately cease having an active sex life once their children and particularly their sons-are married. While there are some exceptions, as a rule cohabitation is stopped when the first son's wife come to live in the household, if not before. There are some cases of older couples maintaining an active sex life or at least sharing a sleeping room after this, but such in neither the ideal nor the statistical norm. Those who do continue to sleep together in old age typically have no married sons, or are couples in which the woman is a younger second wife and the son the offspring of the first wife. Actually in such cases a joint household is rarely maintained for long after the son's marriage.

The cessation of sexual relations between a couple may be gradual and unspoken, but often it is a decision discussed and deliberately entered upon. One woman, for example, described the way that her husband had come to her on the day of their eldest son's wedding saying. "From now on we will live together as brother and sister". Since that day they have not shared a bed.

This practice is rationalised in terms of older people not "needing" sex, and in terms of the "Shame" or "embarrassment" (sharam) that would result if parents were to engage in sex while their son and his wife are also doing so in the same house: "It is a matter of sharam. When the bahu-bete are doing that, now would it look for the sas-sasur to be doing it too? Public opinion seems to be a significant factor in this sense of sharam, for without the custom of married couples having a private bedroom or a double bed (an innovative piece of furniture nowadays routinely included in the sense of sharam for without the custom of married couples having a private bedroom or a double bed (an innovative piece of furniture nowadays routinely included in the dowry but provocative of much amusement among the older generation), it rapidly becomes general family and later, neighborhood knowledge if in older couple continues to sleep together. "People would make all kind of comments. They would say 'Imagine, their bahu has come and still they are carrying on like that. After all we had our time now it is the time of the bahu-bete".

In earlier times, when the village had a farming economy, it was usual for the men of the family to sleep in an outbuilding (gher) and to spend most of their leisure time there as well coming to the main house only for meals, and for occasional surreptitious visit to their wives at night. Even today many families maintain a separate gher where animals are tied and where the older men sit and entertain their guests and carry on interminable card games.

Many of these older men also sleep in their gher-if they do not have one, they are generally assigned a downstairs sitting room, usually the front room of the house, which serves the same general function. The older woman will then sleep in another room with the children, while each young married couple, and sometimes young un-married men, are given a bedroom to themselves.

It is interesting in this connection, particularly to observers of the again process among in Western societies, that awareness of the menopause as a period of physical or psychological stress seems to be quite absent among Raya women. Considerable questioning on this subject from both pre and post menopausal women failed to elicit any not out that the cessation of the menstrual cycle should cause distress in women or the it should be accompanied either by marked physical symptoms or temperamental an emotional difficulties. It is generally felt that if the menstrual periods stop when a woman is still relatively young (i.e., in her thirties) she may become weakened "because of the hat that goes from there to the head at this time". The chief problem otherwise if considered to be the danger to eyesight, which is observed to become poor at around the time of (normal) menopause, and again is attributed to "hear" (garmi) rising to the head. However, cooling foods are recommended as a sufficient antidote.

Many women express relief at the cessation of menstruation, because it is "messy" and a "brother", and (for those who have sufficient sons and daughters) because it means the end of childbearing. Of course, for many women sexual relations have already ceased by this time, for the first son is often already married by the time the mother is forty-five. The emotional upheavals that are associated with menopause in West seem puzzling to my informants, as does the idea that a woman should feel at this time she is "no longer and so on. My inquiries on the latter point were met with hilarity: "Well, he certainly isn't going to go off and get somebody else at this point, is he?" or "He's an old man too, after all what would he expect?"

This is not to say that what in the West are recognised as menopausal symptoms are totally absent for these women as they experience the physiological changes that are taking place in their bodies. But whatever symptoms these women may have they are not associated by them with the decline in their reproductive capacity and are not even regarded as forming a complex, as being related to one another.

It would be difficult indeed to entangle "menopausal" symptoms from others which flow directly from the social-structural circumstances in which women typically find themselves during this time of life. For example, the menopause would tend to coincide roughly for most women with the time during which her children are marrying and new wives are being incorporated into the family. A woman does not need to look for physiological for the tensions and stresses of these years.

And as for the physical symptoms, a person's health is expected to decline gradually as he gets older. Discomforts of the kind that a doctor would associate with menopause are probably taken in their stride as part of this general process of aging. Thus whatever physical or emotional symptoms of the menopause may be present among these women, they are given no cultural elaboration nor considered unique or peculiar to the period we characterise as the "change of life".

Over the years there have been numerous studies evaluating the impact of Structural Adjustment Programmes (SAPs) on third world societies, economies and polities. Currently, apart from World Bank-IMF studies, there are also neo-liberal assessments that generally laud the policy packages typical of SAP. In some cases, earlier critics have turned into committed supporters. Recent critical studies of SAP, liberal as well as radical, have buttressed earlier negative assessments about the viability of these policy packages for "Third World" populations. The South Commission Report was quite unequivocal: "By the standards of the policies forced upon the developing countries by the multilateral financial institutions, many countries had adjusted and others were persisting in the effort. But the result for a large number of them was a decade of development in reverse-neither redistribution nor growth-and a worsening of prospects for future development.

The policies of developed countries and of the international financial institutions they control must bear a heavy responsibility for forcing developing countries on to a path of prolonged stagnation and retrenchment."

The South Commission was not opposed to far-reaching economic reforms or de-bureaucratisation. It was clearly admitted that, "The setbacks of the 1980s exposed the structural weakness of developing countries and showed that appropriate macro-economic policies are indispensable to provide a stable basis for day to day decision-making. The crisis had made it even more urgent to undertake structural reforms in order to strengthen the public sector and its resource-generating capacity, improve tax systems, and create a stable environment in which the private sector can play its role in line with national priorities.

Also it is now very clear that reforms are required to promote exports...to pay for imports....to contribute to the efficient management of the balance of payments. In the adjustment process of the 1980s, these needed reforms were frustrated by an unbalanced international approach towards structural adjustment and by the conditionality prescribed by the international financial institutions...the programme for stabilization and adjustment pressed upon developing countries did not provide for sufficient external support to permit adjustment to occur and endure without choking their growth.

The (structural adjustment) programmes were based on unduly optimistic assumptions about the speed at which structural maladies could be corrected. In addition they were generally shaped by a doctrinaire belief in the efficacy of market forces and monetarist policies. This combination of priorities and policies aggravated the developing countries economic woes and social distress in a number of ways.

The South Commission noted the politico-economic reasons for the countries of the South having to adopt these policies: "The decision-making processes that govern the international flows of trade, capital, and technology are controlled by the major developed countries of the North and by the international institutions they dominate. The countries of the South are unfavorable placed in the world economic system' they are individually powerless to influence these processes and institutions and hence, the global economic environment which vitally affects their development.

Other studies have since confirmed this criticism of SAP policies. A widely cited study by Jane Harrigan and Paul Mosely of World Bank Structural Adjustment Lending, 1980-87 reaffirmed this negative assessment. It found such World Bank lending, which had increased from zero in 1978 to around 30 per cent of the Bank's total lending in 1990 has had a negative impact on GDP growth rates in the 19 countries studied.

This and earlier studies by the authors, showed a negative correlation between the level of World Bank programme aid finance on the one hand, and rate of both policy reform compliance and GDP growth. The provision of World Bank finance and compliance with Bank policy conditions, both had a two-year lagged negative effect on investment. Surprisingly, this study found that, contrary to the claim that the acceptance of Bank-Found conditionalities would increase international capital flows to developing countries by placing a seal of approval on selected LDC governments only in the group of Sub-Saharan countries was there any evidence of a positive net impact of SAP on flow of foreign private finance.

The two year lagged negative impact of SAP on investment as a share on GDP would as the authors noted, "most likely continue to have a depressing effect on GDP growth for years to come". In other words, the negative impact of SAPs on the these countries would continue for years, as the investment necessary for future growth, would have declined because of the contraction caused by reducing the fiscal deficit, subsidies, etc. Studies have shown that these adverse effects on distributional and social welfare indicators, as a whole. As a consequence, less privileged sections including women, have suffered disproportionately.

The World Bank has responded to these criticisms by advocating as it were structural adjustment with a human face. Thus the World Development Report 1991 has a whole chapter on "investing in people" wherein health, education, poverty reduction and the provision of other social services are stressed.

The essentially neo-conservative bias in the report is indicated by its recourse to old theorists. Thus Alfred Marshall's 1890 dictum is cited that, "the chief importance of material wealth....(is) that when wisely used, it increase the health and strength,physical, mental and moral of the human race" But its analysis of the role of the sate is revealing: Authoritarianism often has been seen as a useful if regrettable, expedient for effective policy making in the face of political instability. In fact, in its introductory "overview" the WDR 1991 suggests, " The speed and sequencing of policy reform have often been decisive.... Swift reform may help neutralize the resistance of interest groups opposed to change....Ghana, Indonesia, the Republic of Korea, Mexico, and Turkey seem to show that packages of comprehensive reform, with at least bold changes made at the start of the programme, are more likely to succeed.

The advice is clear. Push through some basic, irreversible reforms, before resistance can be mobilized. Political polarization should be avoided as the record shows: " Democratic governments have a better record than authoritarian governments in countries that are not polarised; the reverse seems to be true in polarised societies".

The WDR 1991 however emphasises the importance of social investment in areas beneficial to women like female education, basic heath and family planning. Thus it notes that, "The results (of its statistical analysis) are quite clear about the importance of educating women. The educational status of adult women is by far the most important variable explaining changes in infant mortality and secondary school enrolments." In its most recent reports, WDR 1992 and WDR 1993, the World Bank while focusing on the environment and health issues respectively, again stresses on the necessity for special provisions for women.

Since the operation of SAPs as studies cited above have shown, actually diminish social welfare and the social safety net for the aged, unemployed women and children, the World Bank prescriptions for women are somewhat superficial and most inadequate. For instance, if as is normally the case during structural adjustment public investment in education declines, women particularly from lower strata will bear the brunt, despite female literacy programmes etc. Similarly the relative decline in public investment in health services, negatively affects women (including the female child) especially from lower strata, more.

Prospects of Indian Women

In India, terms like adjustment, restructuring, stabilisation, liberalisation and deregulation are often used interchangeably. The confusion is confounded by the other tendency to treat all the recent macro-economic policies as something very largely, if not completely, new. As Jayati Ghosh has pointed out, the current so-called economic reforms comprise of two major parts: one a, greater de-regulation and liberalisation of various markets, which is really a continuation of a process initiated in the 1970s and accentuated in the 1980s, and the other a set of contractionary macro-economic polices intended to stabilise the economy and move towards internal and external adjustment, which can be dated around 1990-91.

The conventional description of these reforms as marking a retreat by the state is highly questionable. As Patnaik has stated recently. "Even in the fiscal sphere, where tax-cuts have accompanied welfare expenditure cuts everywhere, there is obviously a specific redistributive design at work a specific kind of intervention embedded within the so-called retreat by the State. In short, the blanket term retreat by the State, is a gross misnomer. What we are witnessing is a transition from one paradigm of State intervention to another... it had an exceedingly important class content.

Patnaik has argued that this shift in state intervention is in general, designed to bring about three important changes in the balance of class forces: first a weakening of workers vis-a-vis the capitalists, secondly a centralisation of capital; and thirdly, a strengthening of financial interests relative to manufacturing interests within the capitalist class itself. While the precise class content of these changes may be debatable, it appears clear that the shift in the state's role in favour of the propertied classes and strata would generally operate against women. Even upper strata women would, give the extremely sexist discrimination against women in India, not benefit from the redistributive aspect of SAP in the same measure as men from the same stratum.

SAP and Urban Women

Any attempt to predict the likely impact of the current economic policies on women in urban India on the basis of experiences of other countries has its limitations. The differences in the domestic situation and the external environment make cross country comparisons hazardous. Yet, some generalisations are possible. A comparative analysis of 12 countries by Horton, Kanbur and Majumdar showed that in all countries there was a substantial increase underemployment and that real wages declined while wage differentials increased.

Another common feature of SAPs is the increased supply of labour largely as a result of the increased participation of women in the labour force. This is particularly true of low-income household to cope with economic crisis. Increased unemployment because of closures and an exit policy leading to increasing male unemployment because of closures also leads to increased female participation, esp, in the lower paid occupations, e.g. poorly paid labour intensive industries like electronics, footwear and garments.

Larger numbers of women have found jobs in the unorganised manufacturing and service sectors, as casual labour, piece-rate workers of self-employed persons. Pushpa Pathak has, on the basis of the experience of other developing countries indicated the likely impact of the SAP on women in the informal labour market. First, she believes that firms in order to reduce wage costs, will subcontract parts of the production process to small workshops or individual home-based workers in the informal sector.

This would mean that more women would work as unprotected wage labour. Secondly in view of declining real incomes in segments of the urban middle strate (the salariat, fixed income groups, etc.) the demands for the goods and service produced by self-employed women may be reduced, lowering the latter's returns. Thirdly, wage labour will find fewer jobs and will increasingly have to settle for temporary or casual employment with no job security, low wages and no other benefits. Given the structure of the labour market, women will suffer more. Lastly the real wages of workers and incomes in all segments of the urban informal sector are likely to decline. But, wage workers and piece-rate workers, of whom substantial numbers are women, will be worse hit. In a study of the likely impact of the SAP on rural women, it has noted the National Sample Survey (NSS) and other data for the 1970s and 1980s indicate a relative stability of main work involvement of rural women and a relative decline in marginal (or subsidiary status) employment. Secondly, secondary data indicates the growing role of female casual labour, in both main and marginal occupations, and in the rural non-agricultural sector. Thirdly, the NSS data show declines in both unemployment and underemployment of rural women workers, while other evidence indicates real wage increases at least until the mid to late 1980s.

Gosh covers well known ground and shows that the fall in public investment in agriculture including in development expenditure the increase fertilizer prices resulting from the cut in subsidies, and the cut in real spending on rural employment generation programmes, will negatively affect the rural population. Moreover, as we have indicated earlier, reduction in health and education, "will all entail declines in the real incomes of rural workers and (their) access to basic necessities".

The liberalisation of agricultural trade, now mandated by the new GATT agreement and internal prices have already led to an increase in foodgrain prices. As far as rural wage labourers are concerned higher food prices represent a decline in real incomes and a shrinking of the consumption basket. Small and medium farmers who are involved in distress sales, and thus may be net purchasers of food at any time, will also be worse of. Ghosh citing other studies also contends that the growth of agricultural processing industries for export will not generate enhanced female employment. The mechanisation that will accompany these new processing units is labour-displacing, esp. as it will replace traditional labour-intensive household industries, e.g. milling and cleaning. Furthermore, since the combination of trade liberalisation and devaluation would make labour relatively more expensive (because of higher food prices), and machines relatively cheaper (because of freer imports), future agricultural expansion is likely to be marked by more mechanisation and labour displacement with deleterious consequences for female wage labour. The Human Development Report 1993 has described "a new and disturbing phenomenon: jobless growth" Even in the developed countries, the HDR 1993 noted, despite an annual increase of 2.4% in per capita GNP between 1965 and 1990, the average unemployment rate is around 7%, and a quarter of the 30 million unemployed have been out of work for than two years. The scenario for the developing world particularly those in the grip of SAPs, is even grimmer.

But for women, not only in India, the situation is especially dangerous. As the Report acknowledges: "Women, a majority of the world's populations, receive only a small share of the developmental opportunities. They are often excluded from education or form the better jobs, from political systems or from adequate health care." They are often excluded from education or from the better jobs, from political systems or from adequate health care. But the social discontent which is unleashed and aggravated as consequence of the economic dislocations caused by SAP may well lead to the political polarization that breads authoritarianism. The consequences of that not-so-unlikely possibility in this country would entail an incalculable cost for Indian women.

Any viable alternative to the SAP would have to be based on an almost radically different model of development: a sustainable development model. The ramifications of such a model were sketched out in the Brundtland Commission Report. The crisis in India today is unlikely to be amenable to any other solution. But this is a very large and complex issue which would require much fuller discussion not possible here.

But the inescapable conclusion is that the suffering caused as a consequence of SAP will be disproportionately borne by Indian women. The measures recommended by the World Bank such as enhanced investment in female education, female health programmes, etc., will be more palliatives unlikely to significantly reduce the suffering of the most vulnerable sections of the population. In any event, as recent experience in

India has shown, budgetary and fiscal constraints will reduce these women-specific allocations to a minimum. Thus the iron rule of all sexist societies will operate: where there is hardship, women will suffer more. Given the extent to mass poverty in India, and its retarded industrial growth despite SAP the future prospects for Indian women under SAP look increasingly bleak.

The post second world war economic scene has witnessed a noticeable change in work participation rates of female workers. This period has also witnessed many technological revolutions which have brought many qualitative changes in the work force and accentuated miseries of the working population. These developments have led to emergence of a different kind of labour process and labour market.

For example, the developed countries drive to cut labour cost has forced them to resort to substitution of highly skilled, highly paid worker by part-time workers. Casualisaion of workers has taken place on a unprecedented scale. More than 50 per cent new jobs in highly industrialised countries were temporary in 80's.

There is general consensus that women are subjected to labour market discrimination and are segregated to low paid and low status occupations. The thrust of the argument is that with the change in level of economic development, the women are pushed to the periphery in terms of productive employment. This phenomenon is referred as 'feminisation' of jobs which contributes to marginalising the economic role of women in the development process. It the past, economic development has adversely affected employment opportunities of female workers.

Now, the main question before us is 'did economic development lead to marginalisation of female workers in India?' The second question posed here is, 'how the structural adjustment will affect the employment opportunities of female workers in India?' The present study will be exploratory in character.

The scheme of the paper is as follows: The next section outlines the various dimensions of Female Marginalisation (FM) thesis. Section 3 highlights the Indian context. Section 4 provides insights of empirical evidence available in this direction. Section 5 deals with main features of Structural Adjustment Programme (SAP) and its impact on female employment in India. The status of women and its contribution to social and economic development largely depends on the availability of employment opportunities for women. In spite of serious efforts of the state to improve the status of women in India, it continues to be unsatisfactory.

The Female Marginalisation (FM) in its generic from contends that the process of industrialisation and economic development are accompanied by marginalisation of women in the production process. The Marxists argue the FM is inherent in the organisation of capitalist production and use of Labour. It is capitalism and patriarchal organisation of society which result in confinement of women to homes and to inferior occupations. The divorce between production and reproduction under capitalism on the one hand and existence of multistructuralist society give rise to segregation and marginalisation of production while, others try to seek explanations in terms of economic, social and cultural fabric of a particular society. Empirical evidence to FM thesis shows an erosion of traditional female role as such and exclusion of women from industrial employment. That is why, the testing of hypothesis becomes difficult. FM can be verified on the basis of following visible dimensions:

(1) FM can mean exclusion of women from productive employment which can be observed either as decline in overall work participation rates of women or diminution in their share in wage and salaried employment;

(2) FM can also mean segregation of women workers in certain specific jobs which are low in occupational hierarchy and less rewarding and low in status and increasing exclusion of either sex from a particular function;

(3) FM may be manifested in concentration of majority of women workers in the marginal occupations, industries and sectors of employment. For example, concentration of women in the informal sectors or in unpaid occupations;

(4) FM may also mean economic inequality reflected through gender wage differentials and casualisaion of female labour force.

It is not necessary that the dimensions of FM have to manifest in order to prove FM thesis. Scott observes that the dimensions outlined above are not different aspects of a single phenomenon. The manifestation of a particular dimension depends upon the stage of economic development. For example, in the initial stage of industrialisation, the first dimension may manifest itself, whereas, in the advanced industrial societies, there may overall increase in participation rates of women accompanied by occupational segregation or feminisation of occupation.

Women's employment in the Indian context

India is predominantly an agrarian economy. The primary sector accounts for nearly 35 per cent of GDP and employs 65 per cent of the main workers. Over the period, the share of non-agriculture sector in GDP has increased but its share in total employment is less than proportionate. It is because the modern sector in India exhibits similar patterns as that of developed countries in economic growth without generating much employment. Are women in India being marginalised in the process of economic development? The answer to this question can be found in participation of women in the general pattern on one hand and sexual division of economic roles on the other. It is in this context that women employment in India is analysed in comparison to employment of men and in total employment.

Women's employment in India has been analysed in the following inter-connected dimensions:

(i) work participation rates;

(ii) status of employment; and

(iii) economic sectors of employment.

Between 1950 and 1985, the overall work participation rates for both the sexes has registered a decline. However, there is a sharp decline in overall work participation of women than men and is more than three times as compared to men. Looking at the age specific work participation rates, the trend in the declining female participation rate is more pronounced. It is seen that the decline in male work participation rate is mainly due to a sharp decline in the economically active population in the age group between 10 and 19. These decline is perhaps due to increasing accessibility to education. The expansion of education may partially explain this decline.

While the corresponding figure for females is 31.1 per cent. The differences in the participation rates between the two sexes show that it is an increasing function of age. The smaller difference in the younger age group is mainly due to decline in male participation rate while, larger differences in the order age groups are due to sharp decline in female participation rates.

Status of employment

Employment by status between 1972 and 1988, the share of women in self-employment and in regular employment has declined. Contrarily, the share of women in casual employment has increased in rural and urban areas. In other words, female employment in India is getting increasingly casualised. This is mainly on account of two reasons. First, in order to avoid provision of maternity and other social and economic benefits etc., the employers recruit women as casual workers. Second, with the increase in the sub-contracting of the production process, the employment in general and that of women in particular is being gradually transferred from the organised to unorganised sector.

The census data makes distinction between Main and Marginal Workers. Marginal workers have been defined as those who have to worked for a major part of the preceding year. In 1991 census, women account for only 16.03 per cent of the total main workers in India.

However, women account for 84 per cent of the total female marginal plus non-workers together 80.18 per cent in rural areas and 91.85 per cent in urban areas are women. This again shows a typical nature of female employment in India. It is generally argued that women in India show reluctance to enter in the labour force, that is why, their participation rates are low. This argument holds good, if unemployment among women is negligible or at lest is lower as compared to men. However, the available estimates of female unemployment are contrary. Unemployment among women is consistently higher than that of men during all periods of the survey both in rural and urban areas.

The major shift in women employment in agricultural sector is from agriculture labour category to cultivators. The cultivator in Indian census means either an employer or family worker engaged in cultivation. The women in Indian context belong mainly to the latter category. It is thus obvious that the status of women between three census periods has marginally shifted from agriculture worker to unpaid family worker. But the share of men in this sector has declined. This may partly be due to migration of males from rural areas to urban areas.

The share of men declined in the household industries while that of women increased between 1971 and 1981 and declined between 1981 and 1991. In non-household industries, the share of men shows improvement between 1971 and 1981 and a decline between 1981 and 1991. The share of women in non-household industry improved during the three Census; periods. The share of women in relatively better paying jab in transport, storage and communication sector shows a decline, while their share in other services after registering a decline shows a marginal increase in the last census period.

The Census evidence points that there are marginal changes in women's employment by sectors whatever be the magnitude of these changes. The evidence suggests that women are sliding down to low paying or unpaid work. Even in the higher paying sector the advancement of women is rather slow as compared to men. Many studies analysing the pattern of women's employment in the manufacturing industries have shown that women are being excluded from most skilled jobs and are concentrated in lower paid jobs and industries.

The empirical evidence shows that there is a plausible ground to argue for a validation of female marginalisation thesis in India. In other words, the overall economic development has increasingly excluded women from productive employment; pushed them into marginal occupations and increasingly casualised women in terms of employment. The dismantling of controls and regulations in the economy are expected to allocated the resources more efficiently than in the past. The big size firms are going to dominate the scene in the future.

The liberalised regime will increase competition in the factory as well as product market. In this process, each firm will try to cut the costs. The immediate response would be curtailment in the level of employment. The process of restructuring is likely to result in closure of many industries. The sickness is also likely to increase in unemployment in both the organised and unorganised sector of industrial manufacturing. Reduced employment as a result of this will affect women both directly and indirectly.

The trade liberalisation and flow of foreign capital is expected to push the rate of industrialisation. Ghosh echoes a gloomy scenario for unorganised sector and holds that globalisation of India economy would mean cheaper imported substitutes for indigenously manufactured goods.

The unorganised sector is the biggest source of female employment. The threat posed by the foreign capital as well as trade liberalisation will seriously affect availability of employment opportunities for women in this sector. They entry of Multinational Corporation (MNC's) such as General Foods, Nestle, Coca Cola, Pepsiocola ad Kellog in agro-processing industries is going to effect women workers where their number is quite substantial. The import of modern technology will lead to cut back in low skill jobs of women on the hand and will push them into low wage regime or undertake more strenuous jobs for the same pay.

India is facing twin crises i.e. Balance of Payments Deficit and the Fiscal Deficit. The debt of the country has reached a gigantic figure of 72 billion in 1992 which has pushed India into the comity of debtor nations. The "debt service" ratio has reached an intolerable limit of 50 per cent.

The Indian rupee has been devalued many times with a purpose to enhance its export competitiveness. Our exports too are unlikely to expand due to stiff competition from China and Taiwan. Further, due to high import intensity and poor quality, the market for India products is not going to expand vastly. The fiscal crisis has led to growing internal indebtedness of the Government. Against this scenario, the prognosis for women it not very optimistic. The general recessionary effect on employment will hit women more, given the bias of the employer, the social constraints placed on them and their obligatory domestic responsibilities. The objective of curtailment of public expenditure is to narrow down the fiscal budget and resort to deflationary measures. This will affect directly and indirectly the volume and quantum of women's employment in the future. This will affect women in two ways. Firstly, some women will be laid off as a part of cut back in production and employment. Secondly, as men lose their jobs, their wives and children will be forced to enter the labour market at vastly reduced wages rates.

If deflation is accompanied by reduction in subsidies on essential consumption, the fall in real income will increase the pressure on women to work for the market. The market has its own logic, therefore, the number of women workers entering the labour market would not be large. All the more, most women who would thus enter the labour force would take more to self-employment than to wage employment. Thus, pushing the women to unpaid or low paid occupation.

The modern technology has always favoured capital and not the labour. The capital has become cheaper than before and this is justified on the ground that industries need technological upgradation. This ultimately will increases the demand for skilled labour of qualitatively new type. Economic restructuring aims at production restructuring and, in turn, involves labour restricting.

Such increase in demand as might arise for the least skilled job where workers would be further exploited as in the case of women in textile and garment industry. Since women have fewer skills as compared to men, it is likely that men may gain in terms of employment in the labour restructuring process. This may result in increased exclusion of women from the production process. Presently, most of the developing countries are focusing their attention on 'Human Led Development'. The provision of health and educational facilities are essential components of tnis strategy. The women would be given prior attention so as to make them equal partners in the development process. The role of state becomes imperative in this direction.

Index